Through Uganda to Mount Elgon

THROUGH UGANDA TO MOUNT ELGON

BAGISHU WARRIORS OF MOUNT ELGON.

THROUGH UGANDA
TO MOUNT ELGON

By J. B. PURVIS

AUTHOR OF "BRITISH EAST AFRICA AND
UGANDA," "THE LUMASABA GRAMMAR," ETC.

WITH A MAP AND 42 ILLUSTRATIONS

T. FISHER UNWIN
LONDON: ADELPHI TERRACE
LEIPSIC: INSELSTRASSE 20
1909

TO

MY WIFE

CONTENTS

9

Contents

Contents

Contents

Contents

need—A Puritan revival—Secular education—Desire for knowledge—Intelligent people—The education problem—Duties of Church and State—Church government—White missionary not permanent—A constitution—Self-support and self-extension—Lack of funds and permanent buildings—The crisis of the nation and the Church—Hope—Questions of Church practice and discipline—Organisation—A division of the diocese

CHAPTER XI

A journey eastward—Kyagwe—Ham Mukasa—A visit to England—Samwili Kangawo—Perfect gentleman—Wayside camps—A view of Lake Victoria and Usoga—Ripon Falls—Whence the Nile springs—A dangerous ferry—A unique welcome—Jinja and its possibilities—From Lake Victoria to Egypt—Agriculture—Road-making—A good centre—Clever thieves—Slow work—Christian revenge—Famine—Hut-tax returns—Value of a paramount chief.

CHAPTER XII

Bukedi—River Mpologoma—Dug-out canoes—Papyrus—Disenchantment—Strange dwelling-places—Lake Kyoga—Floating islands—A spicy experience—Teso country—Clothing despised—Remarkable village fences—Curious ornaments—The care of children—Precautions for benefit of girls—Fear of a mother-in-law—Mission work—Lake Salisbury—A primitive race—Turkana people—Hair-dressing and use of pillows

Contents

Contents

CHAPTER XVI

CHAPTER XVII

LIST OF ILLUSTRATIONS

MAP

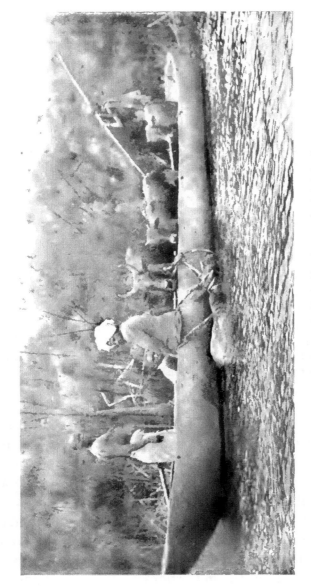

CROSSING THE RIVER MPOLOGOMA IN A DUG-OUT CANOE.

THROUGH UGANDA TO MOUNT ELGON

CHAPTER I

FROM ENGLAND TO THE HIGHLANDS OF AFRICA

A land worth seeing—How to get there—German *versus* English enterprise—The journey—Mombasa—Kilindini Harbour—The native town—Slavery—The enterprise and influence of Missions—Transition—Value of coast-lands—The Uganda Railway—The journey to the capital.

FOR the man who is tired of the beaten track, and who wishes to "see things as they are" in a land which, up to the last few years, was "the Dark Continent"—things that are well worth seeing, since they are all that remain in the world of a primitive simplicity that cannot possibly last much longer—let me commend a visit to our East African Empire.

The "How to get there?" is no longer a

problem, or even a trial, in spite of the fact that
British enterprise played no part in the solution
of the difficulty. Without so much as an effort
on the part of British shipowners, the Germans
have taken possession of East African trade,
and are even polite enough to call at Dover for
would-be visitors to East Africa and Uganda.

Those who prefer a short sea passage have
only to go overland to Marseilles or Naples,
from whence they may reach Mombasa in
fourteen days.

I do not say that German ships are all that
can be desired, more especially to the man who
has not learned to eat pork chop for breakfast,
when passing down the Indian Ocean in the
face of a monsoon; but I understand that
even such food as a German liner can offer
is preferable to the diet of—well, amongst
other things, substantial cockroaches, which
figured so prominently on some of the older
boats that once plied between Aden and
Mombasa.

Even in the matter of boat and diet a
choice is given, though some may think the
choice is between two evils, for whoever
cannot travel by a German line may try the
French, and perhaps prefer it. Here, almost
the only difference between first and second
class is the difference in the price and sleeping

accommodation. The food of first and second class is very similar, and the promenade-deck accommodation is the same.

By either line a very pleasant voyage can be made, giving glimpses of Southern France, Naples, Vesuvius, Stromboli, Messina, Etna, Port Said, the Suez Canal, and Aden—glimpses of life and colour which live in the memory for ever.

With little difficulty it is possible to break the journey at Port Said, and from thence visit the Holy Land or view the sights of Egypt.

For myself, I kept straight on, thankful for the breezes of the Indian Ocean—spicy breezes indeed, since they passed over various cattle-pens placed immediately in front of my cabin window, but nevertheless acceptable after the deadly calm and prostrating heat of the Gulf of Suez.

A little speck in the far distance grows gradually into shape until it becomes to us, after naught but sea and sea and sea, the most beautiful island in the world. The ring-ting-ting of the engine-room telegraph, and the vessel goes slower and slower as we glide into the harbour. A sharp command, the loud rattle of the anchor chain, and we have finished the first stage of our journey to Uganda. Mombasa at last; and all the island seem to have taken a day's holiday to visit the incoming steamer. A shoal of boats rush for the gangway, to be pushed off and off and off again, to sort themselves into the proper order of boarding. First comes the doctor, who, having declared a clean sheet, goes off again to shore, his departure the signal for another rush of boats of all sorts and sizes, with owners of every colour in the rainbow.

"Letters for you from up-country," says some one, and I read to find myself located to Masaba.

"Wherever in the world is Masaba?" thought I, and left a question of geography, which seemed impossible to solve at the coast, to be cleared up when I should reach Mengo, the capital of Uganda, and local headquarters of our mission; and in the interval sought a closer view of Mombasa, interesting always, but doubly so to one who saw it before the younger world had begun to cut, and mould, and shape, and build as it is doing at the present day.

Remembering my first visit in 1895 to the island, with its narrow street of Arab houses, old Portuguese fort, innumerable smells, and crowds of that happy-go-lucky, but useful, species of humanity, the Swahili porter, who, with his jolly smile, seemed to have but two

MASABA CHIEFS ON A VISIT TO THE EUROPEANS.

ambitions in life—the first to find out the
exact state of one's health, with his continual
"Jambo bwana, jambo? u hali gani?" and
the second to convince the new-comer that
to go off into the interior without such a
paragon of usefulness and integrity as the
speaker would be the height of folly; I see
once more the miserable aspect of the island
in those days! The one narrow, evil-smelling
street above mentioned, an English hospital,
and Government House standing lonely and
desolate; the old native town, a mission hospital, and for all the rest—not excepting the
old fort, although it was the home of criminals,
of porters being kept under lock and key until
the very moment of marching, and of the
then Postmaster-General—long grass, trees
and brushwood, the paradise of snakes,
leopards, and occasionally lions, which have
been known to cross the channel from the
mainland.

It was known, of course, that Mombasa was
an island, but very few realised that it possessed one of the most magnificent natural har-
bours in the world, which would eventually
prove *the front door* to the whole of Equatorial Africa, British, German, and Belgian,
and a side-door inlet and outlet to our East
Indian Empire: for here at Kilindini harbour

and township begins that stupendous monument of skill and incompetency, the misnamed Uganda Railway.

'Tis that has proved the magic wand, and changed the whole island so completely that it might now be mistaken for a well-planned botanical garden with substantial exhibition buildings.

All honour to the men who have laboured and suffered and died, some of them, to make this reception-room to our British East Africa what it is, the daintiest imaginable little coral island, with a cathedral, a newspaper, a court-house, hotels, roads, tram-line, and railway station all its own! Indeed, there will be found every requirement for a growing and very much alive little city—every requirement but one.

How pitiable it is that almost the only flag the natives see on ships that steam into that majestic harbour of Kilindini is the French or German! Surely such a promising bit of our Empire should be linked more closely with the homeland ; and perhaps at no distant date it will be done by a subsidised line of British steamers.

Mombasa, as the port of East Africa, is linked to the interior by ties other than the bridge which carries the railway. She sets the pace

TESO HUNTERS FROM THE HINTERLAND.

for the hinterland, and woe betide those men
who have presumed to settle inland if Mombasa is neglected. Yea, woe betide the whole
country and the Government hopes if the
Kilindini harbour is not developed at an
early date! Not Mombasa alone, but all East
Africa, is waiting for a wharf with capacious
go-downs and offices. Mombasa must still go
ahead for the sake of the interior, and it
should be possible for every kind of inquiry
to be dealt with the moment a steamer
arrives.

There is time for a glance at the native
town, with its low, square huts thatched with
palm-leaves, ribs, or mats, to salute the
little, laughing, fat watoto (children), and to
see what Mohammedanism and civilisation is
doing for the recently freed slaves of our
Empire.

Perhaps it will be news to many that the
legal status of slavery in the strip of East
Africa, running ten miles deep, and which
really belongs to the Sultan of Zanzibar, was
only abolished on October 1, 1907. This does
not mean that slavery was totally abolished,
for concubines do not come under the new
Regulations, but it means that a slave-owner
must prove his title to the slave.

In the islands of Pemba and Zanzibar the

slave must claim his freedom before a British court, and prove that he has proper means of subsistence.

Not very long ago the only people who had to face the problem of freed slaves were the missionaries of Zanzibar and Frere Town; and right well they did their work, by turning out what seemed a hopeless conglomeration of humanity into useful members of society—servant-boys and girls, clerks, school teachers, carpenters, builders, brickmakers, and even ministers of the gospel.

This was a great deal to do in the midst of the very lowest type of Mohammedanism, strong chiefly because of its sensuous licence; and it will be readily understood how the sudden spurt of civilisation, the labour demands and moral evils, brought about by the building and completion of the Uganda Railway, combined to almost blot out and make impossible the work of the Christian missionary at the coast.

Yet the C.M.S. agents, under their kindly bishop, stick to their divinity school, industrial work, hospital, boarding and high schools, and, most difficult of all, open-air preaching in the market-place.

The change wrought in the lives of the people at the coast by the Uganda Railway is stupendous, as can readily be conceived by any one familiar with the old method of reaching the interior.

Every load of from 60 lbs. to 80 lbs. weight had to be carried on the head of a porter, and sometimes a thousand men, gathered together from Zanzibar, Mombasa, and the coast strip, would boisterously start off on a thousand-mile tramp, from which many of them never returned.

The railway now carries the loads, and the men are free in a double sense—free from their old slave-owners and free to seek other employment.

Many go off into the interior as merchants in a small way, and as they go spread the superficial Mohammedanism which makes it so easily possible for a man to get rid of an uncongenial wife, and at the same time, without the faintest knowledge of the Koran, obtain some standing in the eyes of the supposedly big people from the coast.

Others are finding employment with such white men as have realised that the coast-lands of Seyidie and Tanaland, though unhealthy, are really valuable, and give better return than almost any other part of Africa when laid under rubber, rice, cotton, fibre, and cocoa-nut cultivation. Perhaps nothing in the world gives a more reliable and profitable return than a cocoa-nut plantation.

We have seen the indications of transition at the door; now let us go inside.

No longer the tramp, tramp, tramp, under the broiling sun, over waterless desert, through fever-laden swamp or foodless country, for we have taken a ticket for Uganda at the cost of Rs.142.5 first class, Rs.71.3 second class, or Rs.23.12 third class, and the journey which took from two to three months can now be accomplished in as many days. And what a journey! Thick forest, rolling plain, howling wilderness, pleasant pasture, hill and dale, mountain and valley, rushing river, rippling stream, roaring lion, English ox, smart official and naked savage, can all be seen in the course of one day, as we are hurried from the sea-level, up and up, to a height of over 4,000 feet.

The Wanyika.

No time now to visit the shy and weakly Wanyika people who live near the coast in their badly made houses, or to feel anything but thankful as the train rushes across the Taru Desert, with its euphorbia, mimosa scrub, aloe, thorn, and stillness of death : once the bugbear of all travellers to the interior by the British

NATIVE-MADE BRIDGE OVER A DANGEROUS RIVER.

route; now not worth considering, except by fibre experts, some of whom have found it so valuable that a decorticating plant has been established at Voi.

From the railway station at Voi there is a good road practically all the way to the snow-capped and beautiful mountain of Kilima-Njaro, and the country is thickly populated and well cultivated by the Wataita people, a branch probably of the Gallas.

These people have brought the cultivation of bananas, sweet potatoes, millet, Indian corn, and sugar-cane to a fine art with their wonderful system of irrigation. For ourselves, we shall rejoin our waiting train, after partaking of our first meal since Mombasa, provided at a very small charge in the Dak bungalow, quite near to the railway line.

How very different from the old days when if one wished for a steak, it had to be chosen from the innumerable herds of antelope or zebra, then shot and skinned and cooked !

Not only the Dak bungalow, but the whole country onwards from Voi, provides a treat, a feast for the eye to the lover of the beautiful and the student of nature. The Uganda Railway has not driven away the game : wildebeeste, hartebeeste, zebra, ostrich, rhinoceri, lions, may all be seen during one short run; and it would be no novelty for a rhinoceros to seek the personal acquaintance of a railway inspector, or for a lion to paralyse the station staff. I well remember two such incidents, and wish I were artist enough to picture to you the face of the Britisher who, almost overwhelmed with the importance of his new position and new white suit, had started off down the line on a trolly propelled by two Indian coolies.

When I met them the rhino had, by way of protest, smashed the trolly and kept the three men some hours shivering and shouting at the top of some trees near which he quietly grazed. There was black murder in the white man's eye, a desire to avenge the loss of dignity and the suit besmeared with dirt and blood-stains, as he begged me to lend him a rifle and cartridges for a short time.

From Voi, mile 103, we continue the journey, and soon realise by the change of atmosphere that we have been ascending all the time. From 70 feet above sea-level at Mombasa we are now over 4,000 feet and again passing through a populous country, Ukamba, with its lofty hills and beautiful fertile valleys. The people, a Bantu tribe, are numerous and industrious, renowned hunters, and trustworthy guides. They are very proud of themselves, and go in for a great deal of ornamentation with beads, shells, brass, iron, and copper wire. They also file the teeth and smear the body with rancid butter and red earth.

We had a rest and meal at Makindu, mile 209 ; but the bracing air has made us ready for another. Our train has crossed the Kapiti Plains at a height of 5,850 feet, and every one is declaring that here is white man's Africa, the land of hope for any overflowing population. Be that as it may, I am hungry, and willing to leave such abstruse questions for another time, since the train has arrived at Nairobi, 327 miles from Mombasa, and 5,450 feet above sea-level.

CHAPTER II

THE CAPITAL OF BRITISH EAST AFRICA

Nairobi—A bad start—Progress—Strong opinions—Knotty
problems—Forcing the hand of the Administration—"Put
the native in his proper place"—The destiny of the
African—Is he capable of mental and moral development?
—The Governor of British East Africa—The settler—
Will he ever be able to make a permanent home in the
Highlands of Africa?—The evils of competition—The
problems of race and colour very pressing—Locate the
white man as well as the black—Is the Asiatic a "settler"?
—The intermingling of the Aryan and Negro—Develop the
country through the native—Organise and educate the
negro—Disintegration of native customs—Taxation—
Rearrange old tribal systems.

NAIROBI, the capital of British East Africa,
5,000 feet above sea-level, and a centre
from which to hunt big game, see natives, and
study problems.

The first problem is how to make the best of
a bad job, for the wise man responsible for
moving the headquarters of the railway from
Mombasa to the Highlands was unfortunately

THE NATIVE AT PLAY.

also responsible for planting it in the middle of a swamp.

Thus the effort to make a beginning in the Highlands got a bad start, and might have proved hopeless but for the grit of some concerned, who have so wrought that what five years ago was a hideously bad dream of corrugated iron is to-day a very presentable Anglo-African town. There is an Anglican church, Roman Catholic chapel, a bank, a couple or more really good hotels, a post office, stores of every description, a well-made main road, rickshas plying for hire, some slight attempt at drainage, and a market that really does credit to the place.

Indeed, there is a great deal more than might have been expected in so new a town, and a great deal more than is good for it, for from the beginning Nairobi has been blessed—or cursed—with men holding strong opinions.

With the building of a house for the Governor began the question of whether Mombasa or Nairobi should be the capital, and since that time it is somewhat difficult to decide whether population or opinions increased more quickly.

The strength of the latter has certainly developed until the tone of one local rag might sometimes be mistaken for an outspoken American. The human element at Nairobi is the one to be considered, and the one that ought to be considered *now* if we do not wish to reap grievous troubles in the future.

It seems almost incredible that whilst here in England, within a comparatively small area, the cry of needy thousands can hardly be heard, in East Africa some five hundred and fifty men are making so much noise that the House of Lords gives pause to listen.   Were it not absurd it might be serious, yet no doubt behind it all lie principles serious enough.

Is "the Colony of British East Africa" a misnomer? If not, who are to colonise it? Well, since the climate is very similar to Southern Europe, the soil rich, fertile, and well watered, European vegetables, fruit, cereals, sheep and cattle already doing well, the answer seems to be, "White men."   And this is the only answer in the mouth of the men in and around Nairobi : the man who is doing well on his farm, and really ought to be encouraged, and the man who has never done well anywhere, but mysteriously turns up in every new African town to hang round the billiard saloon, live on the newest hotel venture, and give gratis his opinion on law and order—a disgrace to his countrymen, a danger to every new colony. There is also another being who answers, "White men!" in a particularly loud voice, namely, the man who hopes to grab as much of the best land for the smallest possible outlay, and sell it at a big price to settlers. Both the latter are men who ought not to be tolerated in a colony like East Africa, and if they could be dismissed I do not think the other would be a difficult person to understand. He is the man who wishes to do the best for himself by honest hard work, and curiously enough he is seldom heard prophesying that the country is going to the dogs. He has built his little house and is far too busy in town or country developing his own business to give advice as to how to make money, run missions, and govern the country.

Still, even he will not believe there is any but the one answer to the question about the East African Highlands, in spite of the fact that there are five times more Indians and twenty times more natives than white men within a radius of a mile from where he stands.

The natives claim the soil ; they have lived there for ages ; they are not the idle, good-for-nothings we sometimes hear them called, and naturally they are surprised when told that the big white man, the Governor, has sold their land to the lesser white man, the settler, who may or may not be disposed to allow the African to remain on the land.

3

One case was brought to my notice where the buyer impudently asked—perhaps out of bravado or wish to chaff the official—if he had a right to shoot on sight any native he caught on his property.

The chaff indicates the trend of thought; not that such men would shoot the native, but that the native ought to be cleared away at the will of and to make room for the white man.

I need not here refer at length to the endeavour made some time ago to force the hand of the Administration on the native question, by unlawfully whipping some servant-boys in the public street of Nairobi immediately in front of the magistrate's office; but I do say, "God help the Governor" of such a country at such a time.

To "put the native in his proper place" simply means, to many who are interested in the question, to put him where he can most easily be called upon by the white man for any assistance in seeking to make a fortune; to be content to acknowledge himself accursed as a child of Ham; and the more accursed the more he strives to remove any indication that he is different to other men.

That the African may have a destiny high and noble, a life to develop on the soil where

BAGISHU GIRLS.

47

found, of course under a more fostering care and tender mercy than those of the man hastening to be rich, has never been considered by many: indeed it is argued that he is totally incapable of mental and moral development; but only a very short journey from Nairobi is necessary to refute such an opinion.

Fortunately the present Governor of British East Africa is a man worthy to hold the position, and he is capably supported by his staff, who recognise their great responsibility to the native sons of the soil.

They realise that they are face to face with stupendous problems which can only be solved by patience, tact, forbearance, and strong common sense, and are not willing to be unduly pushed into one line of action, bullied or frightened into another.

I deeply sympathise with the man who, in the homeland, has turned his little all into capital, and, beguiled by land speculators' tempting advertisements or lectures, has gone out to East Africa, only to find that there are so many difficulties to be overcome before he can settle down, that his capital has vanished.

He is appalled at the length of time necessary to secure land settlements; the unsettled condition of the native question, the incongruity of an English colony in Africa administered under the Indian Penal Code, and administered by officials who have had little or no experience of such administration so far as white men are concerned. The tendency to petty official-ism under such a code galls him frightfully, and he gives up in despair to join the ranks of the malcontents. How well employed would the Colonists' Association be were it to meet the Governor and thrash out once for all the answer to the question at first propounded— Is "the Colony of British East Africa" a misnomer? If not, who are to colonise it? This question once settled, we should have fewer men in East Africa embued with Carlyle's false idea that "the funda-mental question between any two human beings is: Can I kill thee or canst thou kill me?"

Comparing the negro and the white, there is no question as to who is best fitted for the country and which population will grow most rapidly. The negro is at home, the white is not; and, in spite of the fact that homesteads have ap-peared and some progress made in cattle-ranch-ing, it is quite an open question whether the white man will ever be at home in the African High-lands; that he will ever be able to build up here, under the direct rays of the Equatorial

TYPES OF WOMEN AND GIRLS, MASABA, MOUNT ELGON.

51

sun, a strong, contented, self-supporting, permanent, white community.

Take away from Nairobi the official life—civil and military—the parson and priest, the railway staff, general agents, store- and hotel-keepers, the parasites and loafers, and what have you left? Well, the town will have ceased to exist so far as the white man is concerned ; and in the country, on farm and ranch, will be one or two—not more—doing reasonably well.

The evils of competition are too manifest in such a small community, and men are really buying and selling each other, did they but know it.

So long as four millions of blacks are willing —according to some ideas—to remember their right place, and remain hewers of wood and drawers of water for the small, very small, handful of whites, the "lucky" few will be content ; but the colony will still remain undeveloped, the native problem unsolved, and a large section of the whites as discontented as ever.

For the sake of all concerned, let me reiterate that *now* is the time for some master-mind to grip the problems of race and colour, right and prior-right, in our East African colony.

Is it not possible to offer the white colonist and settler a better chance, by setting apart a large portion of the very best land with the most suitable climate, and reserving that, town and country, for the white man only, and administer it under white man's law? Of course it would not be possible for the man with influence to buy the lot, or even the best; but, first come, first served, *if*—and the if is a big one—he be a worker.

Innumerable questions surge up at such a proposition, and undoubtedly great difficulties would have to be encountered and overcome. Would all the labour be done by whites? &c., &c., are questions that would naturally solve themselves, once the principle was laid down that within a certain area was situate and constituted a colony for white men only.

Such a policy would leave the Government free to deal with the next two most pressing questions—the African and the Asiatic.

To take the Asiatic first. No one conversant with Sir H. H. Johnston's purpose and policy, as laid down in his books on British East and Central Africa, can fail to understand that India and Africa are closely allied, in the minds of English statesmen at any rate. And the most superficial observer in British East Africa will notice that the Indian is a factor to be reckoned with in practical politics. Still, I very much

doubt whether he will ever be in Africa that
important factor so many prophesy.

The Indian is the most wonderful merchant in
the world, not excepting the native of Uganda.
He will come to Africa without a single rupee,
get employment from one of his compatriots,
live on a few grains of rice per day, buy native
hoes with his earnings, and with these disappear
into unknown regions to turn up again and
again with loads of skins and hides, until, tired
with journeying, worn out with malarial fever,
and longing for home, he makes his way to that
side-door, Mombasa, and ships for Bombay.

Can this man in any sense be called a settler
or colonist? and are not all the others—merchants, clerks, artisans, and coolies—much the
same? The Money Order Department of the
Post Office supplies the answer by telling us of
the enormous amount of money continually
transferred to India by these *visitors*.

That India has a part to play in our East
African Empire is undoubted, but that Providence has arranged that part to be the intermingling of the Aryan and Negro races may be
gravely questioned.

The great bulk of India's population live in
villages and till the soil; these, if any, are likely
to feel the pinch and require room for expan-
sion. But do they require it? or, what is more

to the point, do they desire it? If so, they have not sought British East Africa as a new home waiting to yield them its harvest.

This being so, we must look elsewhere for the men who will by manual labour develop the natural resources of our colony; and right here comes in the opportunity of the Administration to so distribute, organise, and educate the native element that, with the help of the Asiatic, with whom in many ways the white man cannot compete, we may at once begin a possible and hopeful evolution rather than continue the present chaos, that must inevitably lead to revolution.

"Organise and educate the negro!" Is that possible? Speaking from my own and the experience of many more qualified to judge, I say quite possible, and the sooner it is taken in hand the better. Up to the present moment the whole work of education has been done by missionaries, encouraged but not helped by Government, and the results have been little short of marvellous; but the coming of the Uganda Railway and messengers of civilisation—some good, many evil—before the vast majority of natives had been the least prepared even by Christian missions, have thrown them off their balance. They do not quite realise what part they have to play in the drama of development; and they

feel like boys who have been chased away from
their playground, but hang round perplexed,
ready for any new game, harmless or dangerous.

This latent power for good or evil surely
appeals to England with as much force as the
power allowed to run waste over the Ripon
Falls; and one cannot imagine it will appeal
in vain.

The white and Asiatic elements in British
East Africa are both too small and uncertain
to justify the shaping of legislation to suit them
only; they are both, as a whole, too content to
live on and by the native. And the native,
whose appetite for progress has been whetted,
if only by the desire to obtain a shirt or waistcoat, must have his attention turned to the real
source of wealth—the cultivation of the land for
more than his own needs.

By the introduction of civilisation we have
begun the work of disintegrating the present
social conditions of the African; and it seems
to me a very serious thing to allow this disintegration to go on, whereby all the power of
chieftainship is lost, everything understood as
government annulled, and the native actually
forced from the land of his fathers and left a
huddled, disorganised, and confused mass.

Hut-tax and poll-tax may prove an incentive
to force a portion of the disorganised mass to

seek employment from the settlers, but what of
all the others? We cannot, surely, suppose that
the question will be settled by declaring a certain portion of country " reserve," from which
a native is not allowed to pass without a ticket-
of-leave.

Educate, educate, educate! not by turning
loose among them so many schoolmasters, but
by organising them—on their own clan system
preferably—under trained leaders of men, practical agriculturists and stock-raisers, who might
so use the chiefs and as much as possible of the
old tribal systems, in order (a) to rearrange each
tribe under the changed circumstances; (b) to
settle them on new land if necessary, giving
them plenty of room to expand, *no leave to be
idle*, but every encouragement and help to
develop the resources of their land along
lines laid down by their instructors. Do for
each large native community what the experimental farm at Naivasha does for the white
man, and erect at once industrial institutions
for the training of artisans who will supply
the need of black and white alike. I have no
doubt but that the missionary will be only too
glad to be called upon to supply other education
for which, apart from his evangelistic work, the
Government ought to pay him.

Along such lines there is hope, I believe, for

all, but more especially for the man likely to be forgotten until he becomes a burden, intolerable even to himself—the native of British East Africa—at whom we shall take a closer glimpse before rejoining the train for the Lake.

CHAPTER III

THE NATIVE

Four millions of natives—The Swahili—Arab and African—
Arab influence — Swahili nature — "Black ivory" —
Mohammedan missionaries—Primitive tribes—The Wa-
kamba—Ideas of beauty—Religion—The Wakikuyu—
Their industry — Ornaments — Polygamy — Unrest—The
Masai—"Fierce nomadic warriors"—Nilotic negroes—
Pastoral people—Dress—Warriors—Houses—Women's
work—Engaged—Ear-rings—Sacred objects—The Great
Spirit—A problem.

THE problem of four millions of native
Africans begins at Mombasa and spreads
itself over the whole of British East Africa,
until we reach Lake Victoria.

The Swahili.

At the coast we have that hybrid race already
mentioned, the Swahili, or coast people—a race
brought into existence by the intermarriage of
Arab and African.

A HARD DRINKER AND MEDICINE MAN.

61

Others have dealt with the death of Portuguese and the growth of Arab influence on the East Coast, so there is no need for me to do more than mention the fact—a fact that has had a great influence, not only on the coast life but throughout the whole of Central Africa, for the outcome has been a people and a language. The people, deriving their name from the Arab equivalent for coast, are liberally endowed with Ishmael's wandering propensities, and have become the merchants of the Equator; and it seems difficult to believe that the innocent-looking individual, now buying or selling a donkey, was equally good at bargaining, only a few years ago, for men and women; and that the jester was right who said that *Swahili* is derived from *sawa hila*, which may be interpreted " All same cheat."

Such, however, was the case; the whole of the East Coast slave-trade was carried on by these people until stopped by the power of England.

Curiously enough, whilst the Arabs were able to imprint their personality and religion upon the native, yet the negro element was too strong for absorption, physically or linguistically. The negro type, drawn from many branches of the Bantu race, has held its own, and even forced a Bantu language upon its conquerors or masters.

Pure Arab merchant and hybrid Swahili use the same language, and have made it, by their many expeditions into the interior after "black ivory," the *lingua franca* of Equatoria. The peculiarities of a Bantu language are dealt with in Chapter XV. Such a race as the Swahili, with its negro propensities and Arab cuteness, has great influence as a Mohammedan missionary among the primitive tribes. It has also added very considerably to the difficulties of those working at the coast amongst freed slaves.

Primitive Tribes.

The primitive East Coast peoples, immediately in touch with Mombasa, are the Wanyika and the Wagiryama; few in number, poor in physique and martial ability, very superstitious, but also very industrious in agriculture.

Between the Giryama country and the Somali country, north of the river Tana, dwell the shy and cowardly primitive Wapokomo people, whose customs and manners are very similar to those of the Bantu Kavirondo, which are dealt with later on.

One of the strongest and most interesting peoples touched by the Uganda Railway is the tribe known as the Wakamba, dwelling in the country which stretches from the Tsavo River to the Athi plain. They are a brave and indus-

BAGISHU ABOUT TO OFFER SACRIFICES.

trious people, who would, I feel certain, give a good return for any interest taken in them. Fond of cattle and agriculture, they are also good at making a bargain, and have been more helpful in provisioning passing caravans than perhaps any other inland tribe.

Though not aggressive, they have held their own against would-be oppressors, and for years past have organised their own caravans to carry trade-goods to the coast.

They are not very particular about the amount of their clothing, but are very fond of iron and brass wire, iron chain, and ornaments made with beads and shells. They also seek to add to their beauty by filing the incisor teeth.

The men, armed with bows and poisoned arrows, spears and swords, are mighty hunters, and renowned trackers of game, whilst the women are the most wonderful carriers in East Africa. The load of wood, flour, grain, bananas, or babies, is fastened on the back in the hide sling which hangs from the forehead.

Like most pagan Africans, the Wakamba have but a vague idea of religion, believing in the power of evil spirits, to whom they make meat and drink offerings, and against whose influence they carry charms.

Their custom of circumcising does not seem to have any connection with religion.

The Wakikuyu.

By far the most important tribe in British East Africa is the Wakikuyu: a strong, industrious, and warlike race of Bantu people, related more probably to the western branch of Equatorial negroes rather than to their eastern neighbours, the Wakamba.

These really are the people whose presence near the capital, Nairobi, occupying as they do the beautiful and well-watered country between the river Kidong and the Lossogurti Escarpment to the north of Mount Kenya, has forced the question of white and black, right and prior-right, to the front.

Kikuyu country is situate at an elevation of from 4,500 to 6,500 feet, and is in climate quite sub-tropical. There are evidences that at one time it was a vast forest, which the natives have cleared in order to carry out what is, compared with other native efforts, an advanced system of cultivation, on the best soil in British East Africa.

Although renowned for treachery and turbulence—due, no doubt, to the many attacks made upon them by their cattle-loving and

raiding neighbours, the Masai—the Wakikuyu
are admittedly a hard-working and industrious
people, quite unfamiliar with famine. They
grow bananas, sweet potatoes, sugar-cane, yams,
peas, beans, millet, gourds, tomatoes, and tobacco.
They are not rich in cattle—again, no doubt,
because of the Masai; but under the Pax
Britannica their herds are already on the
increase. They are also bee farmers, and hives
are to be seen in every tree.

Between the Wakikuyu and the Masai there
seems to have been constant warfare, yet,
curiously enough, the Wakikuyu have to a great
extent copied dress, customs, and arms from the
Masai.

The men are content with a goat-skin for a
garment, eked out with the covering of a fatty
red mixture of castor-oil and earth with which
they smear themselves.

The women are more liberally clothed in skins
hanging from the waist and shoulder, the
number of which vary according to the season.
Indeed, except in features, the appearance of a
Kikuyu woman resembles very much that of
her Masai neighbour, because not only clothing
but Masai ornaments have been copied. Ears
are pierced and loaded with iron rings, chain,
beads, gourd ends, pieces of wood, and—since
the advent of civilisation—empty jam tins are

4

seen everywhere fixed in the extended lobe. The men wear a peculiar armlet on the left arm, made of ivory or wood in the shape of a merry-thought bone.

Beads, of course, are used, not only as currency, but for ornamentation; and some very pretty girdles are seen, made of beads sown on to leather, and worn by men and women.

A snuff-box is a usual item of a gentleman's wardrobe, for snuff and tobacco are much appreciated. A Kikuyu man is armed with a spear, sword, knobkerry, sometimes a bow and arrows, and a shield made of buffalo hide, after the Masai pattern, and marked in a similar fashion with a clan mark picked out in colours.

Married as well as unmarried men are warriors, and this being the case, most of the work is performed by the women, who age rapidly.

Like other native races, the Wakikuyu practise polygamy, and wives are bought with cattle; the newly married wife being brought to her husband's village with a semblance of force. She now discards the many ornaments used to attract lovers, and settles down in her own house to lead an industrious and wonderfully moral life.

The unmarried men and the unmarried girls live in houses set apart for them, supposedly under supervision, but there is a great deal of free intercourse between the young people.

The native system of government has scarcely advanced beyond the patriarchal stage, and in many respects they are a people similar to the primitive Bantu we shall meet later on.

Such people are worth considering from an economic point of view, and with them the white administrator might at the present moment do anything.

The idleness and unrest are due to transition; for, as we have seen, clan ties have been loosened, patriarchal authority has had to give way before the Indian Penal Code, and the natives' sociological ideas have been uprooted and overthrown. Before he again enters Utopia there must be a period of individuality, brought about by the kindly help and organisation of the English Government, through such practical education, training, and industrial enterprise as can be given, for the purpose of developing character to rightly use responsibility and opportunity.

The Masai.

A somewhat less hopeful but more interesting people are the Masai, who for many years were as an impassable barrier to those who wished to explore British East Africa. "Fierce, nomadic warriors" was all the description we had of them until the Scotch traveller, Joseph Thompson, gave us a closer view in 1885; and even then those three words seemed to so clearly describe them that there was no anxiety on the part of the travelling public to make a closer acquaintance.

Since that time much water has run over the Ripon Falls, and the more dangerous faculties of the Masai have been so paralysed by the magic of the white man that the most timid inquirer may now approach them with safety.

The Masai are not a Bantu people, but a branch of the Nilotic negroes. Originally in two divisions, each under its own medicine-man, they are now divided into various sections and occupy the country that stretches from Mount Kilimanjaro, in the south, to Lake Baringo in the north.

A purely pastoral people, their custom was —until placed in reserves by the British Government—to move from place to place in search of suitable grazing ground for their vast herds of cattle. Incidental of such nomadic life, it was no uncommon thing for one section to trespass on the ground of another section, with the result that war was declared

—actually *declared*, in civilised fashion, if such a statement is not utterly incongruous. Treachery was only permissible when dealing with those who had not the honour to be Masai.

A Masai, as a rule six feet or more in height, straight as an arrow, splendidly developed, without an ounce of spare flesh on him, his head well balanced, and of a shape quite different to the Bantu tribes around, high cheek-bones and beautiful nose, is a sight well worth seeing, and suggests great latent power and possibility.

This striking individual—the more striking because of his headdress of ostrich feathers, collar of Colobus monkey-skin, with the long white and black hair attached, and his whole body smeared with a greasy red paint that makes him look really formidable—is one of the El-moran, or warriors, and is therefore unmarried ; for the native political organisation is such that when a man marries he ceases to be a warrior.

The section occupying a particular district is subdivided into clans, and on the large shield of the warrior is clearly marked the heraldic device of the clan to which he belongs. Each clan has its spokesman, medicine-man, and political chief. Then come the two divisions of the adult male population—the El-moru, *i.e.*, the quondam warriors who have become benedicts, and as such rank as elders, responsible for the good conduct of their kraal, and the El-moran, or warriors, already described.

The houses are of the rudest possible character, made of bamboo and wattles, twisted and bent into a tunnel-shaped object some three or four feet high, then plastered over by the women with mud and cow-dung. These huts are built in a circle, and if they are to be occupied by the El-moru a strong fence is erected; but if the kraal belongs to the El-moran there is no fence, for as " Britannia needs no bulwarks," so the Masai warriors require no other protection than their own watchfulness.

When a move is necessary the women are responsible for packing all household utensils and the bamboos, &c., used in hut-building, on the donkeys, and transporting them to the new grazing ground, whither the men have driven the cattle. In a Masai home the infants, male and female, are called En-gesa; when boys can walk they are En-aiok; after circumcision they are El-barnode, whilst girls at the same stage are En-doya.

When the males are old enough to carry arms they cease to eat any vegetable diet, and live on beef, blood, and milk. They move

"ENGAGED" GIRLS.

into the kraal of the El-moran, and there
live a life of free love with the unmarried
girls, who, in spite of the fact that the custom is an old one, are nevertheless punished
if they become mothers. The great wonder
is that these girls are able to settle down
after marriage to a fairly moral life.

An engaged girl is easily known by the
length of her hair and by the band round
the head with cowrie shells hanging from a
number of strings, like the married woman of
Palestine with her pieces of money hanging
in much the same way.

At marriage the head is shaved, certain ear
ornaments discarded, and the married woman's
skin garments adopted.

The girls are quite good-looking and graceful, but many seem to be actually deformed
owing to the pressure on arms and legs of
the heavy spiral coil of iron wire.

The ear has been chosen by the Masai as
the chief member for ornamentation, which
means, in some cases, the most frightful dis-
figurement. The lobe is pierced and then
extended until it is made to take a piece of
wood varying in size from two to six inches
in diameter.

There are various forms of salutation used
in the country, one at least not acceptable

to a white visitor—namely, that of spitting. The Masai are quite adepts at sending out the saliva, through the notch filed between the two upper incisors, and of course you must take the salutation in the spirit in which it is given.

The married women do some very pretty bead-work and ornament the gourds in which the milk is kept.   Milk is accounted sacred, and may not be boiled; and no stranger is supposed to receive it either for pay or as a present, but sometimes one has been able to buy a little from a soft-hearted lady.

Grass also is a sacred object, and, when held in the hand, a sign of peace.   A visitor is receiving the most cordial welcome when the Masai touch him with grass.

Ngai is the great spirit of this nomadic people, and to him, who dwells, they say, in the great mountain in the south, they continually pray for help and guidance.

A strange people indeed, and one not easy to deal with as part of the problem before us.   More interesting than the Wakikuyu, but not so hopeful, because they are pastoral and not agricultural.   Yet even with a pastoral and cattle-loving people like the Masai, there is reason to believe that a little expenditure and careful organisation will turn them into settled

and permanent ranchers, willing to sell their
improved stock at the improved prices offered.

Of course, with such a proposal I am knock-
ing right up against the one or two rich
ranchers who at present have it very much
their own way, and would probably not care
to have the native organised, educated, and
helped by Government to beat them at their
own game. Yet it seems to me far more in-
cumbent upon the Government to develop the
native human being, and, by so doing, develop
land and stock, than to neglect the human
element and hand over the land, that has
been the grazing land of the Masai for ages,
at a nominal figure to one or two rich Englishmen, or to a syndicate, for the purpose of
—well, not for the purpose of developing *the
native.*

Though tempted to leave the railway and
push northward beyond Lake Baringo in order
to visit the Suk and Turkana peoples, we
must not do so, but take the next train and
move westwards to the Lake.

CHAPTER IV

FROM NAIROBI TO LAKE VICTORIA

The most beautiful country—The great "fault"—The Mau
Escarpment — Giant timber — A serious rainstorm —
Poisoned arrows—Nandi troubles—A caravan cut up—
Port Florence—Kavirondo peoples—A surprise—The
tropics indeed—The C.M S.—The power of example—The
sight of a lifetime—The day of opportunity for the
Christian Church—Education or Evangelisation ?

LEAVING Nairobi we push on to the Lake
through the most beautiful country of
British East Africa. We cannot leave the
native question behind, for our very train has
been obliged to carry armed Masai to protect
its passengers from disloyal natives that may
be met with.

Having crossed the wonderful Meridional Rift,
or great "fault" as geologists and miners would
term it, which stretches almost the whole length
of Africa, and here at Kikuyu falls almost sheer
to a depth of 1,440 feet, we are soon passing

MASAI WARRIORS GUARDING A TRAIN ON THE UGANDA RAILWAY.

81

over the Mau Escarpment, with its mighty
forests of giant timber that patiently wait for
the axe and saw and ingenuity of man or
enterprise of the Government, to turn the best
of the timber to better account than fuel for
the iron horse, and from the rest provide that
fuel more easily and cheaply than at present.

Already some enterprising individuals are
working in a small way, with the result that
almost every article of furniture may be bought
in Nairobi in a style and at a price that will
compare with anything in England. What a
different journey from the one I took in 1895,
when it was plod, plod, plod up hill and down
dale, in sunshine and shower. One shower I
remember overtook us on this very escarpment,
and I don't suppose it will ever be forgotten
by any of the party.

We were descending Mau on the westward
side and had almost reached a convenient
camping-place when it began to rain. The
cold was intense, the path, bad at any time,
became slippery and difficult to negotiate;
the rivulets became mighty torrents, and the
porters were in despair. We coaxed, we
threatened, we helped with loads, and carried
men; but I believe a dozen succumbed as the
result of that downpour.

From such a recurrence as that the railway

has delivered us, and I, for one, am grateful. The Dorobo people, with their poisoned arrows, are still in the forests, but no longer have we to keep our men in close order lest a stray arrow should find an untimely resting-place. The engine pants and puffs and snorts, and eventually reaches the highest point from which we run down at an increased speed into a totally different climate.

We have reached what for purposes of administration is called the Province of Kisumu, through which the railway was hurried to the Lake by a short cut when the patience of the British taxpayer had almost reached its limit. *En route* it taps the countries of Nandi, Lumbwa, and Kavirondo.

For some time past the Nandi people have given considerable trouble, and at one station there was gruesome evidence of their having paid a visit just before our arrival. Our Masai guard seemed quite disappointed that they had missed an opportunity of displaying their powers; but the passengers were too fluttered by the sight of one dead man to wish for more bloodshed.

It reminded me of my first visit to the Nandi country and of a ghastly experience of their bloodthirstiness.

Our caravan of some six hundred porters

was delayed at the coast for a short time : and a small caravan of some thirty mail-carriers was despatched in front of us. When we reached Eldoma Ravine, a wounded Swahili crawled into our camp and told a tale of awful butchery. He, with the other mail-runners, had passed the Ravine in safety, and had reached the border of Nandi country, where they encamped for the night. The Nandi warriors had watched their every movement, and suddenly swooped down and killed every man but the one who escaped to tell us the terrible story.

Our doctor attended his wounds and he was able to go on with us and point out the scene of his awful experience. It was a ghastly and painful sight, and we delayed our march an hour or two in order to collect letters and valuables belonging to waiting friends in Uganda, and to obliterate the more marked evidences of a savage attack.

Now, however, we are hurried on along the iron road, through the countries of Nandi and Kavirondo to Kisumu, also named Port Florence, after the wife of some official, whom I sincerely hope was not responsible for choosing such a filthy, shallow, fever swamp at which to fix the Uganda Railway terminus.

The population of the Kisumu Province is

roughly computed to be a million and a half, and embraces the peoples of Nandi, Lumbwa, Kavirondo, Sotik, Kisi, and Ugaya.

The Nandi and Lumbwa peoples are related, and belong to the Nilotic Bari group. Both are of a fierce temperament, but the Nandi have given the Administration most trouble, and have recently been removed from the vicinity of the railway into a reserve situate to the east of Mount Elgon. This move on the part of the Government is probably neither more nor less than to restore the Nandi people to their original home from which they were driven by the Masai when that people first invaded Equatorial Africa a hundred years ago.

Kavirondo is populated by two distinct races of people—the Bantu, who are of the aboriginal stock, still found on Mount Elgon, and the Nilotics, who are closely related to the Gang or Acholi Lur people, from whom, legend declares, they separated to seek a country of their own, and having sought to encroach on the land of the Kimam people who occupy the country north of Lake Kyoga, *i.e.*, north-west of Mount Elgon, they were thoroughly beaten and driven through the country, now uninhabited, west of Elgon, right down to the shores of Lake Victoria.

The surprise of a traveller who, fresh from

Europe, has never left the train on its journey from Mombasa, and now finds himself deposited in the midst of a grinning crowd of absolutely nude natives, must be great indeed. Yet that is just what he will find at Kisumu.

Nowhere are the Nilotic peoples very keen on clothing, but nowhere are they less keen than in Southern Kavirondo; and, of course, the question again crops up, What can be done with such a people? Here they are in teeming numbers, very industrious to supply their own scanty needs, rich in cattle, splendid in physique, in no danger from white competition, for, as I said at the beginning of this chapter, the western side of the Mau Escarpment is another climate to that of the Highlands of British East Africa.

Here we are in the tropics indeed, with all the discomforts, all the dangers incidental to a tropical country and climate ; and whilst the white man and Asiatic is able to live and supervise for a short time the work of others, they will never be able to look upon this part of Africa with such longing eyes as to cause the native any anxiety with respect to the land.

The question is, Can we cause him any anxiety at all ? Here is a vast population, touched by the Uganda Railway and the varied influences that represents, and yet quite untouched by any desire for progress in the way that the best kind of civilisation might suggest.

Nothing has been done by the Government to whet his appetite for progress; for taxation, whilst necessary, tends the other way, and no country will develop on taxation alone.

The native of British East Africa has not been utterly neglected, however, for since the year 1844, when the Church Missionary Society began work at Mombasa, the Christian missionary has been striving to improve his lot.

It was the agents of this Society that gave an impetus to the geographical enterprise that eventually led to the discovery of the great inland lakes and the source of the Nile. It was chiefly through this Society's efforts that the Parliamentary Committee of 1871 was obtained, which led to Sir Bartle Frere's Mission to Zanzibar in the following year. In 1874 Frere Town was established by the Rev. W. S. Price, and in 1875 five hundred slaves, rescued by H.M. cruisers, were handed over to him, and housed, fed, instructed, and trained to work for their living.

Since that time the work at Mombasa and Frere Town has been strengthened by additional workers, and other stations have been opened at Rabai, Giryama, Taita, Taveta, Ukamba, Nairobi, Kikuyu, and Kenya. Other sections of the

Christian Church have been awakened to a sense of responsibility and opportunity with regard to this part of the world, and good work has been and is being done by the Church of Scotland Mission established at Kibwezi in 1891 under the auspices of the Directors of the British East Africa Company, and some other missions of more recent date.

All education and industrial training offered to the native up to a little over a year ago was offered by these various missions, first initiated by the C.M.S.

Since 1907 a trading company has been established in British East Africa for the purpose of developing the native products. Being under Christian auspices, the native people come in for a share of attention, but I have not yet heard with what success.

The religious side of the white man's effort to help the native has certainly advanced during the last few years, for thirteen years ago there was nothing being done between Kibwezi and the Lake.

Let us not forget, however, that the neglect by the Christian Church of the various tribes we have been looking at in this and the last chapter, until the opening up of their countries by the railway, and the introduction of good

5

and bad — often very bad — civilisation, has
tended to make the work of the missionary a
thousandfold more difficult than it would have
been a few years ago.

The work of the C.M.S. at Mombasa and
Frere Town has always been somewhat difficult,
but with the great increase of trade it is
doubly so now, for like all seaports the temptations offered to the natives are of a specially
strong character, and we who know our Liverpool, London, Sunderland, and Tyneside will
understand and sympathise with those who are
tempted and those who are seeking to help
them.

It is a sad fact that much of the native
Christianity—if I may so express it—I mean, of
course, the native conception and reflection of
Christianity, has always suffered from the poor
example of nominal white Christians; and this
has been the more marked since the advent of
the Uganda Railway.

Shall I ever forget the sight I saw at Frere
Town and Rabai—which I suppose would be
impossible to-day—when crowds of people who
had themselves been slaves, and others who
were the descendants of slaves, welcomed us to
Africa as the ambassadors of Christ, joined with
us in intelligent worship of the Great God and
Father of us all, committed us by prayer into

His keeping, and prayed that the Holy Spirit would go with us into the very countries from which they themselves had been dragged by slave-traders, and enable us there to preach the gospel of all True Light and Life and Liberty, Jesus Christ?

This is the time of special temptation, special need, and special opportunity. Is the Church to expect the Government to do its duty and yet neglect her own?

Let us remember that Mohammedan traders from Abyssinia are meeting Mohammedan traders from Mombasa, and every Mohammedan trader is a missionary of the false prophet. Mohammedan interpreters for some reason or another are in every Government boma, and Mohammedan interpreters are no less missionaries. These men are not afraid to push into unknown countries, whilst we Christians are in danger of sitting on each other in one or two districts quite near to the railroad. These men are never ashamed or tired of propagating their faith, whilst to the average white man to mention the name of Jesus is supposed to be "bad form."

Now seems the time and opportunity to press in to British East Africa large forces of evangelists with cool heads and warm hearts, capable of co-operating with the Government to supply all necessary education without let or hindrance to their evangelistic misson. Should it ever come to a choice between evangelisation and education, for the sake of some proffered grant, then let the grant and the education go; but of this anon.

At present we are at Kisumu. We have travelled 584 miles, in as many days as it once took us months, and here we are without one man having dropped out; not a worry about food or water, wild beast or savage tribe : a marvel indeed! Let us be grateful and take off our hats to this monument of British enterprise, then turn our gaze upon another wonder for size, grandeur, and beauty—the Lake Victoria.

CHAPTER V

THE LAKE VICTORIA: ITS SURROUND-
INGS AND SCOURGE

First view of Lake Victoria—A sight to enrapture—Waiting
for breakfast—A picture from fairyland—The islanders
of Sese—A voyage of discovery—Life hanging by a thread
—From Uganda to German territory—Baganda influence
—Dangers of the sea—The Bavuma—Steamers—Area and
variety of Lake—A round trip—Sleeping sickness—Death
and desolation—Doctors A. R. and J. H. Cook—Sleeping
sickness means great suffering—Dangerous patients—
Spread of the disease—Cause of the tragedy—The tsetse
fly—The crocodile theory—Is there a cure?—Experiments
—A barrage over the Ripon Falls—Nearing Uganda.

MY first view of Lake Victoria was from a
high hill in Usoga, one morning at break
of day.

Placid and glittering, kissed by the slanting
rays, dotted with innumerable islands, and
backed by mainland that at one point appeared
to be a grassy lawn, at another a cultivated
garden, at another a frowning headland, and

at another an inviting sylvan retreat; it was a picture to enrapture and remember for ever.

At closer range this great fresh-water sea, nearly 4,000 feet above the Indian Ocean, was no less charming, and infinitely more interesting, with quaint inhabitants on its shores and in its waters.

There, within a stone's throw, for all the world like a log of wood, lies a great lazy crocodile, waiting for the breakfast it is all too certain to get, for the cattle will soon come down to drink, and the younger ones are careless. Or, maybe, it has heard the rhythmic splash of paddles keeping time to the spirited chanting, albeit in a minor key, of some delightful folk-song being sung in the distance. It seems to know that we are waiting for the singers, and listlessly follows our example until around a jutting promontory comes into view a picture that might have dropped from fairyland, at which the crocodile immediately vanishes out of sight.

A flotilla of canoes such as we have never seen before, long and graceful, coloured red with earth, and prows adorned with the horns of antelope. Each vessel is propelled by twenty paddlers or more, who, the moment they catch sight of us, put additional zest into both song and work, and send their frail-looking craft skimming towards us.

They are the islanders of Sese, a populous group, situate to the north-west of the Lake; and they are also the subservient sailor-men of Uganda, who have been sent with part of that kingdom's navy to carry us a six days' voyage from the shore of Kavirondo on the east, to Uganda in the north.

They run their canoes into shallow water and jump overboard heedless of danger, until there is a shriek and a tremendous noise of splashing and shouting, to the consternation of the European onlookers, who are certain that some tragedy has happened, until they learn later that only a portion of a man's clothing had been secured by the crocodile. The man was badly scared and the rest were more careful.

All loads are quickly put aboard; the Europeans given places of honour under a thatched canopy temporarily erected in the bow, and the voyage begins—a voyage of discovery.

The traveller is naturally interested in the vessel that carries him, and he is considerably disconcerted to learn in the first place that it literally hangs together by a mere thread. He learns also that these dusky mariners are very human, and immensely enjoy the knowledge

that to suddenly stop paddling and punctuate
their song by a mighty thud with the paddles
on the side of the canoe, which makes it shiver
again, increases the white man's nervousness
about himself, and his respect for their bravery.
These preliminaries, however, are soon over,
and the European enough at ease with men
and boat and sea to enable him to secure such
information as the following :—

It takes fourteen days to travel by canoe
from Uganda in the north to German territory
in the south.

The Basese, from whom the canoe men are
drawn, are the people who inhabit the group of
islands already mentioned. They were con-
quered by the people of Uganda and made
tributary to them.

Baganda chiefs look upon the islands as their
property, and one, with the rank and office of
admiral, is lord over all. He is responsible for
organising the islanders and their canoes into
a navy, to be used by the Baganda on their
many marauding expeditions.

The Basese build the canoes and are allowed
to cut timber for this purpose in the forests of
Uganda. There I have often seen them, hewing
with their insignificant axes giant trees from
each of which they secured only two boards ;
all the rest was waste. The boards were

thinned and bent and sewn together with
the fibre of a palm-tree, which lasts a considerable time, but has been known to
give way and allow the keel board to drop
out at an inconvenient distance from the
shore.

Even with such a liability to dissolution,
the canoe on the Victoria Nyanza is an
advance on the primitive dug-out, still generally used on Lakes Kyoga, Albert, and Albert
Edward.

Nothing will induce our paddlers to face the
open sea; they know its moods too well—its
sudden squalls, its terrible storms that lash
its ripples into mountainous billows that would
at once engulf their cockle-shells. They make
for shore at the first sign of "weather"; and,
of course, the traveller must encamp on land
at night. Here he makes the acquaintance
of Africa's scourge, the mosquito; and more
likely than not he will receive a nocturnal
visit from the hippopotamus which in the daytime is too shy to seek exercise and sweet
potatoes.

Only a passing glimpse of Usoga's luxuriant
shores is possible, but it is necessary to visit
en route the group of islands known as the
Buvuma Islands, lying to the north-east of the
Lake.

Less than ten years ago this group, like that
of Sese, was thickly populated; but whilst the
Basese had become subservient to Baganda, the
Bavuma, being a hardy, warlike, and independent folk, had held their own against the repeated
attacks of the people from the mainland, and
not until the Baganda were assisted by Stanley
and Williams were these islanders the least sub-
dued.   To travellers they were kind, peaceable,
and hospitable.

Other islands were met with, lying off the
shore of Kyagwe, Uganda's south-eastern province, and a great deal might be written about
the flora and fauna of some of these beauty
spots; but, alas! one absorbing interest over-
shadows all others, for the islands and mainland
is in the grip of a terrible scourge—the sleeping
sickness—a sorrowful reason for the passing
away of the old sights and sounds that made
Lake Victoria a scene of never-failing interest.
Another, and happier, reason why the old
method of traversing the Lake has passed away
is that more up-to-date craft are to be found;
and the traveller by the Uganda Railway has
but to step from his carriage on to a hand-
somely found Government steamer—one of four
now plying for freight and passengers between
the railway terminus and the countries bordering the Nyanza.   By one steamer, which leaves

THE HOME OF THE TSETSE FLY.

Kisumu every fortnight, he may, if he wishes,
make a tour of a thousand miles. It will take
him south to Mwanza in German territory, then
west to Bukoba, north to Entebbe, east to Jinja
near the Ripon Falls, and thence to Kisumu
again.

Such a tour will give a good idea of the Lake's
vast area of 40,000 square miles ; the variety in
scenery and vegetation ; whilst the fish, crocodiles, and hippopotami will always keep interest
alive.

By another steamer, which awaits the weekly
" up " train, it is possible to cross direct to
Uganda; and this is now the natural route for
all who wish to get into speedy touch with
the official, business, or missionary life of that
country; but let us linger by the way, and see
for ourselves some results of this awful disease
of sleeping sickness, unknown to Uganda or
East Africa ten years ago.

It meets us at rail-head, and if we travel
southward we find that it has been before us.
It has decimated the population, and is spread-
ing still further south, in spite of every precaution of English and German specialists.
Northward its ravages have been even more
appalling, because of the greater population it
had to work amongst; and as we march through
Kavirondo and Usoga to the Ripon Falls where

we may take the ferry to Uganda, we pass through silent wastes which, less than ten years ago, were teeming with population. The same scenes of desolation and death are to be met with all round the Uganda shores of the Lake, and on all the islands.

The men who made and paddled the canoes have been almost totally wiped out of existence, for not an island has escaped. Death, death, death everywhere; and death preceded by heart-rending suffering.

Writing of one of the Buvuma Islands, situate near to Usoga, the "Uganda Notes" says: "Bugaya is best known as a port of call for the steamers, where firewood is taken on board. At one time the island had a dense population; a few years ago the chief, Muzito, was capable of putting 2,300 fighting-men in the field; and the people were so crowded that each man had his plot of ground marked out for him—a long strip, some three or four yards in width and perhaps half a mile or more in length. These plots were marked off by stones laid in a line, and no one was allowed to dig in another's plot. The stones still remain, a melancholy mark of past prosperity, but the gardens are, for the most part, indistinguishable from a field. The whole island has a deserted appearance. Where, a few years ago, there were 1,900 houses occupied, there are now hardly 200. In one shamba (garden village) there stood 200 native huts; now only 6 of these are tenanted. In another of 170 huts, only 2 remain; in a third of 250 houses there is left a solitary one. In another shamba, high up on a hill, of 70 huts, there is now not a single one occupied. Nor is it that the people have left: they seem to prefer to die in their homes; and very few, if any, have left the island."

The same story is true along the coast of the mainland. Villages I once knew well have passed out of existence, and, where houses remain, the people are dead. In one instance where the huts were standing I approached those having evidences of occupation; indeed, the owner of one sat at the door, and I wished to ask him the distance to the Lake. He sat as a native does in sickness or sorrow—with his arms resting on his knees, and his head bowed down. I gave him the customary salutation and rested my hand upon him, when my boys, in sudden terror, besought me to leave the place. I asked them why, and candidly confess I was somewhat startled when they informed me that the man from whom I was seeking information was a corpse. Alone and untended, he had passed away just before my arrival—the last of his village probably to succumb to the awful affliction from which they all think it useless to flee.

I think I am right in saying that sleeping sickness was first observed in Uganda by the Doctors A. R. and J. H. Cook, of the C.M.S. Hospital at Namirembe, in the year 1901; and from that time these two exceptionally clever and self-denying men have been untiring in their efforts to find a cure and to alleviate the sufferings of their patients.

To many the fact that the patients suffer is a great surprise, because, misled by the name— sleeping sickness—they suppose the people are simply attacked by drowsiness and quietly sleep away.

How very different is what actually happens! Lassitude, drowsiness, swollen glands, severe pains in head and chest; emaciation comparable to phthisis condition; restlessness, pain in stomach and abdomen; hallucinations; inability to control one's actions, so that the patient is liable to become a mental, moral, and physical wreck—a terror to himself and the neighbourhood in which he resides.

In some cases the development of the disease is very rapid, whilst others linger for years after having been declared affected.

It will be easily understood with what anxiety such a plague has been studied by the authorities, and how all concerned have longed for a cure. Everything possible has been done by the Government doctors—noble young fellows who have risked their lives—and, in one instance, Lieut. Tullock gave his life in seeking to trace the course of the disease.

However the disease came to Lake Victoria, all are agreed that it came from the west. It is also generally agreed that the enmity of the various tribes made it impossible for people to pass from one district to another until the European nations apportioned Africa, when the Pax Britannica made it possible for travellers to come in from the west and bring with them, first the jigger pest—which in 1897 had not reached Mombasa, but to-day is busy in India—and then the sleeping sickness disease which has done such havoc, as we have seen, and is now making its way to Lake Tanganyika and the life of British Central Africa.

What causes the tragedy? is the general question, and one not very easy to answer; for the presence in the cerebro-spinal fluid, or in the blood of a patient, of a minute worm-like object —a trypanosome or trypanosoma discovered by Dr. Castellani—which sets up a condition akin to cerebro-spinal fever or meningitis, is really no answer to the idea behind the question, "What is the cause?"

It has been conclusively demonstrated by Colonel Bruce and his assistants that the connecting link between the trypanosome in the patient and the source of the disease is a kind of tsetse fly—the *Glossina palpalis*—about which there can be no mistake, for although no bigger than the ordinary house-fly, it can be picked out at once because of the peculiar way in which it crosses its wings when at rest.

The habits of these flies have been carefully observed by the doctors at great personal risk and inconvenience. It has been found that they live in the trees at the side of a lake or on the banks of a river, and that they lay their eggs on the ground near to the water's edge. It has been proved that, like bees, they "home" to a certain district, and it is hoped that by killing off the eggs, cutting down trees, and generally making a district less favourable to propagation the pest may be cleared out.

Still the question remains, "What is the source of the disease?" The fly carries the germ, the trypanosome is the evidence of the germ having been propagated, but whence comes the germ apart from already infected patients, and, consequently, what is the real cause of the disease?

In the year 1905 I heard that crocodiles had been suggested by some English doctor, and my informant was equally certain that hippopotami were to be taken into account; consequently I was much interested to read that Professor Koch, the German specialist, in his account of the subject before the German Emperor, professed his acceptance of the crocodile theory, *i.e.*, that the fly feeds on the blood of the crocodile and carries from the crocodile to the human being the germ of sleeping sickness, and that the first thing to do is to exterminate the crocodile.

Whether this theory is correct or not, it seems somewhat strange that no effort has been made to exterminate such a pest and menace to human life as the crocodile. For the theory itself we must remember that crocodile, tsetse fly, and native were living close together before the year 1900—then why was there no sleeping sickness? The germ of that disease was probably lacking, and was brought when trade routes and inter-tribal communications were opened by the Pax Britannica. If so, how did it get to the islands first?

Such questions are of far less importance than the next one, namely, How can we destroy the trypanosomes in the patient? English Government doctors, civil and military, doctors from the Liverpool School of Tropical Medicine, the medical missionaries Cook, German and Belgian doctors have all been labouring with patience, zeal, and wonderful self-abnegation in their endeavour to answer this question, and with a certain amount of success, but, alas! without securing a permanent cure. To be inoculated by the fly—*Glossina palpalis*—is to receive sentence of death.

Small doses of arsenic hypodermically injected was one of the first experiments, but it caused the patients a good deal of agony, some of them begging to be allowed to die. An atoxyl, an admixture of arsenic and aniline, was used at Liverpool and London, and then tried in Uganda. This treatment has not only given relief, but has caused the trypanosomes to disappear, for a time, from the blood. Whether, as has been suggested, their reappearance can be prevented and a permanent cure effected by a further administration of a salt of mercury remains to be proved. After long delay the Government decided to deal with the affected areas. Segregation camps have been established and the people removed from the Lake shore. All living in camps are placed under the atoxyl treatment, and the percentage of deaths has been low.

Unfortunately a serious famine has interfered with the good work in Usoga, and thousands of deaths have taken place that may or may not have been connected with sleeping sickness.

All shrubs and trees are being cut down near to the Lake side, and large tracts are being put under sweet potato cultivation. In this way the fly is deprived of its home, and will, it is hoped, die out. The eggs of the fly can only be effectively dealt with by raising the level of the Lake, and although we have not yet reached the Nile, I may, apropos of this subject of sleeping sickness, express the wish that soon we shall see a barrage built across the Ripon Falls, and thus be able to regulate the height of the Lake in such a way as to deal with a pest like the "Kivu" fly by drowning out its young.

Now let us continue our journey across the Lake in what is more like a trim, well-kept private yacht than a trade steamer. Everything on board is spick and span; and the dusky sailor-men move about in an alert fashion that speaks well for the kindness and ability of their officers. On deck and below, all is in such order that the voyage from rail-head to Uganda is far too short. A well-cooked meal, a clean bunk, and a comfortable bath is a great luxury compared with old methods of crossing; and the wonder and expectation of the traveller are heightened when he learns that the brisk youth who oils the engine in such a business-like fashion is only an ordinary peasant lad of Uganda, the shores of which he is fast approaching.

A GOLDEN-CRESTED CRANE.

112

CHAPTER VI

UGANDA: FLORA, FAUNA, AND OTHER THINGS

Beautiful Entebbe — Capital of civil administration—The
native opinion—A mistake—The road to Mengo—No
advance—Appearance of country—A large garden—Cotton
cultivation—Value of cotton export—Climatic conditions
—Extent of Uganda Protectorate—Agricultural possibilities
—Rubber, cultivated and indigenous—A cheap concession
—Timber—Wild animals—A bull buffalo—Death of Dr.
Densham—A native report of a lion hunt—Insect pests—
Mosquitoes and malaria—Value and use of mosquito nets
—Danger of rest-houses—Necessity of change—Protection
against sun—Blackwater fever.

BEAUTIFUL, perfectly beautiful! is the
verdict of whoever views Entebbe,
Uganda's port, from the deck of the steamer.
And, if possible, more perfectly beautiful when
viewed from certain vantage-points on shore.

Well-built brick bungalows, substantial offices,
up-to-date stores, a botanical garden, a bank,
a pretty English church, good roads (in dry

weather), and a Government House, all bespeak the capital, and such it is, for here is the seat of Uganda's civil administration, very beautifully but very mistakenly situate at the end of a narrow promontory from which the untutored native says the white man is ever ready to flee in time of danger.

No doubt the idea of safety was in the military mind that chose the situation; but at this time of day there seems little to recommend it save the fact that the steamer from Kisumu calls once a week. It is not the real capital of Uganda: it is not at all central either for trade or administration; it has cost much to make it tolerably healthy, and it will cost more to keep it so.

The whole promontory, with the exception of the township, which has been cleared of trees and scrub, is infested with the sleeping-sickness fly, and we must travel further inland to gather any true idea of Uganda country.

A broad, well-cultivated road has been made from Entebbe to the native capital of Mengo; and the journey of twenty miles may be done in ricksha, bullock wagon (if you have a day or two to spare), or on foot. At no distant date it will be done by motor-car; but even bullock wagons are in advance of this and other roads, which are only kept clean by repeated cultivation. This means that one length may have a beautifully smooth surface and the next be like a ploughed field.

Streams and swamps are crossed by the most primitive bridges which last but a very short time, and soon become greater hindrances than helps to traffic; and it is no uncommon sight to see stranded wagons, or the traction engine of an enterprising firm, waiting for help to be delivered from the slough that makes the most optimistic business man inclined to despond.

This condition of things is general throughout the Protectorate, and with the exception of an effort to utilise the present native-made roads for the purpose of growing rubber-trees along each side, and to build culverts on the road leading north, no advance has been made on the native idea of providing for pedestrian and vehicular traffic. A month's neglect is sufficient to make one of the present roads invisible, in a little longer it is impassable; and not much more time would be necessary to blot out every trace of an occupation that counts its success by a development of taxation.

Let us not quarrel, however, with the only kind of road at our disposal, but use it to see what can be seen.

Long grass, with an emphasis on the *long*, banana groves, hill and dale, are the predominant features of the district through which we are passing; and these features are common to the whole kingdom of Uganda.

The hills have the appearance of having been sat on before they reached their proper height; and the valleys are as a rule noisome swamps.

Travellers marvel at the wonderful fertility of the country and at the extent under cultivation. It almost appears to be one huge garden chiefly growing bananas and plantains. This is as it should be, since plantains are the staple food of the people; but here and there are evidences that the land is able to produce more than plantains, and may indeed have a future interesting and important to the working men of England.

Huge tracts are under cotton cultivation, to which the natives have taken most kindly. They easily understand its requirements, and it gives a quick return. It has been found that even without European supervision the Muganda is able to prepare the land, sow the seed, and bring a raw material to market, which will compare for length of staple and general quality with any in the world.

So keen was and is the desire to grow cotton that for a time there seemed as if there might be a glut upon the market, owing to the lack

of ginning machinery; but this difficulty has
been quite overcome by the enterprise of two
trading companies which have recently erected
machinery in the native capital to enable them
to deal with any quantity.

In 1904 the cotton export was valued at a
few hundreds of pounds. Last year its value
was at least £50,000.

The soil, rainfall, and general climatic conditions of nearly the whole of Uganda Protectorate—which stretches from Mount Elgon in
the east to the Mountains of the Moon in the
west, and from Gondokoro on the Nile in the
north, to the German East African frontier
on Lake Victoria—seem to specially fit it to
become one of the best cotton-producing countries in the world. It is not necessary to
labour the advantage such a thing will be to
Lancashire.

The castor-oil plant is in evidence everywhere,
as is also the tobacco plant, but neither of them
have yet been taken in hand by experts with
a view to development and exportation. The
same may be said of coffee, which can be seen
growing in the various banana gardens, and
growing so well that berries from an untended
plant were declared very fair quality on the
London market.

Ground nuts and chillies are grown in great

quantities, but chiefly in the east and north-east parts of the Protectorate.

The country is rich in fibres, but probably for lack of patience there is no cultivation or preparation of these, for which from £30 to £100 per ton might be procured in London.

On every plantain grove there may be seen the tree from which the natives strip the bark which, when beaten with their hard-wood grooved mallets, dried in the sun, and sewn together, is used as the clothing of the people.

Here and there we get a glimpse of garden stuff that reminds us of the homeland, and cannot but marvel at a soil and climate that does so well for cabbage or cactus, tobacco, or tomato.

We have already seen the rubber-trees planted at the roadside, but there are also trees and vines indigenous to the country ; and one syndicate, the Mabira Forest Company, has secured the right to deal with a large tract of land in the Province of Kyagwe, on which they estimate there are 2,000,000 *Funtumia elastica* trees from which they expect at once an annual return of £137,000.

I understand that this concession was made in the first place for a few hundred pounds.

Other companies have been formed for the purpose of working rubber plantations, and one or two private settlers are at work putting in trees; but they will have to wait from five to ten years, according to the kind of tree, before they can expect a yield of latex.

Uganda is not very rich in timber, but there are three or four very good kinds available for all general local needs, and our journey takes us through the exquisite little forests from which these are procured.

Here probably for the first time we come across the wild animal life of Uganda: perhaps only an impertinent little rascal of a monkey with his short grey coat, brown tail, and lively chatter, but not unlikely a leopard, lion, or buffalo may be met with, in spite of the large amount of cultivation and population.

On my last journey to Mengo, the native capital, a solitary bull buffalo dashed across my path, quite near to a native village. He had been driven out from the herd, and was consequently a very dangerous character—an animal to beware of, yet much sought after by sportsmen. It was just such an animal that killed an able and promising official of the Administration, Dr. Densham, whom I knew well in Usoga, and whose brother is well known in the town where I am now writing this.

It seems almost incredible that the king of beasts should also lurk about the capital, but within the last few months two lions were killed without a day's march, and I append the story of the hunt given in *Uganda Notes* by Ham Mukasa, who wrote that quaint book, "With Uganda's Katikiro in England."

"We were told that the lions had roared the last night from Kasai in Bukerere, Kajungujwe's place At first we did not believe that, but the next morning the people who came from Bukoba told us that they had seen their footmarks on the road at Kasai. But on August 1st they (the lions) walked hard a good journey, and reached Mukono and went by the road which goes from behind my fence and leads to the market. They reached the place where my cows live, about 260 yards from my fence. Then they found the cows in the house by themselves; the herdsmen were not there, they were waiting for food in the fence so that they might go back to the cows.

"At half-past eleven my big dog Blanco barked loudly, so I understood that it was the lions. We were at table, H. Luganda and I, and I told him that my dog was raising alarm for the lions, for they had come, and I heard a voice like that of a door which is knocked; but when the herdsmen were going back they met the lions in the middle of the road eating the cow which they had killed, and they roared very loudly to make the herdsman run, but he did not run, for he had a little boy with him, and the lions were two. Then that herdsman for his bravery did not run, he lifted his arm, the lions ran away from the cow and he raised the alarm and we all heard him.

"Then all my boys went at a great rate and found the cowman standing where the cow was which was killed. The lions had eaten all the chest and entrails and lungs, the stomach only was left. Then the boys went into the house in which the cows live to see whether they were all killed. They found one cow hiding at the end of the house with her calf, and they brought her from the house and they could not see the others and we thought they had gone mad and we would see them the next day, so we stopped (searching).

"But when I came out of the house I went there with my gun and two boys and I stood where the cow was which was killed while the boys were looking for the others. Then H. Luganda saw me and said, 'Sir, do not stand on the cow that is lying in the road.' In that time the lions were with me, one on my right and the other on my left, lying on the sides of the road in the jungle. One of them was lying eight yards from where I was and the other ten yards. They were quiet and did not breathe hard, but my big dog heard them and started twice and looked either side. It was very dark and it was going to rain. Then I beat my two drums in the way of war drum beat. All the people who live near came and I took them to see that they (the lions) had killed the cow, and we found them eating again. When they (the lions) saw us they ran away, and we left the cow which they had killed in order that they might eat a good deal and not go far away so that we might hunt them the next morning. Then I told all the people that when they would hear the drum the next morning they should be ready for hunting.

"When the morning broke the drums were beaten and all the people did what I told them; they came before me and said they would do their best to kill the lions. I sent to the doctor at Kyetume to ask him whether he would go for hunting. Then he sent Mukusu, and gave him a large Masai spear. Then Mukusu brought people from the Camp at Kyetume, about a hundred men or more, and they saw the lions in the little wood which is near my place. Then I stayed in the market-place and Mr. Baskerville found me there when he came to congratulate me about what had happened last night; and he was sorry he could not go with us to hunt for he had work to do in the church, for it

was Sunday. So he remained to take prayers
with the women and children, on that day all
the teachers were hunters. Y. Kaizi and
H. Luganda were with the hunters, and the
Sunday service was held by Mr. Baskerville,
and it was he who prayed for us on that day.

"Now when I was sitting in the market-place
many people came with their hunting nets, then
I appointed Mukusu to dress (distribute?) the
people so that I might go after him. While I
was there Captain Gray came with two guns.
Then we looked for them (the lions) very much
and we could not see them, and Dr. Gray was
tired and went home at 1 o'clock in the afternoon, for there were many pigs in the forest
and we could not tell the lions' footmarks from
the pigs'.

"When I saw that the people were very tired
and every one thought in his own way and
were disputing with one another that the
lions had passed (but they were left behind us
where we thought that they were not) then I
sent S. Mulowoza to examine well, and when
he came back he told me that they were
behind in the little wood. Then I told all the
people to go home for the darkness was drawing
near, at half-past five, and I told them that if
we could not kill them (the lions), the next
morning we would take out food with us and go

after the lions to Unga, where they came from. And they all agreed to that and went home.

"At ten o'clock in the night the lions came out of their hiding-place and went to the cow-house where they had killed the cow and peeped into it, but it was empty, and they went down and passed by my station at Nasuti. When they reached the little wood which is in front of the station they went in there and stayed there till half-past three when they went up in the circle road which leads to Kauga and reached the porters' compound, they passed quite near the porch, four yards from the house to the place where they passed. And they went down into the forest Lyajah and across the river to Kirowoza and they reached the place known as 'Balimumperamukyalo' in the Sekibobo's garden where there is a little wood in which they made their den. There were many little animals, about ten; perhaps they were going to eat them.

"I sent my men who are very clever in tracking animals, and I appointed my headmen whose name is N. Siga and they tracked them and saw closely the place where they had left some of their fur. Then one of my men whose name is I. Kisajaki came back and told us all that they had seen. I was at Kauga, my old *embuga*, and I told every chief with his people to promise before me whether they had determined to kill the lions. After their promises I asked them to discuss how we should hunt the lions, for they had run away from us the previous day because of their cunning. Then every one said what he thought was right, while I was silent to see if they were all right. When they had spoken I picked out what were right and I drew them a map and I prepared the people in lines so that they might fight well against the lions. Then I stopped every one to advise me and they did what I told them. Then I appointed Namutwe to line them up. But the chiefs had few people, a lot of them came afterwards and found us hunting.

"When we reached the place where the lions were I prepared the people in their places, and during that time Dr. Rendle of Kampala arrived. Then afterwards we planned to cut off a part of the place where the lions were, and I sent Siga and four beaters with him and they went and cut off the part of the place where the lions were. But when they had walked eighty yards they found the lions sitting under a tree, and they both roared and the men attacked them, and the lions left them, one went on the right, and the other went on the left. Then the fighting began, the elder lion came direct at us without turning back, and we all aimed at him.

7

When he saw us he seemed as if he was told not to come to us, then he went half right and fell into the net. My man Kapere speared him in the chest and the spear went in one foot and one inch. When he rose up Sabagabo fired at him and Kopolo ran after him. When he turned to fight then he fired at him in the shoulder and he fell dead. He was wounded with forty-six wounds and he was killed at a quarter to three.

"This made us braver and happier, this was killed about twenty-five yards from the place where I was. I was afraid before, then I took heart.

"The other lion went up to Mukito's side and they shouted loudly when he tried to fall on to the net, and they stopped him and then he returned to us. He was afraid to come near us and he ran about twice before us like a dog. In that time you could not think that the lion was as big as a heifer. When I was going to aim at him while he was standing in one place thinking what he was going to do, the men who were with me objected saying that if I left my place the lion would pass there, only I should choose another instead of me. Then I chose Yoeri for he knows very well how to shoot, and he was made Corporal when he was with the Police. He went with Mulondo to shoot the lion where he was and he could not see it at first because of the shrubs, but when he examined well he aimed at him and shot him in the chest and the shot went through the skin on the other side. And he fell there and when he got up for his great strength he roared in a low tone like a leopard. And soon he rose and came in a great rage and fell into the net and fell on a man named Kijoje and bit his hand, but he did not hurt him badly for he was no longer strong because of the wound. When the lion was running Namutwe shot him and he fell and was speared with eighty-four spears by the people. He was killed at three o'clock in the afternoon and fell on my left hand about thirty-five yards from the place where I was. And they told us that there was a third lion, and we went back to the place where the lions were, but there was no other, they had heard the thunder!

"We also killed nine small animals and a big snake in one place.

"HAM MUKASA, SEKIBOBO."

Not a bad article surely from a native pen!

The traveller need not anticipate much danger or inconvenience from wild animals, for as a rule they seem quite as anxious to get away from a human being as he does to keep clear of them. His real danger is from the multitudinous insect pests that infest the countries west of the Mau Escarpment and make them utterly impossible for white colonisation.

Chief among the pests is the mosquito, which is responsible for more sickness and deaths than anything else. Far too long, for lack of scientific knowledge, it has been accepted and treated as nothing more than an inconvenience, but now men are well aware that the species of mosquito known as the *Culex anopheles* is the medium by which the minute animalcule named Malaria is transmitted from the blood of one person to another.

There is no need to expatiate on the symptoms of malaria—the less travellers know about it experimentally, the better; and the only way to keep clear of it is to keep clear of mosquitoes. Do not sit out on an unprotected verandah after sundown, and do not sleep without a net.

Of course I mean that the net should be let down each evening; it should have a small mesh, and it should not be torn. Such advice is not superfluous; for I well remember sharing the room of a friend, and in the dead of night being nearly frightened to death by a series of terrible howls close to my ear. I was confident that a leopard had got in and collared my friend, until I heard him calmly assure me that it was only his dog had put its head through a hole in the mosquito net, and could not withdraw it.

That was evidently the chronic condition of that mosquito net, for on another occasion I heard him recounting to a new-comer an experience he had with a large bat. It wakened him, and when he sat up it was hanging to the inside of his net. His disgust seemed unbounded when the new-comer suggested that the mesh of the net must be rather a large one.

Another real danger meets the traveller as he passes through Uganda, and meets him where he least expects it, viz,, in the sheds that have been most thoughtfully erected in the various wayside camps as shelters from the sun's rays in the heat of the day. These rest-houses were undoubtedly a great boon to the traveller; it was perfect luxury to find the shelters ready in storm or heat; and they became so popular that some Europeans ceased even to carry a tent, and used the rest-house by night as well as during the day, until it was proved that the common occurrence of Spirillum, or relapsing fever, amongst Europeans—a fever seldom fatal but exceedingly trying because of its frequent recurrence and high temperature—was due to the bite of a tick which was found to infest these shelters.

These same camps are overrun by another scourge—the jigger; that nasty little insect which burrows under the toe-nail, forms a sac, lays its eggs, and causes a good deal of pain and inconvenience to the individual.

Like sleeping sickness, this pest has travelled from West Africa; but let us hope that sleeping sickness will not make such rapid progress on its journey. Thirteen years ago the jigger was six hundred miles from the East Coast of Africa; to-day it is working havoc in India.

Ants—myriads of them meet one at every turn: white ants, black ants, red ants. Rats, big and little; mice of various sorts; flies that seem to be made in all sorts and sizes; bees, wasps, and hornets innumerable, and all warranted to sting without provocation; spiders, that strike terror to your very soul, seek close acquaintance; whilst lice are larger in Uganda than perhaps anywhere else; and the fleas are renowned for their ability to jump and power to make their presence known.

Snakes are uncomfortably common; we have seen them drop from the ceiling and peer from the walls of our mud house, yet I have never known a European attacked by one.

The croaking of frogs, and the " cheep, cheep " of countless beetles and other insects give warning of the closing day when bats and owls and

wheel birds come forth to assist the mosquitoes
keep the night-watches.

To many, the insect life is more trying than
the climate ; and both together make it imperative for the white man to seek a change after
very few years' service.

The atmosphere may seem all that is desirable,
but imperceptibly one loses energy, becomes
"nervy," and susceptible to any disease going.
It is well, therefore, to take plenty of exercise,
keep the head, eyes, *and body* well protected from
the sun, understand, as far as possible, tropical
diseases, causes and cures, and so keep clear of
insect life which may be responsible for some
other diseases not yet understood.

One such disease is that known as Hæmoglo-
binuric, or blackwater, fever, which has recently
been rather common with a high percentage of
fatal results among Europeans.

The real cause of this fever is not known ; but
it has been suggested that frequent attacks of
malarial fever predispose the patient to blackwater fever. Another suggestion is that the
constant use of quinine is responsible for the
breaking down of certain blood-vessels in the
kidneys.

Against these are the statements of reliable
men who declare that they have never had
malaria but have had attacks of blackwater ;

and for the second suggestion, that only by the constant hypodermic injections of large doses of quinine was the temperature lowered and the blackwater stopped.

Although no positive cure has been declared, it is interesting to note that out of thirteen cases, Dr. A. R. Cook, of the C.M.S. Hospital, Uganda, lost only one, and that one hopeless from the beginning because of complications. His brother, Dr. J. H. Cook, has been equally successful, and their medicine and method of treatment have been supplied to every mission station, Anglican and Roman Catholic, throughout the Protectorate.

THE KING OF UGANDA'S OFFICIAL DRUMMER.

134

CHAPTER VII

UGANDA: ITS PAST CONDITION

The amazement of travellers—Stanley's expectations—Con-
centrated cruelty—Mtesa's smiling welcome—The people
of Uganda—System of government—Social life—The
Bahuma—Native wine—The other side of the picture—
Mtesa, the causer of tears—Mwanga, a cruel son of an evil
father—Alexander Mackay—"The dark places of the
earth"—Effect of missionary effort—Expulsion of missionaries—Murder of Bishop Hannington—Growth of
Mohammedanism—Influence of native Christians—
Rebellion, capture and death of King Mwanga—King
David—Light and liberty.

FROM the days of Speke and Grant to the
present moment, every traveller who
enters Uganda is amazed.

To reach it he has travelled through other
countries and seen many peoples, but none just
like these. From the coast to the Lake it was
more or less chaotic, untutored savagery; but
now he is face to face with a highly developed
system of feudal government as an oasis in the

desert. This struck Stanley on his first visit, and he never ceased to wonder and express his high hopes and expectations of such a country and people ; and it is no exaggeration to say that could he have had his great desire to revisit Uganda, he would have realised how much his hopes and expectations were fulfilled.

Little, however, did the Christian world realise in the year 1875, when Stanley sent his memorable challenge, that behind the smiling welcome of King Mtesa there lay a concentration of cruel savagery unknown to the barbarian peoples so utterly despised by the Baganda.

The picture presented was that of an enlightened King whose very name meant "the arranger of affairs," presiding over a well-ordered and industrious population of Negroids, *i.e.*, a people neither wholly negro nor wholly Hamitic, but an admixture of the two.

The whole country was divided into provinces, and at the head of each province a chief appointed by, and directly answerable to, the King. These chiefs formed the Council of the country, and were presided over by the King.

The provinces were subdivided, and held in such a way that every piece of land and every soul could be accounted for. No one was independent, for each was owned by some one else who had powers of life and death.

The marvellous completeness of an organisation that could, at the sound of the King's war drum, transform the whole adult male population into an army ready to march whithersoever his Majesty commanded, was no more wonderful than the ordinary sights and sounds of this country as seen by the early travellers and missionaries.

They saw an alert and intelligent people of a colour ranging from light brown to jet black ; with good physique and generally well-proportioned bodies, except in the case of some women whose enormous hips and breasts were supposed to be signs of beauty.

There were no signs of mutilation for the purpose of adornment, such as is common among the surrounding tribes with their filed and missing teeth, elongated ear-lobes, perforated lips, tongues, and noses, and cicatrisation of the body.

With the exception of the little girls, who wore a plaited waistband of coloured grasses, the whole population was clothed with graceful and becoming garments made from the bark of a wild fig-tree. The work of stripping the bark, beating it with grooved mallets of hard-wood, drying it in the sun and then sewing the pieces together, was that of the men, who, because of this labour, have quite naturally taken the position of the nation's dressmakers.

The men were also responsible for the fighting and house-building, whilst the woman saw to it that the food supply was never short. The wife was the gardener of the family, and right well she did her work, skilfully tending the plantain grove which surrounded her little hut made of poles and thatch, and also cultivating the sweet potato, Indian corn or maize, peas, beans, and other vegetables necessary to make a change of diet.

With great care and cleanliness the green but ripe plantains were peeled, tied in leaves and boiled in the earthenware pot, then turned out and mashed—squeezed would be a better word—into a hot mass of pulp, which was served on fresh, clean leaves strewn on the ground.

No woman sat and ate with her lord and master, but received his commendation if the mass was good, and any pieces he might pass to her as she stood behind him. His feast was for himself and any male guests he chose to invite, and the women fed together with their children.

Politeness was noticeable as a marked trait of the Baganda character, and little courtesies between a man and his wife or wives were never neglected. The ladies turned out to meet and welcome their lord returning from some raid in Usoga, Unyoro, or Toro; and from the congratulations heaped upon him it might have been supposed that he, and he alone, had won the battle.

"Webale! webale nyo ge! kulika musaja wange!" ("Well done, very well done you! bravo, my man!") resounded on every side; to which the gentleman replied "Awo!" ("Thank you!").

The man on his side never forgot to congratulate his wife on her cultivation and cooking; and these courtesies played an important part in the native life.

Some of the houses seen were of the most primitive character, resembling nothing so much as a haycock; but others, though of a curious shape to the eyes of a European, were always of great interest because of the beautiful way in which they had been thatched—a branch of work for which the Baganda have always been rightly famed.

Fowls, goats, sheep, and cattle seemed plentiful; and for the safe keeping of the first three the children were held responsible—not the progeny of the householders, for the Baganda, supposing it impossible to exact obedience from their own offspring, send them to be brought up by friends or relatives, whilst they make themselves responsible for the children of others and really bring them up very well.

The cattle were herded by a tribe of Hamitics, called Bahuma, who were practically slaves to the Baganda though related to the rulers and aristocracy of the neighbouring countries Unyoro and Ankole.

Apparently the people had all that heart could desire, and more than was good for them, for vast quantities of bananas were used to provide, not only the "Mubisi," or un-fermented sweet *wine* of the country, but also the intoxicant known as "Mwenge," made by adding millet seed to the "Mubisi."

To outward seeming, then, the picture was one of happy contentment. That slavery was customary, and that women were looked upon as inferior beings, was well known ; but it was inconceivable that the picture had another side almost too revolting to imagine or describe.

Mtesa and his chiefs were guilty of the most demoniacal practices, which account for the fact that the name by which he is known throughout the country to-day is not "Mtesa," the arranger of affairs, but "Mukabya," the causer of tears— a very appropriate name for the man who sold justice (!) to the highest bidder, brought cruelty to a fine art in the maiming of his victims, and wantonly murdered people to appease a passing whim or the spirits of his ancestors.

Never was the scripture, "the dark places of the earth are full of the habitations of cruelty," so fearfully illustrated as in the history of Uganda, and that within comparatively recent years, although we speak of them as the bad old days.

Succeeded by his son Mwanga, the natives and the missionaries hoped for better things, but were doomed to disappointment. Weak, cowardly, and vacillating, the son proved himself all too worthy a successor to his cruel father, and the burden of the people became almost more than they could bear.

For some years I was in daily contact with a man who had been Mwanga's playfellow, and bore the marks of such dangerous intimacy. He had been entrusted to collect the King's revenue in the Province of Kyagwe, and on his return a discrepancy was discovered between his statement and that of the district chief. Certain sheep and goats could only be accounted for on the supposition that the King's messengers had had a right royal time on the homeward journey. Undoubtedly a dereliction of duty, but hardly sufficient to warrant the cutting off both ears of the chief messenger with a sharpened reed.

One of my best native teachers was a man named Erisa, or Elisha—a big, fine man, who remembered Alexander Mackay, that splendid missionary, who did so much in his own quiet, plodding way to lay the foundation of the Church's successful work in Uganda. He remembered Mackay building the first brick house with panelled doors which were the wonder of all; but when I asked him to examine the house I was then building, it was most pathetic to see him *feel* his way over it. He was blind; his eyes had been gouged out and an ear cut off at the bidding of Mwanga, because the King's drink, for which Erisa—then an unbaptized youth—was responsible, was not ready to hand when his Majesty called for it.

Both these cases constantly before me, and another which may still be seen, made me thank God that the time had arrived when such barbarities were impossible.

The third case was that of a woman whom I saw trying to hoe some sweet potatoes. There were others assisting, who willingly threw down their hoes to see and touch the white man. This particular woman stood back from the rest, until I intimated my desire to speak with all, when she drew near and shocked me by the awful sight of a woman indeed, but one without hands or lips. These had been cut off by her owner for some trivial offence, and there she was, pitiful to behold, as, ashamed of her condition, she endeavoured to do a woman's work.

May I once more say "the dark places of the earth are full of the habitations of cruelty"? And such cruelty that, in comparison, the above cases are as nothing.

The missionary toil of early days was beginning to take effect, and the King, realising that the minds and lives of his immediate followers were being influenced by the Scriptures and the teaching of the missionaries, issued an edict to the effect that all reading must cease under penalty of death; and then began the trial of strength between light and darkness, right and wrong, cruel oppression and progressive liberty, which lasted as long as Mwanga was on the throne.

The old tortures and mutilations became more numerous, and to these were added the brutal murder of those who continued to read the Gospel in spite of the King's edict.

Of course, many fled the country and took their faith and teaching to the people of Ankole in the west; but others remained and sealed their faith with their blood.

The missionaries were made prisoners, thrown

into a small thatched hut, left without other food than the few bananas given to them by kindly passers-by, and finally taken down to the Lake and sent adrift in native canoes, after Walker had been stripped of his clothing.

I often wondered afterwards, when visiting King Mwanga along with one of these victims, now Archdeacon Walker, just what was passing in each man's mind. Mwanga certainly never seemed comfortable ; and how could he, remembering not only his treatment of Gordon and Walker, but also his murder of Bishop Hannington ?

With the expulsion of the missionaries, he seemed quite certain of the death of Christianity and the growth of Mohammedanism, or at any rate such crude and cruel features of Mohammedanism as appealed to him. Yet, strange to say, he had to depend upon the very lads and young men whom he had threatened with death and driven into exile to fight his battles and protect his throne and person from the Mohammedans who made periodic bids for the capture of the country.

For four years I lived in and near the capital of Mwanga ; was constantly in touch with him, and know something of the influence which the same lads—grown up as men, and, because of their reliability and integrity, made chiefs in the country—had over the life of the King.

He writhed under it, yet realised that for the stability of the country it was necessary; but eventually their determination to go a step further than the freedom of slaves and the extinction of cruelties was too much for his personal lusts, since they compelled him to expel from his presence the base characters who encouraged him in drink, treachery, and nameless vice. He rebelled against them and British influence, and the sequel was a lonely death on one of the Seychelle Islands.

So ended the conflict between light and darkness. The last representative of Uganda's pagan kings was buried in a far-off land, without the extravagant "Kitibwa" (honour) so dear to the heart of a Muganda.

No interminable procession with costly cloths to throw into the grave. No massacre of near relatives. No building of a national mausoleum on the site of the house in which the King had lived. No moving of the native capital to a place chosen by the new King. No processions such as he rejoiced to have, when the opportunity was taken by the new King, not only to view his predecessor's tomb and relics, but also to sacrifice a number of his followers.

How vividly I have heard men who accompanied Mwanga on one of the visits he paid to his father's tomb at Kasubi, describe with what pleasure he gave an order to his gun-bearers to follow him, carrying their loaded guns over the shoulder, and at his word pull the trigger and allow the charge to plough its way through the mass of humanity in the rear!

All this has gone, and not only because of the passing of Mwanga and his like, but because the Baganda as a nation have changed their point of vision. The "Lubare," or devil-worship, responsible for gross superstitions and much suffering, is now scarcely known in the kingdom.

"Le roi est mort, vive le roi!" ("The King is dead, long live the King!") And for once the people really meant what they cried : for their "Kabaka," or King, although only an infant a few months old, had been baptized Daudi (David), and was to be brought up a Christian.

Long ago the directors of the Imperial British East Africa Company presented King Mwanga with a chair which served as a throne, and took the place of the one made by the native carpenter. The latter chair, with that of his father Mtesa, King Mwanga gave me just before he rebelled against the British Administration, and they are both now used in the study of the Bishop of Uganda.

H.H. KING DAUDI (DAVID) CHWA (+).

To those who really knew Mwanga, nothing was more incongruous than to see him on his new throne, for just above his head was the carved motto, " Light and Liberty." The donors undoubtedly had their vision of things which to-day are being fulfilled, and the evidences of great advancement are thrust upon us as we make our way to the native capital of the present King, Daudi Chwa.

CHAPTER VIII

UGANDA: ITS PRESENT ADMINIS-TRATION

No Uganda Railway—Porterage system—No relief for British taxpayer—Sir H. H. Johnston—Provincial chiefs—Pax Britannica—One Governor suggested for East Africa and Uganda—Tropical diseases—Native development or revenue—King David at home—Native parliament—Regents—Sir Apolo Kagwa, K.C.M.G.—Native capabilities and possibilities—Chamber of Commerce and Labour problem—Road-making—Waste of labour—Transport facilities—Need for technical education—Military service—Strategic position of Uganda—The Right Hon. Winston Churchill and the Baganda.

ON nearing Mengo, we are surprised at the numberless porters leaving the capital for outlying stations, with loads of every description. We soon realise, however, that " Uganda Railway " is a misnomer; there is no railway in the country, and porterage is almost the only method of transport. I advisedly say " almost," because one or two private traders have recently introduced the bullock wagon with results far from satisfactory to either wagons or bullocks.

A closer acquaintance with the present system of government convinces us that the porterage system is only one indication that Uganda cannot be said to have advanced under British Administration—advanced, I mean, in such a way as to relieve the pockets of the British taxpayer, and, at the same time, so as to develop native character and self-support.

We have seen that in the days of King Mtesa the country was organised on feudal lines, by which the heads of provinces had power to try, fine, and, under certain limitations, kill.

This form of government was slightly altered by Sir H. H. Johnston when British Commissioner; and it cannot be claimed that the recent order whereby the Provincial, or Saza, chiefs are allowed to hold Courts and try cases is a development. It simply gives back an authority and standing which was taken away from them when, under the British Administration, they were turned into hut-tax collectors, for which they received the salary of £200 per annum.

This latter arrangement turned the revenue into the official coffers for the payment of salaries European and native; and the Muganda who forgets the real benefits of the Pax

Britannica (my typist wrote Tax Britannica, a mistake almost too good to correct), and complains that the white man is eating up the country, is told how much more English money is spent on administration than is received from native sources. Perhaps, like myself, he realises the lavish generosity of England, but thinks that it is too lavish in the wrong direction; and believes that the small kingdoms of Uganda, Unyoro, Toro, and Ankole could be more easily, beneficially, and cheaply administered by an English Adviser to the native kings; a Government land officer, a commercial agent, an English Accountant with various native clerks, all directly responsible to one Governor of British East Africa and Uganda, than by the building up of an intricate Whitehall system of bigger and lesser fleas who must be supported, development or no development.

We must not forget that Uganda is not, and probably never can become, a white man's country; neither can the Asiatic hope to make it his home. The climate may be temporarily possible for both, but in spite of the statement of such an authority as Sir Patrick Manson, K.C.M.G., &c., that tropical diseases are not climatic, one may be allowed to say that without a tropical climate the intermediaries which transmit the germ-causes of tropical diseases

could not exist. They do exist, and indeed thrive
under the conditions found in Uganda, and until
those conditions are altered, as, for instance, the
doing away with plantain-trees—a thing not to
be dreamt of—we shall have mosquitoes, and
if mosquitoes, malaria and all that malaria
means to the white and Asiatic.

Bearing this in mind, we naturally think that
development and not revenue should have been
the watchword from the beginning—development of native resources for and by the native
under European supervision. I am well aware
that such a suggestion is pooh-poohed by many ;
first because they think it wrong, and second
because they think it impossible.

A glance round the capital of Uganda will
convince all who hold such opinions of their
mistake, for on every hand are evidences that
rapid strides have been taken to bridge the
gulf between primitive barbarism and Western
civilisation.

Large, well-built, and in some instances
beautiful houses top the plantain groves; keen
and varied business is carried on in the markets
under the direction of a native superintendent.
Here a butchery department, there a grocery
store, hardware of every description, tailors busy
at work with hand and machine making clothing for men and women, carpenters turning out

chairs and tables that would do credit to any British workman, all bespeak advance in the social life of the people, through crowds of whom, well dressed and orderly, we make our way to the hill from which the capital takes its name.

Here we meet the little King David, a boy of eleven years, who succeeded Mwanga, and although the "Lubiri," or reed-fenced enclosure of the King, has much the same appearance as in the old days, yet the moment we have been announced by the King's official drummer and passed through the various courtyards into the inner court, we perceive the great change which has taken place.

A snug-looking, brick-built bungalow has taken the place of the reed and grass monstrosity inhabited by Mwanga; and the visitor is ushered into a scrupulously clean sitting-room, very simply furnished after the European style. There is no longer the sight of dirty, wicked-looking loungers, popping up from every corner like vermin from their holes; or the continual sound of lewd and ribald songs, discomforting the visitor but giving pleasure to the King, who was quite capable of delaying his presence in order to impress the European. The shy, pleasant-faced lad who now bids us welcome has been trained in a different school and is doing credit to his teachers.

KING DAVID LEARNING THE MYSTERIES OF A KODAK.

Simply dressed in the flowing Arab robe which has been adopted as the dress-garment of all the chiefs, the boy-king carries himself with dignity, which on occasion he can shake off, and enjoy as any other lad a game of footer and hockey, or a spin on his Sunbeam cycle. He is also fond of riding his pretty little white pony: to European eyes a more dignified method of transit than the native custom of sitting astride the shoulders of a huge Muganda.

His education was begun by a native school-master under the direction of a missionary of the C.M.S.; but the British Government has for some years past provided him with an able English (Scotch, surely!) tutor, a graduate of Cambridge. Under him Daudi has made rapid strides in all the elements of a sound education, and is especially proud of his ability to understand and converse in English.

On the same hill and in the King's enclosure is the native parliament house, where the chiefs assemble to discuss the condition of the country and promulgate laws, which may or may not receive the sanction of the British Governor. At present, and until he reaches the age of eighteen years, the "Kabaka," or King, is a minor; and three regents are responsible for the government, receiving for this an additional £200 per annum. One of these regents, the

"Katikiro," or Prime Minister, presides over the parliament, except on such occasions as the young King is brought in for the purpose of training. The Prime Minister, a capable-looking giant, was a notable figure at King Edward's Coronation, and has since been made a Knight Commander of the Order of SS. Michael and George. This man, risen from peasant rank, is the virtual ruler of Uganda, and responsible, perhaps more than any one else, for the great desire to advance along Western lines which has taken such a hold of the people.

There is a native proverb to the effect that the strength of a sheep is in its tail; that behind all forward movement there is some one or something giving a powerful impetus; and this is undoubtedly true of the Katikiro, Sir Apolo Kagwa, K.C.M.G.; but of this power we shall speak in another chapter, since my object here is to point out not only the advanced desires of the natives, but their remarkable capabilities and the possibility of making them immediately responsible for every branch of administration, with only a comparatively small outlay for European supervision.

What would be lost by such an arrangement?

The collection of taxes is already in the hands of the native chiefs, and they are also responsible for the roads and markets. The Indian

SIR APOLO KAGWA, K.C.M.G.

159

Penal Code is made possible by the help of native laws, although by such an arrangement there is a grave danger of too much law.

Nothing has been done by the Administration for the industrial training of the people. All education is carried on by missions, chiefly by the agents of the C.M.S., who also do the bulk of the medical work among the natives. We have in Uganda and neighbouring kingdoms comparatively as strong, if not a stronger, European staff of civil servants as that set apart in British East Africa for native work; and yet we have a letter like the following sent by the President of the Uganda Chamber of Commerce to the Acting-Deputy Commissioner:—

"I am desired by the Chamber of Commerce to forward you the following on the question of the critical and defective supply of native labour in Uganda.

In accordance with your suggestion a circular was addressed to every member of .the Chamber asking for opinions as to cause, effect, and remedy, and though no unanimous views are held as to remedies, yet the opinions are generally as follows:—

Native labour in almost every South African colony is inadequate to the supply. But as regards Uganda in particular.

CAUSES.

1. The natural richness of the country and the cheap and plentiful food and clothing supply.

2. The indolent life led by all Africans not subject to forced labour and oppressive legislation.

3. The increased demand for labour for industrial and trade purposes as well as for porterage, especially for through Congo carriage of loads.

4. Want of primary technical agricultural education.

5. Encouragement by Government and missionaries of local agriculture whereby the peasant is able to produce all he wants in the way of money from his own garden, as is seen by the great increase in the cotton-growing industry.

6. Absence of labourers who formerly came here from German territory.

7. Monthly payment of wages of a sum so nearly coinciding with the hut-tax.

8. Dislike of the peasant to work in the towns owing to the increased cost of living. The majority of men who came to earn money for hut-tax arrive generally entirely unprovided with money or food, and unless helped by friends, or they receive posho, practically starve themselves for a month, and feeling

this enforced punishment so severely that immediately they have received a month's pay return to their homes.

9. Sleeping sickness mortality preventing the growth of the population.

EFFECTS.

1. Persistent shortness of labour supply.

2. Gradual and regular increase of wages.

3. Loss to Government and merchants by delay.

REMEDIES.

1. Immigration. Inquiries have shown that large numbers of men are available in the neighbouring German territory. At Bukoba alone I am informed that five thousand men could easily be obtained at a day's notice. Would it not be possible to induce the Government of German East Africa to allow indenture of natives for work in Uganda under due safeguards for their return to the colony, and a payment by immigration agents to that Government corresponding to the amount of the hut-tax payable to the colony.

2. A census and registration of the adult native population through the chiefs and registration for six months by employees. The right

given to chiefs to punish by fine natives for not keeping to engagements or absconding.

3. A weekly wage experiment has shown that when the peasant receives a weekly wage he requires no posho, spends more, lives better, and is consequently a longer time in saving up sufficient money to enable him to pay his tax. The payment of posho and a wage at the end of a month is an encouragement for him to return to his country.

4. Encouragement given to minor native chiefs to exact rent, or labour in lieu thereof, for the house and land occupied by the peasant.

5. Improved roads to allow increased transport facilities by bullock wagon, which would relieve many thousands of men from Safari who are now merely beasts of burden. A calculation has been made by one of our members long resident in Uganda that at least 50 per cent. of the labour of this country is non-productive, and utterly wasted, in porterage, in water-carrying and in road-mending or making on an altogether primitive and wrong system.

6. The provision of primary technical schools for agriculture, trade, road-making, &c., which would help to induce the males, and especially the younger generation, to desire a more regular manual labour."

It is not necessary to agree with every point
in the letter to realise its value, as emphasising
the fact that there is a serious breakdown in
the general administration of the country—and
a breakdown, not in spite of, but more probably
because of the dual form of administration ; the
Western as represented by English officialism
not daring to Westernise enough, and the feudal
as represented by the native "Lukiko," or Parliament, holding things together.   Indeed, without its capable co-operation the present peaceful
organisation would undoubtedly collapse.

One really striking statement in the letter
is—" A calculation has been made by one of our
members long resident in Uganda that at least
50 per cent. of the labour of this country is
non-productive and utterly wasted in porterage,
water-carrying, and in road-making or mending
on an altogether primitive and wrong system."

No greater condemnation than that contained
in this passage could have been passed upon a
native administration ; but this is passed upon
the British, and deservedly so, for I believe that
if a man like " Bwana Tayari " (Sawhili name,
meaning " Mr. Ready," and used by the natives
when speaking of Mr. George Wilson, C.B.,
Deputy-Governor of Uganda) had been allowed
to generally superintend and direct the gradual
and natural evolution of the feudal system, we

9

should not have had what is now acute—a native labour problem.

The "wrong system" of road-making can be seen in operation throughout the Protectorate. Hundreds of men, women, and children are required in the first instance to cultivate the portion of the country that has been pegged out as a proposed road by one of the white officials. It may be ten yards wide or it may be thirty; it may be straight or it may be crooked; it may satisfy one official and be left to die by another, who will call upon the chief to do all over again elsewhere what is after all only a heart-breaking job, for such a road must be constantly kept weeded to prevent its being lost sight of.

Naturally the people soon get tired of such unending labour, and many of them leave the homes of their fathers because situate near a road; and large tracts of land, once well-cultivated gardens, have been given up to long grass and leopards.

Now, and not the dim and distant future, is the time to improve the roads, for every year the native is in touch with so-called civilisation brought in by the Uganda Railway, makes him more difficult to deal with and more expensive to employ.

Each chief and people of a district in the

Uganda and adjoining kingdoms, as well as in the country of Usoga, where the natives have been under European influence for some years past, might be made immediately responsible for the construction and maintenance of macadamised roads. The time spent in breaking stones by a few hundred men in each district would eventually prove an enormous saving in time, temper, and labour. Attempts have also been made to utilise certain waterways for the conveyance of merchandise ; and there again the "wrong system" was seen at work. At one time large gangs of men have been employed in cutting down papyrus and clearing away the sud ; but gradually the workers disappeared, and the work was allowed to drop until the growth was as thick as ever, when the labour of clearing was begun all over again.

Definite and sustained effort is badly needed in order to perfect transport facilities, and were it made known that all taxation would cease for one year in any district occupied with roadmaking, with proper punishment of harder labour for individuals refusing to do their part, the transport problem would be solved, because wheeled traffic would be really possible. Another very important point touched on is the lack of technical instruction. Not a single penny has been spent by the Administration on technical instruction. Had this been done not only would the males of a younger generation have had a keener desire for regular manual labour, but the present generation would have solved, and will even now solve if taught how, the most pressing problems. If the idea behind British administration in Uganda is not the farming of taxes, but the true development of the native and his country, then I plead most earnestly that technical schools for the teaching of trades and agriculture be established by Government in each district, and that every boy *and girl* be compelled to attend for no less a period than three years.

The calm way in which the Government relegates this and all other education to the Christian missionary, making suggestions here and requests there, would be most amusing—in the face of an education problem at home—were it not deplorable. In a country like Uganda and neighbouring kingdoms, where there is native desire for advancement, and organisation already in existence to enable the head of the State to deal with each individual, and a very substantial revenue, it is the duty of the Government and not the privilege of missions to spend money in seeking to develop this side of native character. The writer would be sorry to convey the idea that he does not recognise the inestimable value to Uganda of England's protection, brought about in the year 1894 through the influence of the C.M.S.; but we must not forget that there are certain compensations given in return, which lay responsibilities and obligations upon the protecting Power.

Out of a computed 19,600 square miles, the British Administration took as its own under the 1900 agreement 1,500 square miles of forest land, and claimed control over 9,000 square miles of uncultivated land, which really means that we have taken more than half of the land for being willing to protect the remainder, and then of course we make the remainder pay as much as possible of the cost of protection.

For 1907 the receipts for the whole Protectorate, from hut, gun, and poll taxes were between £50,000 and £60,000. Besides this amount there were import and export, road and wharf dues, registration fees, licence fees, &c., &c., bringing the total to a goodly sum, the expenditure of which—with additional grants from England—provides not only interesting reading but material for serious reflection.

Some £6,000 is returned annually to the King and chiefs of Uganda under the above-mentioned agreement, whereby, as we saw at the beginning of this chapter, the chiefs became in return simply hut-tax collectors. To this, as we have seen, the Administration has found it necessary to add much of their old feudal power, and to-day there are no more hard-working, painstaking, and loyal men anywhere than the Saza chiefs of Uganda; yet I have heard men gravely discuss whether we are justified in paying these chiefs their £200 per annum, which is £50 less than the allowance to a raw assistant collector fresh out from England.

In my own mind the doubt is whether in a Protectorate like Uganda, with such native material ready to hand, infinitely more capable than raw youths from England of doing collectors' and magistrates' work, we are justified in paying any but native officials, with, of course, the exception of white leaders as I have already suggested.

If only in addition to the £6,000 spent on stipends to the King and chiefs, an additional £10,000 could be spent annually for the next ten years on providing a commercial, technical, and industrial training for picked youngsters drawn from the whole Protectorate, how much more good it would do than, say, the building of an expensive military system; and surely such technical training is far more important.

The letter from the Chamber of Commerce failed to mention that whilst in England the wages of a private soldier—including everything

—are about equal to those of a labourer, in Uganda they are about three times as much; so that a careful native who joins either the police—who do military work—or the regular army, can, during the first term of service, save as much as will enable him to pay hut-tax and meet all his needs for many years.

Thus we have a native problem growing more pressing and difficult every day; and is it any wonder?

The strategic position of Uganda is another valuable asset of England, and it must be held; but it would be wiser and cheaper in the end to hold it by Sikhs only, than at this stage of Uganda's history to enlist the native, and, by an unhealthy rate of pay, jeopardise the development of the country.

Let it not be thought for a moment that my criticism of a system means a criticism of the British official, or a suggestion that he is at all incapable. As in every class of men, there are no doubt good, bad, and indifferent officials; but my experience is chiefly of the good. They are men who find a system in existence and try to make the best of it; but would it not be better for them and for the Protectorate if the system were altered so as—to quote the Right Hon. Winston Churchill, who, as Under-Secretary for the Colonies, recently visited Uganda—"to organise scientifically, upon a humane and honourable line, the industry of an entire population, and to apply the whole funds of their labour to their own enrichment and elevation "?

The British official would still be required to open up the vast regions north and north-east of Uganda, leading right away beyond Lake Rudolph to the borders of Abyssinia.

INTERIOR VIEW OF MENGO CATHEDRAL.

ST. PAUL'S CATHEDRAL, MENGO, UGANDA.

174

CHAPTER IX

THE SIGHTS OF MENGO

FROM the King's hill, although not very high, interesting and picturesque glimpses of the capital can be secured.

Behind us lies the Lake ; and soon, I have no doubt, the port of Uganda will be Munyonyo, a place not more than eight miles from Mengo, safe for shipping, and more suitable and convenient in every way than Entebbe, which is more than a comfortable day's march from where we stand.

Here, outside the King's fence, we can see

the little hill of Kampala, which was the first Government station in the country; and curiously enough, because of this, the name of the little insignificant hillock now occupied by a Commission sent out to inquire into the ravages of Specific Disease has been made the postal and geographical name for the native capital.

Some years ago the local administrative centre was moved from Kampala because of its unhealthiness, to Nakasero, a high hill near, on which is built the English fort. Here also may be seen European and Indian traders, catering for the taste, inclination, and need of native and white man, with every conceivable article.

Near the foot of the same hill is built the factory of the Uganda Company, which was floated to take over and develop on practical business, yet Christian, lines the industrial work of the C.M.S., for which more money could not be spared.

With such a philanthropic aim it secured the practical sympathy of many Christian people, and also received considerable help from the C.M.S., who allowed one of its missionaries to transfer his services to the Company as manager, which at once gave it a unique advantage over ordinary concerns.

On the whole it has done a good work, though not quite on the lines expected by many; but no doubt any failure to develop its industrial work actually on the lines of a Christian Mission has been due more to the force of circumstances than lack of inclination.

If for nothing else, the Uganda Company deserves well of England, because of the impetus it gave to cotton-growing before any one else had moved in that direction; and a visit to the factory, built at great expense—the greater because the first of its kind, and all such ventures must pay for the privilege of handing, down experience—is both interesting and instructive.

A complete cotton-ginning plant, worked by steam-power, controlled by the Baganda under the superintendence of Englishmen, can be seen in operation, whereby the whole process from seed extraction to bale-pressing is carried out without a hitch; reflecting the greatest credit on the manager who was responsible for its erection.

This and other factories have now taken their place as an accepted part of Uganda life, and crowds of natives come in from long distances with loads of raw cotton, for which they receive about a penny per lb.

Some two years ago there was such a rush of

cotton that the agents feared they would have to refuse it for lack of storage room. Tons came in every day, and might have continued to come in even with a greater rush had a casual examination not proved that the Baganda were not such innocents as the management supposed. A penny per lb. for raw cotton leaves a fair margin for all expenses, and a good healthy percentage besides ; but when quite three-quarters of each lb. is composed of stone—well, some one is likely to "see trouble," as the Baganda express it.

It was so easy to put a lump of ironstone in the middle of a bundle which was merely weighed; and the consequence was that a good many stones were bought at cotton price !

It was also comparatively easy to walk round the building with the load of cotton which ought to have been deposited inside ; consequently a goodly number of Baganda walked round the building with their loads and resold them to the innocent agent at the scales !

There is also a printing department at the works of this Company, and I hope the ancient borough of Stockton-on-Tees, with which I am at present connected, is justly proud of the fact that it has provided the superintendent of this department. Each month I receive a little journal from Uganda—for that country has now two newspapers, or at any rate monthly pamphlets which serve as such : one, *Uganda Notes* for Europeans; and the other, *Ebifa Ebuganda*, Uganda news for natives, ably edited and published by Mr. C. J. Phillips, a member of the C.M.S.—admirably printed by Baganda boys in the works of the Uganda Company.

In another shop of the Company, and in sheds throughout the capital, native men and boys are at work upon boards that have been sawn in the forests by other natives, and brought to Mengo for sale. These are speedily made into tables, chairs, doors, shutters, frames, desks, and bookshelves, and turned out in fairly good style, though lacking that finish which bespeaks the master-hand : a fault for which the lack of long apprenticeship is responsible.

Not far from the factory the Company has its store for the retailing of imports ; and this, per-haps, is the only department to which any exception can be taken. It may be argued, with some show of justice, that this department brings a professedly philanthropic enterprise, which has received unique advantage over other trades through the help rendered by the C.M.S. and its agents, not only into competition, but into unfair competition, with other traders ; yet in this department the Com-pany and the country have been fortunate in securing the services of a manager who remarkably carries out in his own life and work the primary aim of the Company, namely, to try in the course of ordinary business to influence and elevate the native.

To the right of Nakasero, and where we stand, can be seen the hill of Nsambya, the Uganda headquarters of St. Joseph's Mission : a branch of St. Joseph's Society for Foreign Missions founded at Mill Hill, London, by the late Cardinal Vaughan.

The first Bishop of this Mission left London with four priests in May, 1895, the same month in which I left with others to begin our journey. The priests reached Mengo in September of the same year, and we arrived at the end of October, having travelled round the Cape of Good Hope.

This Mission has over twenty thousand baptized adherents, many of whom were passed over to it with the portion of Uganda allotted to its Bishopric from the jurisdiction of the French Algerian Mission of the White Fathers, whose local headquarters are very prominently and substantially built on the hill of Rubaga, situate on our left as we stand at the King's Gate.

This latter Mission has had an interesting, aye, even exciting time in Uganda, for it is the one whose adherents clashed with those of the

C.M.S. in Lugard's time over the question of whether the country was to be French or English; and it is almost pathetic to think that its reward has been the French Ecclesiastical Coup, from which I understand it only managed to save its Algerian property by its transference to lay holders, and the setting up in the capital of Uganda of another Roman Catholic Bishopric with which it has had to share its honours.

Apropos of Roman Catholicism in Uganda and East Africa, I was recently asked why the C.M.S. had not a working agreement with lines demarcating spheres of influence. I explained that this was done for the Mission in the Soudan by the Government, but with us since Government has not marked off spheres, and since the C.M.S. was first in the field, it would be impossible: the Romanists would not agree to any such arrangement. I gave a very striking example of Roman Catholic nonconformity—or at any rate disunion—which is even now going on near Lake Naivasha, where certain priests have appeared from the Somali coast, and are threatening the Bishoprics of the Uganda and Zanzibar Roman Catholic Bishops, who are doing their best to keep them out.

To return to our stand outside the King's Gate; we see right in front of us the English Cathedral on the hill of Namirembe; and a weird yet striking edifice it looks, with its three thatched pinnacles, all in a row, like the prongs of a giant's trident. Thither we now make our way, and find it the centre of activity, for the hill is the headquarters of the C.M.S. Uganda Mission, whose agents are to be found at Wadelai, in the north, Nassa, in German territory, to the south, beyond Ruwenzori in the west, and beyond Mount Elgon in the east.

The present cathedral is the third which has occupied the site during the last few years. The two former were miniature forests; for innumerable poles were planted in the ground and used to support the woven canopy of poles and reeds which carried the thatch. They were very useful buildings, but risky; for no pole seemed beyond the appetite of the white ant, and the result was a somewhat speedy collapse.

The building we are now viewing is a tremendous advance on its predecessors, though scarcely a permanent structure. It is made of sun-dried bricks, and is altogether the work of the natives under European supervision. Externally it is not a thing of beauty, but a glance at the photograph of the interior on p. 174 will show that its lines and proportions are bold and noble.

The ordinary Sunday morning congregation

is a sight worth seeing, for often there are not less than two thousand people, old and young, rich and poor; some on chairs, others on stools, skins, or straw mats. Only the chancel is provided with seating, so that the general congregation, white or black, must bring their own seats if they wish to be raised above the level of the floor. May the system long continue!

Many beautiful skins of leopard and antelope are seen being carried to and from the church; and this reminds me that recent writers have said that the Baganda are noted tanners. They are nothing of the kind; the Baganda do not know how to tan, but they are remarkable skin-dressers, in the process of which they make a liberal use of a knife, a stone, and butter.

The congregation is summoned by the beating of a drum or drums—a very important factor in the life of a Muganda.

In the old days the King's drum was sounded to summon men to war; and so perfect was their organisation that its sound and summons was passed on from hill to hill, so that before evening every warrior in the country was under arms and on his way to the capital, there to receive the appointed general, who would lead the army wherever the King wished

10

them to make a raid for cattle or human beings.

The sound is still passed on, but now from Namirembe, the hill of peace; and at its summons full sixty thousand people assemble to render homage to the King of kings, or to go forth among the very nations who hate the Baganda for their past oppression, to make known to them the Gospel of light and life and liberty.

The morning service may seem somewhat lengthy to a European, but he will not fail to be impressed by the reverence of the congregation, their bright and hearty—if to his ears unmusical—singing, and by the large number of communicants.

One or two native clergymen assist at the service, and it is no unusual thing for a layman to preach the sermon, which I can assure you is of fifteen minutes' duration—and more.

The visitor will also be interested and amused at the process of evolution evident in the attire of the congregation, and he will understand that such absurdities are bound to show themselves even at solemn times and in sacred places, when a nation unused to such things is suddenly given the means of displaying its most fantastic tastes in colour and shape.

WEDDING PARTY OF BAGANDA LEAVING CHURCH.

A glance at the accompanying picture of a wedding party leaving church will show that their taste is not always extravagant or unbecoming. The only thing at all objectionable is the lady's tarbooch, or Turkish cap—one stage in the evolution which I am confident will soon pass away.

The cathedral is surrounded by other buildings, in which the ordinary work of schools, preparation for baptism and confirmation, and the training of teachers is carried on.

There is a fine school for girls, another for women, and another for boys, all built of sundried brick ; besides which there is an imposing structure of the same material used as a theological hall, in which the teachers and clergy are trained.

The work carried on in these buildings is of an extensive, interesting, and useful character, beginning at the very bottom of the ladder with A B C, and going right on to the higher branches of theology.

On one day of the week all this teaching ceases, and the members assemble to take part in a missionary meeting, at which natives, who have been labouring in distant corners of the Protectorate, tell of their work.

Not a detail is omitted. The number of sermons preached, the attitude of the people, the kindness or otherwise of the chiefs, the dangers encountered, the presents received, the amount of food eaten, are all retailed with an exactitude most amusing to a foreigner ; but besides this there is in some of the addresses a deep spiritual tone which is the real life of the movement.

At the close of the addresses an offertory, more varied in kind than the English mind can conjure up, is made : bananas, sugar-cane, eggs, fowls, goats, sheep, cattle, shells, beads, pice and rupees are all given, and it is no uncommon thing for natives to offer themselves for work in distant and difficult places, although I think this is not now so usual as at one time.

On the side of the same hill is the C.M.S. Hospital, which was founded in 1897 by Albert R. Cook, M.D., B.Sc. Lond., B.A. Camb., who was soon afterwards joined by his brother, J. Howard Cook, M.S. Lond., F.R.C.S. Eng., M.D. Lond., D.T.M.H. Camb.

To reach the hospital we pass the little plot where lie the remains of Bishop Hannington, Pilkington, Hubbard, and others of the C.M.S. Mission, and De Winton, Thruston, Macdonald, Densham, and others of the Administration. Noble souls, all of them !

What memories surge up as we pass their

resting-place! We live over again the night in 1897 when news came in that Thruston, Wilson, and Scott had been taken prisoners at Luba's in Usoga by the Soudanese soldiers who had refused to follow Colonel (now General Sir J. C. R.) Macdonald on his journey north with sealed orders, and had marched back from the Ravine Station on to Uganda.

These men were ever a bad lot, having rebelled against the Egyptian Government, and when serving Emin Pasha had held him prisoner until relieved by Stanley.

With their leader, Selim Bey, they were enlisted in the Lado Enclave by Lugard, and placed in charge of the Uganda border forts, where they were a greater curse than any number of enemies might have been, since under Selim Bey they were a Mohammedan menace to the peace and stability of Uganda, until they were enrolled as Imperial troops.

But their old nature was too strong for them, and now from the fort at Luba's near the Nile they had despatched messengers to all the soldiers throughout Uganda, calling upon them to kill the white men and take the country for Mohammed. These emissaries had reached the lines at Kampala, and we were warned that before morning we should probably be attacked and killed. In the event of no attack we were to make our way to Kampala Hill next morning and there help to disarm the soldiery who could no longer be trusted. We did so and succeeded; but in the meantime grave things were happening at Luba's, for the rebels there, having been repulsed by Colonel Macdonald, had brutally shot their three white prisoners, Major Thruston, Mr. Wilson, and Mr. Scott.

Then came the news of the fruitless attack on the rebel fort by the brave Protestant Baganda (most of the Mohammedans were wavering or had already thrown in their lot with the Soudanese rebels, and many of the Roman Catholics had thrown in their lot with the rebellion of King Mwanga in the west), and of the death of Captain Macdonald (the Colonel's brother) and Mr. Pilkington.

It fell to my lot to speedily build the first hospital, to meet the wounded who were sent by canoe, and get them carried to the capital, where Dr. A. R. Cook worked day and night, ably assisted by the Mission ladies, to alleviate the terrible sufferings, that had been intensified by a long delay *en route*.

Graves had to be dug for the Europeans killed in Usoga, a coffin made for Pilkington's body—the Government made others for their own men—and then there was that last sad and solemn scene when they were laid to rest "in sure and certain hope of the resurrection to eternal life, through our Lord Jesus Christ."

The roses are blooming on their graves, and sweetly speak of life, yet we cannot help but linger, and picture it all again; but now let us wend our way outside the wall and down the hill to the hospital.

The first branch of the medical work met with is the dispensary, known as the "Wellcome Dispensary," a substantial and very useful building where cases are diagnosed, medicines dispensed to thousands of out-patients, for whom evangelistic services are held in a verandah at one end of the building.

The hospital itself is a more pretentious structure with wards, pathological laboratory, and operating-room that will compare very favourably with a similar institution anywhere.

Bodies and souls are well catered for, and here, if anywhere, can be refuted the nonsensical argument that it is unfair to speak to natives about their souls when their bodies are in need of healing.

The Baganda patients soon realise that but for the fact that the doctors and nurses are impelled by the love of God in Jesus Christ to care for them, they would never have come out to the country; and if their Christian doctors and nurses had not come, who else would have thought of them?

The doctors are perfectly fair to every patient. All are taken in and attended to; and if there happens to be a Roman Catholic, the Mission to which he belongs is communicated with, and they are allowed to help him spiritually. That such work is appreciated by the Roman Catholics may be evidenced by the fact that they have more than once sent donations to the funds.

After a walk through the wards we make our way round the hill to the Mengo High School—a feature of the C.M.S. work at the capital.

Inside the usual reed fence is a large courtyard, along the sides of which are built boarding-houses for young chiefs, or sons of chiefs, who are removed from the evil surroundings of home and placed in this school to receive a sound mental, moral, and spiritual training.

The ability shown by the majority of these youngsters is remarkable, and will compare favourably with that of lads at home. In some subjects there is not the least doubt but that the black can "lick" the white boy hollow; thus proving that, given opportunity, the Baganda, in spite of their colour, might be made anything.

BISHOP TUCKER OF UGANDA IN CAMP.

The three R's, English, physical exercise, swimming, cycling, tennis, footer, Bible and Prayer Book, are all taught and excelled in.

There is another important school called the King's School, situate at a place called Budo, some distance from the capital, and some of the boys from the Mengo High School pass into the other on scholarships; but enough of this subject for the present; let us pass on and complete our round.

We began with the capital of British Administration, the home of the Governor, and made our way to the native capital and home of, the King; and we close this chapter at the palace (!) of the Bishop of Uganda— Dr. Tucker, who has just completed the eighteenth year of his episcopate—a native-made wattle and daub, thatched bungalow, well-worn, weather-beaten, and ready to fall, but still tenaciously held by his Lordship, as an example of what will suffice whilst more important things are being attended to.

CHAPTER X

THE WORK AND INFLUENCE OF MISSIONS

True Socialism—The life of women—Native missionaries—
Condition of the Church—Appalling numbers—Numerical
not necessarily moral strength—Danger of numbers—
Danger of civilisation—The housing problem—Superficial
character—Evil living—Johnston's opinion as to Uganda's
need—A Puritan revival—Secular education—Desire for
knowledge—Intelligent people—The education problem—
Duties of Church and State—Church government—White
missionary not permanent—A constitution—Self-support
and self-extension—Lack of funds and permanent buildings
—The crisis of the nation and the Church—Hope—
Questions of Church practice and discipline—Organisation
—A division of the diocese.

THE missionaries of Uganda have always
striven to implant in the native mind the
corporate idea of one family in God; and the
truly socialistic because Christian idea of man's
duty to his fellow-man. Their work has lifted
woman from a position of degradation and

scorn and made her accepted throughout the
kingdom as the equal of man. It has made
family life as sacred a reality to many as it is in
England; it has increased the value of human
life and given to individuals, once thought too
insignificant and loathsome to be noticed, due
recognition as men and brethren. Indeed, no
one who knows the African nature, or who has
carefully compared the condition of Uganda
before the introduction of missions, with its
condition at the present day, can help but
declare its firm conviction, that we are face to
face with a modern miracle.

To see men clamouring to leave home, friends,
food, security, and chances of advancement to
go to unknown and inhospitable countries in
order to preach a Gospel which to them was
more precious than life, and for which they
received little or no remuneration, was enough
to convince the hardest sceptic of their sincerity;
yet this was a common sight a year or two ago.
The wonderful Church—building and people—
now existing in the country of Toro near the
Mountains of the Moon is due in great measure
to the pertinacity, sincerity, and intrinsic goodness of one such man; but the question is often
asked, "Are the Christians of Uganda willing to
do the same to-day?"

In some instances Yes, emphatically. No

more striking instance of self-sacrifice can be given in the world's history than that of the woman teacher who, hearing that the people of a certain island were dying of sleeping sickness and were without any physical or spiritual assistance, offered herself for the work ; and although efforts were made to dissuade her from undertaking such a task, she insisted on going to live and, if need be, to die (eventually she did die of sleeping sickness) for her fellows—but generally speaking the answer must be No.

There is still life, strength, and effort of a high character; but there is a change in the attitude of mind and will, due very largely to the changed economic conditions brought about by the introduction, *viâ* the Uganda Railway, of elements which have turned the attentions of men into channels, not only other than religious, but even irreligious, and have created demands that are looked upon as development but do not really mean progress.

In the year 1886 there were two hundred baptized members of the Church of England in Uganda, and two adults were baptized that year. To-day there are more than sixty thousand baptized members, and six thousand baptisms take place annually.

Such numbers are almost appalling because of

the responsibility of those in authority; they
represent progress of a kind, but is it progress
indicated by such vital godliness, high moral
principle, general self-sacrifice and missionary
effort as might be, and ought to be, expected
from a young and healthy Christian Church
still full of its first love? In my own mind
I am convinced that it is not, and for some
years I have endeavoured to study the cause
or causes of such a condition of Christian de-
clension.

In the first place, the very numerical success
of Christianity has constituted one of its
gravest dangers. It grew from beneath just
as in the time of the apostles, but it gradually
became the religion of the rich and powerful,
with the result that the followers and depen-
dents of the rulers thought it the right and
honourable thing to seek baptism.

Every precaution was and is taken to test
their mental, moral, and spiritual fitness, yet
only those closely concerned know how impossible it is to say who ought or who ought not to
be accepted.

The man who has not a Christian name and
who cannot read and write is looked down on
by his fellows; consequently Christianity is the
popular religion of the country, and is paying
the price of all popularity in being too general,

weak, and shallow, rather than deep, strong, and lasting.

With God all things are possible, and we have no reason to doubt the value and deep reality of the three thousand added to the Church on the Day of Pentecost, but as a general rule large numbers are superficial; and in the Christian work in the kingdom of Uganda large numbers have been general.

I have already spoken of glorious work done; of the power of the Gospel message in the lives of many; so I cannot be misunderstood when I refer to facts on the other side, which every missionary deplores and endeavours to combat.

Secondly, it seems to me that although the Gospel had a good start in Uganda, making whoever really accepted it purer, happier, more unselfish and useful, yet it was working these wonders among a people more useless, selfish, weak, superficial, and cruel than any with whom we have been hitherto familiar. This being so it is foolish to expect that an ignorant people of naturally weak, shallow character and low standard of morality would not suffer from the sudden presentation by the Uganda Railway of Coast, Indian, and European civilisation.

They have suffered terribly, for the storm of

temptation has been most severe; and one of the saddest features of the case is, that at the very moment when pastors and people need to be drawn very closely together, to understand each other, and learn to grapple with perhaps the one great crisis in the nation's religious history, the new ideas of housing have taken such a hold upon European and native, as to prevent their being thrown together as they were a few years ago, when privacy was at a discount and fellowship all important.

The alertness of the native mind, but also its superficiality, has made them jump at the concrete parts of the missionary's teaching upon the necessity for bettering their social condition; and they have to a large extent given themselves up to the questions of building, banking, sleeping, cooking, clothing, and eating to the exclusion of the development of moral principle.

Professedly Christian men openly speak about the infidelity of their professedly Christian wives, declaring that there is no such thing as faithfulness among the women of their country: we know there is much faithlessness amongst the men, and sleeping sickness is not the only scourge responsible for decimating the kingdom—the kingdom which at one time had a population of nearly two millions, but to-day is little more than six hundred thousand, the population of Liverpool. Venereal disease is working sad havoc everywhere, so much so that a special commission has been appointed to deal with the matter.

It is not very difficult to get a wrong and exaggerated view of such a subject, and such it seems to me was presented to the United Services Medical Society, and reported in the *Lancet* of October, 1908.

In his paper Colonel Lamkin states that in some districts as many as 90 per cent. suffer from Specific Disease; and that it produces infant mortality to the extent of 50 or 60 per cent.

The first place in the cause of the epidemic is attributed to the interference by Christian teaching and teachers with the tribal laws and customs of the people.

On both these points the Drs. Cook, who know all there is to know about Uganda and its people, traverse the Colonel's paper; and show very conclusively that the ravages of the disease have not affected more than 19·4 per cent. in the most populous district; whilst on the second head they insist on the word *civilisation* rather than Christianity as the potent cause of the trouble.

It may not be out of place to emphasise here

my strong belief in the power of the Gospel of Jesus Christ, not to create such licence as is responsible for the terrible evils mentioned above, but to guide and regulate the liberty, all too hastily given to the Baganda, into right and useful channels.

This emphasis cannot be better illustrated than by the words of Sir H. H. Johnston, who not long ago was Commissioner in Uganda :—

" If the Baganda are to be saved from dying out as a race—and I cannot but believe and hope they will—it will be entirely through the introduction of Christianity and the teaching of the missionaries, both Roman and Anglican. The introduction of monogamy as a universally recognised principle now amongst all people who desire to conform to mission teaching may be the salvation of Uganda, strange to say. The people through this teaching are now becoming ashamed of marrying girls who have led a bad life before marriage. The appreciation of female chastity is distinctly rising, while at the same time young men find debauchery no longer fashionable, and endeavour to marry early and become the fathers of families. If ever a race needed a Puritan revival to save it from extinction it is the Baganda, and if ever Christian missions did positive and unqualified good among a negro race this good has been accom-

11

plished in Uganda, where their teaching has turned the current of the more intelligent people's thoughts towards the physical advantages of chastity " ("The Uganda Protectorate," p. 642).

Surely we have at once in this quotation any answer necessary to Colonel Lamkin's indictment of missionary work, and also the only hope for the future. God grant that the "Puritan revival" may not be long delayed !

I am also firmly convinced that the present stagnation in the religious life of the people of Uganda is connected with the tendency to side-track the Church and its agents along the line of secular education.

There is an insatiable desire for knowledge on the part of the Baganda, and they are people of undoubted intelligence, far more highly developed than that of the surrounding tribes ; and I recognise the need for such education as will lead to the useful occupation of minds and bodies of such a people no longer given over to constant warfare. Up to a certain point the C.M.S. has given such education ; for all its work in Uganda, whilst primarily evangelistic, has of necessity been educational of a very practical character ; so much so, that not only has every candidate for baptism learned to read, but I dare

PHYSICAL DRILL AT MENGO C.M.S. HIGH SCHOOL.

to say that had there been no church on the hill there would have been no factory in the valley.

In its High School at Mengo it has also sought to meet on its own terms what seems to me any need for higher education; since its teaching is of such a character that, although it is carried on amongst youths who have been baptized, it is definitely evangelistic. From beginning to end it is an effort to remove young chiefs, and the sons of chiefs, from immoral surroundings, and to strengthen their mental and moral faculties through the influence of Gospel teaching.

The tendency of the times, however, is to demand from the missions educational work not primarily evangelistic, but such as will supply the requisite number of clerks, cooks, and carpenters.

There is no reason why missionary teachers should not be used to give such training to the Baganda if they or the Administration pay for it, and thus allow for the provision of other missionaries to do the work for which the Missionary Societies exist, and for which vast districts with far greater populations than Uganda are waiting. But there seems every reason why the C.M.S. should not give way to the popular cry, and set aside laity and clergy provided for out of funds gathered for evangelistic purposes, to build up a general elementary education system throughout the country, or a higher educational system amongst youths already baptized, confirmed, and possessed of as practical, workaday an education as the average youth in England, and who may never give the Church's need one iota in return.

This latter system appears to be the trend and danger of one mission school recently begun in the country, and I sincerely trust that the idea will not grow; for the condition of Uganda is not analogous to that of India, where educational work is often the only means of reaching a large population with the principles of the Gospel.

The freedom of choice in their life's work offered to the students of such a school is undoubtedly ideal; but the payment of teachers ought not to fall upon missionary funds, *i.e.,* upon those who have not as good educational advantages for their own boys, and who are really poorer than the Baganda whose teachers they are asked to pay.

The work of the Mengo High School, already referred to, if strengthened and developed so that *all* who wish to pay for the teaching, *and the teacher*, might send their sons and daughters (there are a number of poor lads being paid for by the native Church, chiefs, and friends at home—and this might be extended), and with a special department with higher teaching as preparation for definite missionary and ministerial work, is, with a theological college for teachers and clergy, all the education work the Church need trouble about. More than this will at present hamper missionary extension, and in time lead to difficulties such as are now threatening the Church at home, for history has a way of repeating itself.

Let it not be thought that I deprecate the value of true education; but I do not wish the good to take the place of the best, and therefore say, let the State authorities take up at once their own responsibilities, and in the name of God's only-begotten Son, who has given us our marching orders, let the Church do its work of preaching the Gospel; for that, and that alone, was the cause of success in Uganda.

Another element of danger to the Church of Uganda, and reason for the present colour feeling, lukewarmness, and general down-grade tendency manifested by many Christians, is the supposed lack of sympathy and confidence shown towards them by their white teachers.

I need not emphasise the word *supposed;*

that will be taken for granted by all who have come into touch with Uganda missionaries; but as in a former chapter I expressed my firm conviction that with very little British help the people of Uganda and surrounding kingdoms might be made to cheaply govern themselves, with results as good, if not better than those now forthcoming, so here I declare that I feel very strongly the time has come (if the opportunity has not already passed away) to give the native Christian of Uganda a good deal more say in the management of his own Church affairs.

Circumstances make the man, and since God has allowed the circumstances of marvellous missionary success, and the formation of a native Church, I cannot help but think He has, somewhere in Uganda, the native leaders necessary for such a Church if only they were allowed to lead.

The Church, like the Government, will suffer if the white man has a wrong idea as to the purpose of his presence in the country. *Permanence*, whilst the first thought with regard to his work, should be the very last thought in the missionary's mind with regard to himself, and woe betide the Church, goodbye to all native development, where the missionary, because of a mistaken idea of native ability or the danger of native responsibility, undue attachment to his own particular work, language limitation, or the circumstances of married family life, settles down to the "country rector" sort of life, where the work could be done as well if not better by a native pastor.

"Failure," says some one,—"utter failure." Failure, yes, that is to be expected again and again, for by failure the Baganda will learn; but not "utter failure," for all the evidence goes to prove that where the Muganda has been trusted with responsibility, he has done extraordinarily well, but that where he has been a factotum to the white man he has been more or less a failure.

Happy the day for Uganda Christianity when the white men give all pastoral work into the hands of natives organised and directed for some years to come by an itinerant over-pastor or archdeacon. Such a move would at once set free some experienced clergy and laymen to push out as pioneers to untouched countries, and would hasten the establishment of a self-supporting and self-governing Church, as well as kill the present native attitude of "Why need I worry, work, pay, or be present? —the white man is responsible for everything."

These problems have long been in the mind

of Uganda's Bishop, Dr. Tucker, and he has
striven incessantly for years to form a native
Church with a constitution which places the
native in such a position that he may one day
become the head of his own branch of the
Anglican Communion.

This constitution, accepted by native and
European, is now in operation, and from it we
may expect great things, since it seeks to
develop independence, place responsibility upon
the right shoulders, and make the Church self-
supporting and self-extending.

In the matter of self-support the Baganda
have in the past nobly responded in order to
meet every need; but I believe I am right in
saying that at the present moment the financial
condition of the Church is something worse
than "from hand to mouth."

The innumerable calls for teachers, and the
magnificent response, have been met by native
funds; but the demands of the speedy growth
and magnitude of the work have prevented
those in authority from giving that attention
to the organisation and development of the
material side which the Church now requires.
And at the very moment when we are thinking
of religious independence for the Baganda,
we are brought up somewhat sharply by the
facts that the coffers are empty; with the

exception of one in Toro, there is no permanent church building in the country; and the crisis of the nation and the Church is upon us through the mental, moral, social, and spiritual balance of the people having been upset by the too sudden presentation by the Uganda Railway of the material side of civilisation.

It will take some time to readjust their point of vision; and in the meantime, God grant that their attention may not be wholly taken up with cycles, watches, cutlery, clothing, houses, and Company shares!

A dull picture, probably: but I am wholly optimistic with regard to the power of the Gospel. I am also perfectly certain that the Christianity which withstood the persecutions of King Mwanga will live through the present critical stage of transition, and will emerge numerically smaller, no doubt, but brighter, stronger, and more real than ever before.

I have not yet seen Bishop Tucker's book recounting his past eighteen years' experience, but I have no doubt he there refers at length to the constitution of the Church in Uganda, so I need not speak further of it here. We are part of the English Church, so of course our services are the same; but I have often been asked about the nature of the elements used in the celebration of the Holy Communion; and would explain that red wine is used in the cathedral church, and wherever else men have it; otherwise a native substitute is used. Personally I think this diversity of use a great pity, and wish the national drink of Uganda could be sanctioned; for as I do not believe that the efficacy of that blessed sacrament depends upon the *time* of its celebration, so I think it very unwise to convey to a nation's mind the idea that its efficacy depends upon the *colour* of the material in the cup, and so force them to begin an import which will not eventually be confined to Church use.

That the *material* itself is not the important factor may be argued from the diverse use in the English Church at home. In one Church there may be used an insipid mixture of coloured sugar and water, and in another a cheap poisonous port, neither of which ever saw a grape; so I cannot think that a universal use in the Church of Uganda of the unfermented native wine—a drink made from bananas— would be at all wrong or inexpedient.

"The best and purest Wheat Bread that conveniently may be gotten" is used at the capital and wherever else flour is procurable, and a person can bake it; but there are times when it is not procurable, and I cannot think that under such circumstances the injunction "that all things be done to edifying" is more reasonably carried out by the use of a questionable biscuit than by the use of "such (food) as is usual to be eaten," viz., a baked plantain.

Is this not an occasion when, according to Article 34, "Tradition . . . may be changed according to the diversities of countries, times, and men's manners"?

Another common question refers to discipline: "How do you deal with professing Christians who continue to live in flagrant sin?"

At one time we dealt with them by exhortation and expostulation, and when these failed they were excommunicated. But now such a thing is almost impossible, owing to the fact that we have no working agreement with the Roman Catholics, who will receive those who go over from the Anglican Church. In my first district there was a chief who had led a clean and good life until he was baptized into our branch of the Church. Then he began to go back, and became, what he had probably been before preparing for baptism, one of the biggest rascals it has ever been my lot to meet. I did my best to help him, and got kindly natives to deal with him, but all to no purpose;

so I warned him that there was nothing left
but excommunication. His case was to come
before the Central Church Council at Mengo
on a certain Saturday, and he left his country
place a day or two before to go up to the
capital. On the day when he ought to have
appeared before the Church Council to show
reason why he should not be publicly excommunicated he was parading the capital laden
with rosaries, medallions, and crucifixes, declaring that he had found a better religion than
ours, having become a Mufalasa, *i.e.*, a French-
man. Although leading a wretchedly bad life,
he had been received into the Roman Catholic
Church—a thing which could not have happened
had there been a working agreement between
us to deal with such cases.

The feeling that we should be driving them
to the other side, and probably the fear to lose
some of those in authority, is responsible to
some extent for the general weakening of
Church authority consequent upon the disuse
of excommunication.

The present Bishop of Uganda, with the
assistance of men like Gordon, Walker, Pilkington, Baskerville, and others, has done
a glorious work, which is now at the parting
of the ways; and much depends upon the
Church's rulers as to what the future will be.

The size of the diocese is detrimental to real progress, for it is impossible to give it adequate supervision, and to keep in close touch with and supply the varying needs which require unwavering continuity of purpose.

An Executive Committee does not meet the need, for it is no part of the native Church; and members, because of the pressing needs of their own districts, or because they are totally ignorant of the needs and exigences of work in other parts, are not always able to give that adequate consideration necessary to develop a work which requires chiefly tenacious continuity of purpose.

The Bishop, as head of the Church, is the one to give close attention to the development of its constitution, with its ideas of self-government, self-support, extension, &c., and if the present or future Bishop of Uganda is to do this, his work must be considerably minimised by division and the formation of another diocese between Uganda and Mombasa.

The new diocese should extend from Nassa to Abyssinia, and from Usoga to the Kikuya Escarpment, and would contain more than six millions of inhabitants whose language and mode of living mark them off very definitely from the peoples of Uganda, Usoga, Unyoro, and Toro.

Mount Elgon district would be the very centre of such a diocese; therefore strengthen and develop the work at that centre—a distributing base convenient in every way.

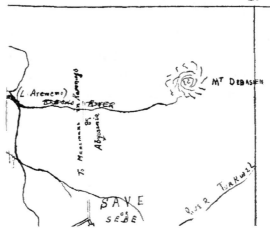

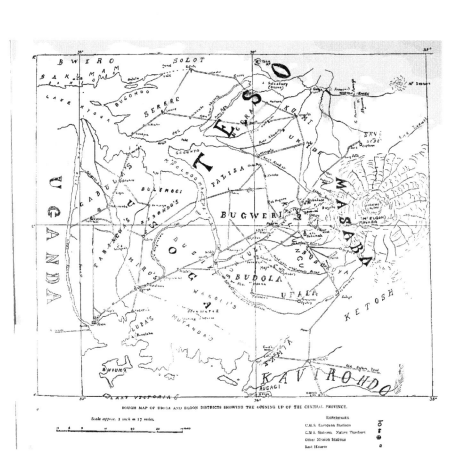

ROUGH MAP OF USOGA AND ELGON DISTRICTS SHOWING THE OPENING UP OF THE CENTRAL PROVINCE.

Scale approx. 1 inch = 17 miles.

REFERENCES

C.M.S. European Stations

C.M.S. Stations, Native Teachers

Other Mission Stations

Rest Houses

CHAPTER XI

THROUGH USOGA

A journey eastward—Kyagwe—Ham Mukasa—A visit to England—Samwili Kangawo—Perfect gentleman—Wayside camps—A view of Lake Victoria and Usoga—Ripon Falls—Whence the Nile springs—A dangerous ferry—A unique welcome—Jinja and its possibilities—From Lake Victoria to Egypt—Agriculture—Road-making—A good centre—Clever thieves—Slow work—Christian revenge—Famine—Hut-tax returns—Value of a paramount chief.

OUR journey must be continued; and having seen what there is to see in Uganda, and having ascertained that Masaba is a country situate on the slopes of the extinct volcano, Mount Elgon, our next businesss was to get there.

It might have been reached direct from Port Florence, the terminus of the Uganda Railway, by marching north through the part of Kavirondo occupied by Nilotic people, and on through the Bantu people at Mumia's. This journey in itself would be a revelation and education to many; but having crossed the Lake Victoria, I prefer to take you from Namirembi, directly east, *viâ* the birthplace of the river Nile, through the country of Bishop Hannington's martyrdom, the scene of sleeping-sickness ravages, and on into regions until this last year or two unknown.

After waiting for loads long delayed on the railway, then again for porters to carry them, we set off through Kyagwe, the eastern district of Uganda, a most beautiful country with the road running through well-tended banana gardens and ideal tropical forests.

The native head of this district is Ham Mukasa, the intelligent Muganda who accompanied the Katikiro, or Prime Minister, to England for the Coronation of King Edward. No traveller to Uganda should miss the opportunity of coming into touch with this chief, or his friend Samwili (Samuel) Kangawo, chief of the district Bulemezi, north of Mengo. He will be astonished to find such intelligence, strong character, perfect gentlemanliness, real goodness, and deep religious feeling, without a suspicion of cant. He will also learn, on passing through Kyagwe, that its chief is practical in his administration, stern in the suppression of lawlessness, and just yet merciful to offenders.

As we approach his place we are met by
runners who give us their chief's greetings,
and soon we meet the gentleman himself;
for he has ridden out some distance on his
cycle to welcome us, and, with his retinue,
he escorts us to his house for rest and refresh-
ment.

English chairs, or chairs made in Uganda
from an English pattern, are provided for the
guests, and tea is served in proper style, during
which the wife and child of our host are
presented to us, and crowds of natives
assemble to do honour to their chief's guests.

Kindness, tact, and courtesy seem characteristic of this man, and as an illustration
let me say how well I remember his staying
in my camp until very late at night in order
to help mend a bicycle that had met with
an accident on the way.

Our pleasant visit to this chief was all too
short; we found him interested in the spiritual
and social welfare of his people, keenly anxious
to help the poorest person in his district, and
not forgetful of the welfare of his guests and
their porters. Messengers were sent off in
front of us, to warn the people along the
road of our approach, and requesting them
to provide food for the porters, for which
they would be paid.

We had three days' march after leaving Ham Mukasa before we reached the Nile; and twice we slept in the camping-places prepared for the use of travellers. As a rule these places are fenced off in order to provide some protection against thieves and wild beasts. There is a place for the European's tent to be pitched, a rest-house for his men, and sometimes a little thatched place in which the traveller may sit during the heat of the day— an undoubted boon, but, owing to the prevalence of the tick, responsible for conveying Spirillum fever, they have become veritable death-traps.

Pushing on still eastward, we reach Nyenga, and get an exquisite glimpse of Lake Victoria, backed by thickly wooded Usoga. From here it is a rapid descent to the lakeside and more particularly to the interesting spot where the water dashes over the Ripon Falls to form the Nile.

Undoubtedly the traveller will be somewhat disappointed if he expects to see the water falling from a great height, but he will not be disappointed in the amount rushing over. The prettiness of the scene immediately near the Falls has been recently considerably modified; for the dread scourge of sleeping sickness has made it imperative to cut down all trees and bushes that lined the banks of the stream.

In the pool above the Falls crocodiles and hippopotami abound, and since these are a menace to the users of the public ferry between Uganda and Usoga, it is allowable to shoot them without having procured a licence. No doubt the powers that be realised that the ferry, crossing as it did, until quite recently, very near to the Falls and without any protection in bad weather, and carried on by means of the laced native canoe from which the keel-board has been known to fall when crossing, was danger enough to the traveller. Perhaps the time is not very far distant when not only will the crocs and hippos be cleared from Napoleon Gulf, but a small oil launch will run from shore to shore; and even now the spicy feeling of possibly drifting over the Falls might be taken away by drawing a wire cable from Uganda to Usoga.

We must deal, however, with things as they are, and sit down on the Lake shore until a few canoes have been collected together. With gentle persuasion and much force the mule is pushed and lifted into one, a milch cow into another, the loads into another, and ourselves into a fourth. The native porters, firmly believing they will be safer with a

European, make a rush for our boat, with the result that we are all but swamped, and another half-hour is wasted in adjusting, shouting, and threatening before we can leave the shore of Uganda.

One notable crossing I made recently at this ferry was with the Rt. Rev. Dr. Tucker, Bishop of Uganda, who was leaving Uganda to visit the vast regions forming the eastern portion of his diocese. He was expected at Jinja to confirm the many candidates, young and old, who had been prepared by the Rev. T. R. Buckley, B.A. L.L.B., now Archdeacon of Usoga; and remembering how short a time it is since Bishop Hannington was murdered in this very district, the reception accorded to his successor seemed nothing short of wonderful. As our canoes approached the shore of Usoga, we could see Buckley with his school lads, the sons of chiefs, and practically all the chiefs of the country waiting to welcome their Bishop (even the old man Luba, who had killed Hannington, though dying, was represented), and with the others helped to send up a good imitation of a British "Hip, hip, hurrah!" when the Bishop stepped out of his canoe.

It seemed hardly credible that this could be the country of Usoga, and these its people.

THE VENERABLE T. R. BUCKLEY, B.A., LL.B.

Only a short time ago it was subject to the tyrannical rule of Uganda, whose meanest peasant despised the Usoga people, and looked upon them as lawful game, yet here were men and women escorting us from the ferry to the Mission station, whose faces had quite lost the crafty, hunted, and fearful look so often seen on the downtrodden African; whilst in its place could be detected calm strength and dignity, thanks to the work of such Government officers as the two Grants, Boyle, and Cubitt, and missionaries like Buckley, Wilson, and Skeens. "The persevering, patient, quiet life of Buckley, living there among the natives in his £30 mud-house, has done more for us fellows and for the country than any outsider can ever know," said a Government officer to me; and to see the native chiefs around him, and their attitude to each other on that day of the Bishop's arrival, enabled me to understand what the officer meant.

As we looked from chief to chief we soon realised that the sleeping sickness had been no respecter of persons; this one and that one well known to us had passed away, and vast districts through which the Bishop and I had travelled years before, and found teeming with population, are now as howling wildernesses.

Jinja is an important place, and likely to become more so, for it is the Government headquarters for the Central Province of the Uganda Protectorate. It is healthily and beautifully situated, overlooking the Ripon Falls and the Napoleon Gulf. The Uganda Railway has recently completed a very good pier, along the side of which the Lake steamers are berthed when they call each week to take off the large exports of ivory, hides, skins, ground nuts, and pepper.

There is very little doubt but that soon we shall have here a large power station, certainly to supply all local needs, and, let us hope, to be used to open out the countries lying east between Jinja and Kisumu.

It is now possible to travel from Jinja down the Nile to Unyoro and on to Egypt. This route was followed by the Right Hon. Winston Churchill on his recent tour through East Africa and Uganda. The Government propose to run a railway from Jinja to Kakindu, a place on the Nile about forty miles north, where a small steamer will meet passengers and take them on through Lake Kyoga to Unyoro. A survey party has also actually started to map out a line from the Nile through Masindi in Unyoro to Butiaba on Lake Albert Edward, thus bringing Jinja

into direct communication with the Congo
Free State.

Usoga has a far richer soil than Uganda,
and even now the natives are experimenting
with cotton-growing; but unfortunately there
is no one to buy it from them after it is
grown. Perhaps soon we shall see gins and
baling presses here at Jinja, with such water-
power at hand, and the steamer only a few yards
off ready to receive shipments for Europe.

A beginning has been made with rubber-tree
planting, but already two planters have died
from blackwater fever; and men taking up
such work should never live and work alone,
for by working in pairs it might be possible
to arrange for change and rest when necessary,
instead of having to succumb as much to worry
and work as to fever.

The position of Jinja will always prevent its
becoming a great native centre on account of
the food difficulty; and since we must leave, let
us push on eastward to Iganga, the natural
capital of the country, where once there was
a Government Boma and where again, I have
little doubt, will be set up the headquarters of
native administration. Iganga is only eight
miles from the Lake; it is very central, thickly
populated, has a good food supply, and from
it native-made roads running in all directions.

Nowhere in the Uganda Protectorate has there been a greater waste of native labour than on the road running east from Jinja through Iganga. A necessary waste, maybe, under the circumstances, but a waste nevertheless, and it must be gratifying to native and European to know that the Government intend to spend £2,000 this year on a properly made road.

Unfortunately, the sleeping sickness seems specially busy in this centre, and the Government has recently opened a camp for patients. The C.M.S. agents have done a good deal of work amongst the sufferers, but since little relief and no cure is possible the work is specially difficult.

The C.M.S. has had a station here for some years, and a wonderful work has been done among a people despised by the Baganda and notorious for many evil practices.

The Baganda are clever thieves, but are not to be compared with the Basoga.

Some years ago, before the Uganda Railway was built, when about to travel down country I had occasion to encamp for some days in Usoga for the purpose of buying food for my porters. I knew the people were given to stealing, for they had actually taken the rifles from some of the Indian soldiers who were

sent up to Uganda after the Soudanese rebellion, but as there was nothing of great
value in my camp I hoped we should be
unmolested.

All went well until the food supply was complete and preparations made for an early start.
Each porter retired to rest with his bag of meal
under his head, but before morning every
vestige of food had been taken and my tent
rifled. I begged the men not to make an out-
cry, but to rest until the morning and then go
on with the packing and preparation for the
march as if nothing had happened. I was busy
at breakfast when a princess and acting chief
appeared and commiserated me on my losses;
I was sure the ruse was working and that we
had found the thieves, for how otherwise could
they know of the matter? And you can imagine
their consternation when, instead of allowing
them to leave my camp immediately after con-
doling with me, I declared my intention of
taking them on to the nearest Government
officer. For very shame they dared not bring
back the meal and cloth stolen, but they
immediately offered to pay the value in goats
and sheep.

This thieving trait in the character of the
Basoga has been developed under proper
teachers organised by the chiefs, and I am

thankful to say it is dying out under the stern measures of the Government and the influence of Christian Missions.

Iganga has always been a trying station, and the Europeans have suffered a good deal from thieves, wild animals, and disease. The Mission ladies have often had attempts made to enter their house at night-time; leopards repeatedly walk across their courtyard, and not long ago, whilst I was there, a sleeping-sickness patient was carried off by a hyæna or leopard from a hut within the compound. On another visit I found one of the ladies who had been waiting upon this very patient down with blackwater fever, to which she succumbed after only a few days' illness.

Slow, dull, and trying for missionary and administrator this work in Usoga; but already the reward is wonderfully encouraging. Thousands under instruction, many showing evidence of mental ability that will compare favourably with that of the average boy or girl in England. A large number of capable native teachers, a number of promising candidates for the ministry and young chiefs who would have sunk only too readily into the slough of their forefathers are being mentally, morally, and physically prepared for the task of ruling their districts in accordance not only with England's laws, but

SEMEI KAKUNGULU.

238

also that authority responsible for England's greatness—the Word of God.

Such is the revenge of the C.M.S. and Christian England on Usoga for the murder of Bishop Hannington; and this revenge must have appealed to the most bigoted heathen when, as a climax, the son of the murdered Bishop baptized the son of the murderer "into the name of the Father and of the Son and of the Holy Ghost."

Even as I write, the news has reached England that Usoga has been visited by a famine and some thousands of people have died in spite of the efforts of Government officers and missionaries. Such a condition of things will continue, I presume, until the resources of the country are so organised that every nerve is not stretched to secure big hut-tax returns, but to teach the people that they need not succumb at the first prolonged drought.

It is interesting, too, to note that although Usoga is sometimes held up as an example of what can be done in the way of hut-tax returns without any definite payment to chiefs, such as we have seen prevails in Uganda, it has been found necessary to take a capable and influential Muganda chief—Semei Kakungulu—and set him as president over the other chiefs, to develop in the minds of the Basoga the more advanced, yet ancient, methods of the Baganda, based on the feudal system.

It would be infinitely cheaper, quite as efficient, and undoubtedly practicable, were Semei Kakungulu made absolute paramount chief of the Central Province and an Administration set up in accordance with the idea already proposed for Uganda and neighbouring kingdoms—*i.e.*, Semei Kakungulu and the native chiefs, under the direction of a capable white adviser, would do the work of the present junior officials.

CHAPTER XII

ON THE MARCH IN UNKNOWN LANDS

Bukedi—River Mpologoma—Dug-out canoes—Papyrus—Disenchantment—Strange dwelling-places—Lake Kyoga—
Floating islands—A spicy experience—Teso country—
Clothing despised—Remarkable village fences—Curious
ornaments—The care of children—Precautions for benefit
of girls—Fear of a mother-in-law—Mission work—Lake
Salisbury—A primitive race—Turkana people—Hair-dressing and use of pillows.

UNTIL quite recently Usoga was the limit
of the Baganda marauding expeditions,
and beyond that the vast countries stretching
away to Lake Rudolph and Abyssinia were all
denominated by the one word Bukedi, a word
corrupted by the Baganda from Ukidi, the name
of a district in the Teso country, and conveying
to the Baganda mind a great land inhabited by
dangerous, naked savages.

I have journeyed into these countries from
rail-head at Kisumu, from our last resting-

place, Iganga, going directly east, and also from Iganga, going north *via* Kamuli on to Lake Kyoga, and thence in canoe to Bukedi, or, more explicitly, Teso.

Let us now march directly east, my wife having taken her place in the hammock I made to help her along.

In three marches from Iganga we are at the side of a great expanse of water which the natives at this point call Mpologoma, or Lion. This water has been described as a backwash of the Nile, and it has also been mapped as a swamp, but after careful observation I have been able to map it as a river, and one of the chief rivers to carry off the waters from Mount Elgon to Lake Kyoga and thence to the Nile.

Former travellers may well have supposed the River Mpologoma a swamp or lake, for where it is touched in Usoga by the ordinary trade route it is one mass of papyrus, through which the natives have cut a passage for their dug-out canoes.

This passage has recently been declared a Government ferry, which means, I suppose, that the natives will still have to provide the means of transit and pay for the privilege of doing so.

It is a source of amazement to stand at the river-side in the early morning before the sun

has looked over Mount Elgon, when a silence
which can be felt reigns supreme, to hear your
cries for boatmen come back to you with a
hopelessness that suggests death and desolation, and then to see a weird figure standing
erect on a small piece of wood, across which
the water pours, shoot out from the high-
growing papyrus, paddle himself swiftly to
within a few yards of you to comfort you
with the assurance that large canoes will soon
be on the spot.

The meaning of the word *soon* is undoubtedly
relative, for to the African it may mean two
hours, a day, or even longer; still, since "all
things come to him who waits," even the giant
dug-out canoes on the river Mpologoma appear,
brought from their hiding-places in the papyrus
by numbers of men and women who have
sprung from no one knows where.

Every one seems to talk at the same time,
and there is a babel of language, for there
are porters from Masaba, Uganda, and Usoga,
whilst the boat people speak a dialect quite
their own. Each one knows better than the
other how to induce a mule to enter a canoe,
and the result is chaos with good promise of
disaster; but at last every thing and being has
found boat-room, and some of the canoes have
already disappeared down what looks a long

lane, but is really the ferry cut by the natives through the papyrus from bank to bank of the river.

The traveller has no doubt settled himself to utilise the forty minutes crossing by thinking of the wonders of Africa and wonderful ways of the African. He has been intensely interested in the canoes, the men and women, some of the latter with babies hanging on to them as they paddle and chant their way across the stream; and he has also been interested in the way the men jeopardised their lives in fighting for a place in the canoes. How true these porters are to their charge! And he begins with admiration to study the faces of the men in his canoe.

He is encouraged in his study by a smile which greets him from the end of the boat; but that same smile quickens him into mental and physical activity more effectually than the myriad mosquitoes that have left their resting-places in the papyrus to claim blood-relationship with the new white man, for by a lightning process of deduction he concludes that since that smile belongs to the mule-boy then the mule has been sent on alone to be pulled and mauled, and perhaps lamed, on the opposite bank by the men who do not understand it.

He looks round and recognises men who

HOUSE BUILT ON THE RIVER MPOLOGOMA.

245

ought to be with their loads in other boats, and fails to recognise the men who so carefully deposited loads that as far as possible always travel with the European. The loads indeed are near, but will have to wait half an hour on the bank-side before the porters told off to carry them arrive.

The traveller soon realises, if he has not already done so, the philosophy of the Kiswahili "Pole, pole" ("Slowly, slowly"); and of the Luganda proverb, "Akwata mpola atuka wala" ("He who goes slowly reaches far"); and having comforted himself with the thought that he will arrive *some time*, he settles down—as well as the mosquitoes will allow him—to pass the time profitably.

This at any rate was my experience; and having heard a rumour to the effect that the people lived in the papyrus, I got the rowers to take me out of the usual route to see the chief of these men and women of the river.

The canoe was made to wind in and out among the high-growing reeds; and then with a sudden push through what seemed an impossible barrier, we were amazed and delighted to find ourselves floating in a clear expanse of water, at the far side of which stood, as if also resting on it, a large-sized, comfortable-looking native house, out of which a dog came

13

to bark at us, whilst the children, affrighted at the sudden appearance of a white man, stood at a safe distance within the doorway and gaped.

No island or mud-bank near, it seemed inconceivable that any house could be in the vicinity; yet here was one, and I afterwards found many more.

The natives explained to me that in years gone by there was no security in the countries bordering this great river. Their forefathers were constantly raided, and were eventually forced to seek shelter in the marshes and rivers.

Some ingenious man found that by cutting the papyrus level with the water, and then sewing the stems together, he was able to make a substantial and safe surface upon which it was possible to build a house safe from the land robbers, and from which terms could be dictated to those who wished to cross from one side of the river to the other.

Quite a strong community of these river dwellers is to be found on the Mpologoma; and whilst it is marvellous how they have withstood the mosquito pest, it is most pitiful to know that the sleeping-sickness fly has reached their dwelling-place, and most of them are probably doomed to die of this awful plague.

It was a pleasure to go in and out among these people whenever I was at the Mpologoma; and through the kindness of a Muganda chief I had a little church erected near the river to which some of them came to read, hear, and learn of the love and peace of God.

The river is known by different names in different parts of the country, but I have carefully traced it from Mount Elgon, and have given it on the map on pp. 220–221.

Having crossed it on the road running directly east from the Nile and Iganga, we have a journey of some forty miles to travel before coming to our Masaba Mission station situate on the foothills of Mount Elgon; and since the intervening country is somewhat uninteresting it will not be amiss to retrace our steps and take the reader north from Iganga across Lake Kyoga, formed no doubt to a great extent by the river Mpologoma; at any rate fed by the Nile, Mpologoma, and connections from Lake Salisbury, which acts as a reservoir for much water from Mounts Elgon, Dabasian (Kokolyo), and Teso.

It seems to me that when dealing with the Nile supply too little notice has hitherto been taken of the water pouring into Kyoga from these mountains.

Great floating islands of papyrus are a

feature of Lake Kyoga, for the rush of the rivers Mpologoma, Naigombwa, Abuketi, and Agu seems to prevent any thick growth in the water, which is here quite expansive.

The crossing is quite a spicy experience, especially when the headman of the canoes, in order to extract a compliment, informs one that the canoe in which we are sitting turned turtle on the journey from the other side, and was only saved by the skill with which he and his fellows got it and themselves alongside a floating island.

In fear and trembling our porters land on the shores of Bukedi, as they call it, but really in Serere, a district of Teso, a large country stretching from Lake Kyoga to Lake Rudolph, and occupied by a Nilotic tribe of people.

We are, indeed, in a strange land: houses, people, language, cultivation, all differ from anything met with elsewhere in the Uganda Protectorate, south of Acholi country, and even the white man can sympathise with the nervousness of his porters.

Remarkably tall men absolutely naked, and women with bead and iron belts from which hangs a fringe behind and in front go stalking past; and large companies can be seen at work preparing the ground for the sowing of millet, the chief item of food. So there are certain evidences of a large population, but not a house can be seen until some friendly native escorts us behind the thick screens and defences formed by the cactus plant, and there in peace, safety, and comfort is seen the patriarchal family with all they require.

As an additional defence the doorways of the houses are often made so remarkably low that people and cattle are obliged to kneel to enter. This custom has developed a condition of chronic white swelling, or housemaid's knee, among many of the men, women, and cattle ; and it is a most peculiar sight to see people and cattle walking about with a great swelling on each knee.

Polygamy is the usual custom of the people in these regions, and the favourite wife can generally be distinguished by some special mark of favour. In one group I photographed the chief's favourite was wearing an iron chain apron, and was looked upon as a great swell.

The rest of the ladies in the group had vied with each other as to how many rings they could wear in nose, ears, lips, and tongue, and one young girl seemed very proud of the fact that she had five rings in her tongue, which she shyly kept out whilst I was taking the photograph.

The men are equally fond of such adornments

to ears, nose, and lips ; and further north they enhance their " beauty " by allowing their hair to grow, and then working into it thick potter's clay, which looks and feels almost like an unnatural growth. Into this clay they stick ostrich feathers, which add considerably to their already great height and striking appearance.

Nowhere else in Africa have I seen the care bestowed upon infants which is to be met with in Teso country ; and one picture explains what I mean. The tall mother has been on a journey, and her infant is resting in a very nicely made skin sling on her back. To protect the child's head from the sun a gourd has been prepared, and can be seen in the picture hanging from the mother's neck and covering the baby's head.

The pictures of a Teso house and grain store will enable the reader to understand how careful these seemingly wild people are to make provision for the future.

Care is taken to protect the unmarried girls by making it compulsory for all young unmarried men of a family or village to sleep together in a hut set apart from the rest ; and it is said that after these youths have retired the elders prepare the ground in such a way that trespassers are easily traced. This, how-

TESO HOUSE AND GRAIN STORE.

GRAIN STORE IN THE TESO COUNTRY.

253

ever, is only done when flagrant advantage has
been taken of the custom of the country for
girls not to refuse when solicited.

When being taken round one of the villages
by its chief, I was interested and amused at
seeing a practical illustration of the awe with
which a mother-in-law can inspire her daughter's
husband. ʼ✔

The man was describing to me how that he
was the head of his village, that men and
women helped to till the ground and gather
the grain; that sweet potatoes and bananas are
also cultivated, but the bananas are not eaten
for food but used for making drink.

He explained the necessity for guarding
themselves with the strong cactus fence against
the Kimam or Kimama people to the north—a
people of less striking physique than the Teso,
Koromojo, and Turkana tribes, but much more
formidable fighters; and when in the middle
of his explanation he suddenly stopped, gripped
me by the arm and led me off at a rapid
pace in the opposite direction. I was certain
then some of the enemy had appeared. At the
gate, however, he stopped in his flight and went
on with the conversation as if nothing had
happened.

Naturally I was inquisitive, and pressed him
for an explanation, when he pointed in the

direction from which we had come and uttered the words "Mother-in-law." I chaffingly suggested that his description of things could not be correct, for he had told me that he was head of the village, and here he was afraid of his mother-in-law. He smiled, somewhat grimly I thought, but would not be persuaded to return by the same route. The lady was on the outlook for us, and at the same time anxiously endeavouring to protect herself from the shame of being gazed upon by her daughter's husband. A curious custom no doubt, yet one perhaps which makes for peace.

For the past five years Baganda teachers have been working amongst these people with encouraging results. Archdeacon Buckley and I have baptized young men from Miro and Bululu, on the shores of Kyoga, and have found them bright and intelligent ; and two years ago some Teso lads from Kumi, near Lake Salisbury, were baptized by a Muganda clergyman whom I had placed there.

One of these lads came to live with me and teach me his language, but sickness intervened and I was invalided to Europe.

Since then the C.M.S. have appointed a European and his wife to live at Ngora, the centre of this Southern Teso district, with a million of people, where the first white woman

TESO MEN AND BOYS.

257

the natives had ever seen—Mrs. Crabtree—was
the wonder of the age ; and where the present
lady, if not driven out by malaria, will prove
a tremendous influence for good. The perfect
friendliness of the people at Ngora may be
gathered from the fact that many were daring
enough to brave the unknown powers of the
camera.

Near by is Lake Salisbury, known to the
natives as "Bisina," a not very beautiful or
expansive sheet of water except in the rainy
season when much of the surrounding land
is inundated.

I was able to trace the distinct double
connection between Lakes Salisbury and
Kyoga formed by the rivers, or arms, Agu
and Abuketi, marked on the map on pp.
220–221.

Fishermen and hippopotami hunters from
Nsoga paddle up one or other of these arms
into Salisbury.

Lakes Salisbury and Gedge are really one
sheet of water in the rainy season.

From the shores of Lake Salisbury we got
a glimpse of Mount Debasian, called Kokolyo
by the natives, rising some twenty miles
away to the westward like three huge jagged
teeth.

Through the glass its cliffs and precipices

look inaccessible; yet perched on the very top of them are the dwellings of a people whose language and habits differ considerably from those of surrounding tribes.

This people, sometimes called Tegetha and Tepeth, are to be met with again on Mount Moroto, near Manimani, in the north; and since they are undoubtedly of Bantu stock, their presence so far north, and surrounded as they are by powerful Nilotic peoples by whom they are respected, is a striking phenomenon. I have often longed to visit them, and hope the opportunity to do so may come; but at present must content myself with the interesting question as to whether or not they are remnants of a great Galla invasion which passed over the Lake Rudolph district down to the south and south-west as far as the Ruwenzori Mountains and Lake Albert.

Away in the north, between Lakes Salisbury and Rudolph, dwell the powerful Koromojo and Turkana clans, blood relations of the Masai, closely allied in customs and manners to the Suk people of Lake Baringo district, and akin in language to the Teso people among whom we are now travelling.

Like the Teso, the Koromojo and Turkana men eschew clothing of any kind. They are big, strong, brave fellows, renowned as fighters,

but vainer than the most frivolous woman
with regard to trinkets and style of hair-
dressing. A Turkana warrior is a sight to be
remembered, with his long hair thickly inter-
twined and hanging from his head exactly like
a very thick, black doormat with the corners
rounded off.

Where the hair is not long and thick enough
to form of itself a sufficiently prominent head-
dress, it is encaked with potter's clay in which
ostrich feathers, red berries, and pieces of reed
are stuck, giving to the wearer a really terrible
appearance.

The difficulty of sleeping with such a
permanent head-dress is overcome by the use
of a small wooden pillow, made with two
prongs to stick in the ground, and the top
carved to receive the neck of the sleeper. In
the daytime it is carried on the arm of the
owner by a thong of rough hide, and is always
conveniently near when a seat is required.

For many years past Koromojo, Turkana,
and Dobosa, or Toposa, have been open to the
trader and ivory hunter, and indeed one might
truthfully say have been under the supremacy
of the ivory hunter—settlements of Arabs,
Swahilis, and Baloochis. Now and then the
depredations of these rascals have been
suddenly ended by the swoop of a marauding

party of Abyssinians, but from either party
the natives suffered grievously and still suffer,
for there is no attempt to administer what is
a fine and promising district.

Life in some parts of Koromojo and Turkana
will always be somewhat difficult, especially
in the hot season when water is scarce and
sometimes disappears altogether; so that milk
and blood have to be depended upon by human
beings, and the wants of the cattle supplied
from any underground accumulations of water
that may be found by digging.

At present ivory is the chief export from
these districts, and some idea of the number
of elephants to be met with may be gathered
from the rich haul represented by the accompanying picture.

There seems no difficulty in persuading men
to undertake hardships for the purpose of gain
—one young fellow is said to have cleared
£8,000 profit in about nine months; but how few
men there are—at the present moment none—
willing to answer the call of this vast district,
to use the present grand opportunity, before the
Swahili traders have forced Mohammedanism
upon the natives, and before the evils of civilisation have ruined them, to go in and win the
whole district for Christ!

What a glorious work might be done at

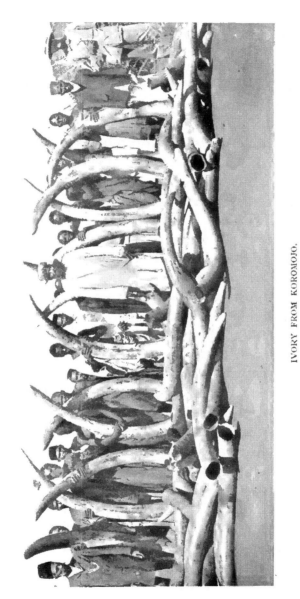

IVORY FROM KOROMOJO.

Manimani by a few earnest and practical young fellows—a clergyman, a doctor, and a couple of laymen !

Even Abyssinia recognises the opportunity, for not two years ago five Abyssinians travelled down from their own country through these districts to my station on Mount Elgon, and begged me to go back with them and see the many peoples by the way in need of a missionary. Four of these men claimed to be Christians, a remnant of the old Coptic Church —in this instance an example to more enlightened professors of the Christian religion.

I was too ill to move far from my own station, and in any case the work at Mount Elgon had the prior claim, but I hope the time is not far distant when men from England will be forthcoming to take up such a challenge as these Abyssinians gave.

At present we must turn our backs on the north and continue our journey southwards towards the great black mass we know to be Mount Elgon.

CHAPTER XIII

MASABA: COUNTRY, PEOPLE, AND CUSTOMS

A cool camp—The largest extinct volcano in the world—Mount Elgon and its foothills—Masaba—Primitive customs—Caves and cave-dwellers—The wildest people in Uganda Protectorate—Native customs—Circumcision—Patriarchal government — Clan system — Land laws — Heirship — Marriage laws and customs—Dress of married women—Clan marks—Ornaments—Protection of girls—Punishment of wrong-doers—Clan fights—Native courtesy—Spirit of independence — Jealousy — A father's curse — Curious customs.

IN the middle of the hottest season it is possible to sleep comfortably at our last camp, Nabowa, or Napowa, for the cold winds from the largest volcano in the world have been blowing over us, and we rise refreshed to see a sight interesting and pleasing.

Right in front of us, apparently quite near, rises the extinct volcano known—no one knows

why—as Mount Elgon. Its foothills stretch
away vast distances to right and left, and
appear on the north to join the peculiarly
shaped mountain Debasian, or Kokolyo.

As a matter of fact the crater of Elgon
must be some thirty miles from Nabowa, but
at a distance of fourteen miles there rises
abruptly a hilly plateau some 7,500 feet above
sea-level, and this with a cloud hanging over
its top at first sight appears joined to the
crater.

All the hill region is known as Masaba, and
until the last few years it has been quite
cut off from the outside world.

There, on the hill in front of us, are men
who offer sacrifices as in the days of Cain and
Abel, and procure fire for the purpose probably in the very same way as those ancients
by the rubbing of sticks.

On this western side are to be seen caves,
which, though now only used as hiding-places
in times of danger, were undoubtedly at no
distant date the usual dwelling-places of the
Bagishu.

Away to the south-east of Elgon the caves
are still in use, though the bolder spirits are
beginning to build in the open.

I have not the least doubt that the caves
are originally natural, but have been enlarged

to meet the needs of growing families and herds.

A belt of "Kalungu," that is, uninhabited land, almost surrounds Masaba, and gives the country an uninviting appearance; but no sooner has this been crossed than Masaba is seen to be a land of plenty, beauty, and, because of its primitive simplicity, a land of wonder.

The long elephant-grass of Uganda and Usoga is absent, and as far as the eye can reach almost every foot of ground seems to be under cultivation, whilst innumerable clusters of houses are visible in every valley and on what appear to be inaccessible hills.

We left the last Government post more than twenty miles west of Masaba, but nowhere else in Africa did I receive a more hearty welcome or meet with a more kindly disposed people than in this country, where the people were living as they had lived right along from the past ages, and are described by the late Commissioner of Uganda, Sir H. H. Johnston, as "perhaps the wildest people to be found anywhere within the limits of the Uganda Protectorate. They are wilder even than the Congo dwarfs."

Such a character almost appalled one, but

AN OLD MASABA PATRIARCH.

four years of life among them proved them not only very kindly but very capable of development.

A primitive, pastoral, Bantu-speaking people, they are known as Bamasaba or Bagishu, but distinguish themselves as a race apart from others by the name Basani, *i.e.*, men, whilst all men of uncircumcised nations are called Basindi, *i.e.*, boys.

There is an annual festival of circumcision, when all youths who wish to be recognised as full members of the clan, warriors, and men to be reckoned with, parade, dressed in war dress, and march from village to village to make public their brave decision.

They are *fêted* by young and old for days before the actual operation, and they visit the sacred grove of the clan, and, having made their offerings, receive through their witch-doctor the blessing of the spirits.

The final operation is carried out by adepts, who receive a fowl from each lad.

This operation is performed in public, not in one centre, but in various places situate as near as possible to the homes of the young men concerned.

Each patient has to stand forward, grasp a young sapling with both hands, and stand without flinching whilst the foreskin is cut

14

away. On the least show of cowardice the patient is fiercely beaten with sticks by the onlookers, but at the close of the operaton is treated with great care and consideration until better.

A house is set apart for the young men suffering, and they are carefully tended night and day until better.

As a rule, the youths are nude until circumcision, after which they wear a skin apron.

The form of government has only reached the patriarchal stage; and this explains the reason for the independent village life found in Masaba. Ten, twenty, thirty, and as many as a hundred houses are clustered together, sometimes fortified with a strong mud wall and deep trench; and in these dwell the wives, sons, grandchildren, and other relations of the chief man, who is the old patriarchal head or son chosen to succeed him.

The old patriarchs long ago took clan names, and instituted the clan system whereby the land of the country was fairly apportioned and settled on a satisfactory basis.

Each clan owns a definitely marked strip of land running towards the principal mountain heights.

Each adult male individual of a clan can claim a piece of this strip. No land is ex-

changed, but any individual may sell his
land, and often does sell a portion of it. No
chief may interfere, for the Masaba chiefs
are not chiefs in the feudal sense and do
not own the land more than any other householder. Each male has an independent right
over his own land, and no chief can turn
him away, as is the case under the feudal
system.

The land is hereditable, and on the death
of the father, if married sons only remain,
they share alike. If married sons and young
children are left, the eldest son takes charge
on behalf of the young male children. He
and the other married sons may share the
cattle with the children, but the land is kept
for the children.

If there is more than one wife, and each
wife has children, the male children fall
heirs to the land cultivated by their own
mother.

If there be only one wife, with issue of sons,
the sons divide the estate.

The heir to the chieftainship—*i.e.*, representative of the family—is elected by the
male relatives of the deceased, and is always
a son.

A person may change his clan to enter the
clan of his mother, and he may succeed to

land in both the clan of his father and of his mother.

Members of the same clan do not intermarry.

The clan feeling is very strong, and each individual is intensely loyal to the call of the clan in time of need. An insult offered to the humblest individual is offered to, and will be resented by, the whole clan. Consequently the clans are often at variance. Their petty jealousies prevent any cordial co-operation or amalgamation, even in time of direst necessity, and this makes missionary and probably any other kind of work among them very difficult.

There is little doubt, however, but that this condition of the people has been of some assistance to the Government, for such a thing as organised opposition is quite out of the question.

The strongest patriarch, or chief, is the man who has been able to procure the most cattle, and with them buy the largest number of wives, for each of which he would have to pay from two to ten head of cattle, according to age and condition.

The suitor for a lady's hand approaches the girl's father and discusses the price of his choice in cattle. These negotiations often last a considerable time, until at last the bargain is struck and the cattle paid over.

For the space of three months not a sign is given that the arrangement is complete ; the woman is still in her father's house, and things go on as usual in the house of her suitor.

At the end of this time the lady's father kills a goat, and friends—except the prospective bridegroom and his clan—and relations are invited to partake of a feast at his house, after which a procession is formed, composed of the bride-elect, escorted by thirty unmarried girls of her acquaintance, the foremost of whom carries the head and skin of the goat which formed an important item in the recent feast.

Before and behind these females march young men, decked out, like the girls, in all the glory of beads and iron wire.

Behind all come some men, related to the bridegroom, carrying earthenware pots full of strong drink made from grain. The more common drink made from bananas is not used on these occasions.

On arrival at the house of the bridegroom a mimic war takes place, to convey the idea that the two clans are fighting for the lady.

If the bridegroom-elect is still uncircumcised the bride and her retinue stay for two days to cultivate whatever plantain garden the gentleman owns.

If, however, the bridegroom-elect is, from the Bagishu point of view, a man, they stay three days, eating, drinking, working, and playing.

Anything of an unseemly nature is strictly taboo; and as the man and woman most closely concerned are not yet married, they stay apart from each other.

At the end of the second or third day the bride-elect returns with her retinue to her father's house and there remains for one or two months, after which another goat and fowls are killed, plantains cooked, strong drink brewed, and every preparation made for a great feast.

Married men are sent by the bridegroom with jars for the drink and baskets for the food. The procession is once more formed, this time without the young men, and the lady is brought to her husband.

Friends and neighbours and all who will from far and near, except the father and mother of the bride, assemble to eat the marriage feast, at the close of which the bride, now arrayed in the symbolic dress of a married woman, is

escorted by the bridegroom to her future home.
A house and grain store are provided for each
wife, and as a rule the women settle down
after marriage to a quiet, loyal, and fairly industrious life, cultivating, cooking, bringing
firewood and water, counting and restringing
her beads.

The distinctive dress of a married woman is
a fringe of light-coloured string, made from
plantain fibre, tied round the waist at the back,
then gathered together, passed between the legs,
and tied to the string in front.

There is also a small black string fringe,
without which no well-bred woman will approach her husband to serve food or even be
without in a man's presence.

There is no distinctive dress for the younger
women, but they are strictly careful to wear a
piece of cloth or leaf or plant.

When the young men are considered old
enough to marry, and become full members of
their clan—*i.e.*, at from sixteen to eighteen
years of age—they are circumcised; and the
young women, on attaining the age of from
fourteen to sixteen years, are marked on the
abdomen and forehead with the tribal marks,
cut after having been perforated by some old
lady of the clan.

Sometimes the wounds fester and form one

large keloid which looks very like a doormat tied to the abdomen.

It is also customary for the women to perforate the lower lip and gradually enlarge the hole until they are able to wear, comfortably, I suppose, a piece of wood half an inch in diameter or—the height of ambition—a large piece of white quartz two or three inches long.

Both men and women are fond of ornamentation. They wear beads of every kind, shape, and colour, and whatever coloured bead is the fashion becomes the currency for the time being. Necklets, bracelets, and anklets of iron and brass, some of them exceedingly heavy, are greatly sought after; waistbands, too, of ostrich eggshell, cowrie shells, and iron are very popular, and hippo teeth, rams' horns, leg bells, shell and monkey-skin hats are worn to add dignity to festive occasions and to inspire awe in time of war.

At the age of about ten years both boys and girls leave the house of their parents and take up their quarters in houses provided for them, girls in one house, boys in another.

I have already referred to the care taken by the non-Bantu people in Teso to ensure the safe keeping of their girls at night-time. The people of Masaba are not so particular; there are certain penalties attached to wrongdoing, and

MUGISHU WOMAN WEARING LIP STONE.

279

if the young people are foolish enough to brave them they cannot complain of the punishment.

A father who has been given cause for suspicion will hide himself in the grass near the house of his daughter and wait night after night until he knows for certain whether his confidence has been betrayed.

Woe betide the guilty youth! The whole village is aroused, and the elders, with all the male relatives of the girl, fall on him with sticks and beat him until he wishes he had never been born.

And here let me state a fact, hardly comprehensible to Western minds : in nearly every case of solicitation the girl is the culprit.

When without a marriage according to native custom a child is expected, the girl is severely punished by her father or brothers ; indeed, their anger often leads them to the length of spearing her, after which they will bring her to the European to be doctored.

There is no idea of shame in the question, but the marketable value of a girl drops on account of her condition, and instead of the marriage allowance being from four to ten head of cattle her relatives can only get from two to four.

There seems no great difficulty in finding a

husband for such a girl, and I have not the least doubt but that the reduced price tempts suitors.

The child, which to the native mind is illegitimate, goes with the mother and becomes the property of the husband.

It might have been supposed that in the event of the child being a girl a larger number of cattle would be demanded and gladly paid; but no, the woman and her child go for the smallest possible price without a sign of festivity or joy; and we may take it for granted that the voice of the nation has settled this and other unwritten laws for the social welfare of the whole community.

Much of the trouble between clan and clan is caused by unsatisfactory marriages. It is an understood thing that if a wife leaves her husband and returns to her father without having borne a child, the marriage is dissolved by the father returning to the husband all the cattle.

If a child has been born the cattle are returned less one killed to give a feast to the wife's friends and relations. But if there are a number of children the cattle are not returned.

It is undoubtedly difficult to get any African to return cattle that have been in his possession, and the above marriage laws often lead to squabbles and even serious feuds because a wife

CHARGE OF BAGISHU WARRIORS AT MASABA, MOUNT ELGON.

has left her husband to return to her old home, and her father is too strong for the husband, who dare not even go near to claim his own.

As a rule the wrongdoers and the wronged person are supported by their respective clans, and this sometimes leads to a regular battle, such as I have witnessed more than once.

The men of each clan arm with spears, knives, sticks, bows and arrows, and meet for battle on the boundary.

Charge after charge is made, heads cracked, and spear-wounds given, and it may be a man on each side killed; but this does not often happen, except in a drunken brawl.

As a rule the clan fights are carried out with the utmost good-humour, and when either side is tired; the others are quite willing to stop fighting until their opponents feel refreshed; they would not think of taking a mean advantage under such circumstances.

If a man is speared, his friends are allowed to carry him off the field, and unless there is bitter hatred between the clans the fight is not continued on that day.

No clan would dream of molesting a woman belonging to the opposing force. She might with perfect safety walk between the combatants, and is even allowed to pass in safety through the enemy's territory, taking her husband's goats or other possessions to some place of safety.

Indeed, considering the conditions of life in Masaba, it is a wonderful fact that women are very much respected. They hold a much higher position in the country than was the case only a few years ago in Uganda, and is to-day in Usoga and other countries in the Lake district. The Masaba women do not rank with the goods and chattels, but receive respect in youth and honour in old age.

The spirit of independence has been markedly developed in the people, no doubt owing to the fact that the nation is not organised under one head, and the consequent necessity for each person to look after himself or herself. A child will defend with its life its own small property, perhaps a single fowl, and dare its father to use it for himself. A wife will deeply resent any claim of ownership over her made by her husband, yet will be strictly loyal to him until he begins to neglect her claims and rights.

It is sometimes necessary for the husband to assert himself in a manner painful yet salutary to his wife; but when the woman has been in the right, and has taken steps to defend herself, her methods are usually

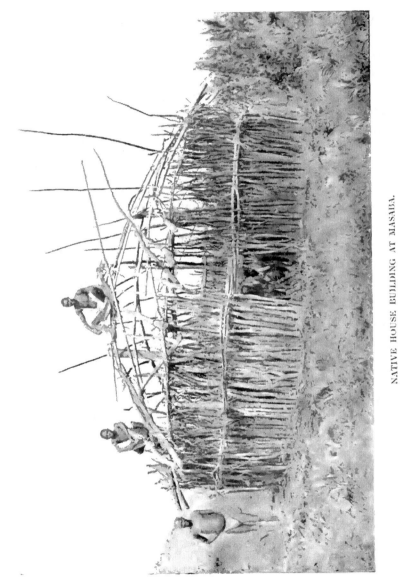

NATIVE HOUSE BUILDING AT MASABA.

288

so drastic that an operation or funeral is necessary to the husband.

Such cases I have had brought to my notice, and must confess that in one such I found it quite difficult to impress the lady with the wrongness of sticking a knife into her husband's back, within an inch of his spine, for she was quite convinced that he deserved it, and had an idea that I thought so too. She promised, however, not to do it again, and gladly left her husband in my care until cured.

The system of polygamy is not responsible for the amount of domestic trouble it is generally supposed to engender. Each wife has her own house, the framework of which is built by the man and his friends, whilst the lady and her friends carefully mud the walls and beat the floor. Outside this house are one or two grain stores, where the lady stores up the last grain harvest as a safeguard against a prolonged dry season when the banana supply gives out.

Sometimes, however, a spirit of jealousy creeps in between wives, and then nothing goes right. Each wife is on the watch for any act of the husband that can be construed as favouritism, and the slighted one begins to plan revenge.

In one case the husband was made to suffer, when, after a day's outing at some drinking party, he returned and demanded admittance to the house of his slighted wife. They quarrelled as to who should open the door, they fought when he got inside, and when, overcome with drink, he sat down dozing at the fire, the woman was so carried away by her mad passion that she crept up behind and killed him there with his own axe.

In another case, the two women came to extremes after bickering and insulting each other for weeks. The favourite wife invited the other to fight the matter out fairly before witnesses, but the witnesses happened to sympathise with the other wife; consequently they held the favourite whilst the second wife tried to cut her head off with a large knife. The woman was terribly cut, but she got off and raised her clan, who first of all sought the weak husband and murderous wife before bringing the injured woman to be attended to at our dispensary.

Although the spirit of independence is so marked, even in the young, there is no lack of parental authority. This is no doubt due to the power of a father's curse. The word "Kutsuba" is dreaded, for to "Kutsuba," or curse, one's child is the severest punishment a father can bestow. The son so dealt with becomes a wanderer, not because his father has cast him out, but because he believes in the power of the curse, and by the action of his own mind brings upon himself what his father's words would have been totally incapable of—utter destitution of health and wealth.

He roams from place to place, unable to fix his attention for long upon anything. He takes pleasure in nothing, and even when married he will leave his wife and all belongings and periodically disappear.

This punishment is given to a son for gross impertinence to or for threatening a father; and to a daughter for marrying without a marriage arrangement, *i.e.*, before her father has received the usual number of cattle.

In the daughter's case the punishment falls heavily upon her husband and herself, for she will either be childless or her children will die at or soon after birth. Case after case has been pointed out to me where my informants declared the curse had indeed had this effect, and one couple I know quite well have recently taken steps to have the curse removed after losing three children, one after the other. Such is the influence of mind over matter.

The removal of the curse is effected by the son or daughter, as the case might be, bringing to the father a goat or sheep which is killed and eaten by the two most nearly concerned in the matter, and all their friends and relations. During the feast the father takes the contents of the animal's stomach and with them smears his son or daughter, who goes forth to show all the clan that the curse has been removed.

Many of the Masaba customs, such as the one just mentioned, are exceedingly curious, and the people cannot give or suggest a reason for them. They have another, well worth mentioning, the meaning of which is, I think, quite conceivable to European minds.

When two clans have been engaged in war, and each has tried in vain for the mastery, they decide to make a compact which no man or woman would dream of breaking.

A dog is brought to the boundary and there cut in two, where so many fights have taken place. One half is placed on the land of one clan, and the other half on the land of the other clan, and the warriors of each clan march in procession between the two halves, which are then spurned by both parties.

There is much hand-shaking and merriment, and from that time the clans are friendly.

There is little doubt but that the idea at the root of this custom is the wish that whoever breaks the compact may have an end like the dog—disowned, cut in two, and spurned.

CHAPTER XIV

LIFE AND WORK AMONGST CANNIBALS

Lost near Mount Elgon—Quaint figures—Clothing despised—
Invalid missionaries—A cheap house—Human hyænas—
The place of departed spirits — Burial customs — The
gathering of the clans—The coming of Roman Catholics—
Laying out a station—Native kindness—Progress—A
unique church dedication — Variety of work — Healing
powers of nature—First baptisms.

IN September, 1903, my wife and I found
ourselves hot, hungry, and very tired,
struggling through banana gardens in the
country at the foot of Mount Elgon, and
making for a hillock which seemed to be
further away every time we caught a glimpse
of it.

Our porters had lost the way and we were
alone, yet not as much alone as we could
have wished, for almost at every step we
took we had evidence of company that at
the time was not much to our liking.

"A TALL IMPRESSIVE FIGURE" NEAR MOUNT ELGON.

295

A tall, impressive figure, naked but for a dressed goat-skin, and armed with one or two spears, would stand and look at us, utter a few words that were unintelligible, and then disappear. Then a group of men and women with less clothing than we had ever conceived it possible for human beings to wear in public, forced their attentions upon us, but were unable to make us understand their welcome or direct us to our destination.

A few more miles had been covered, and the hill we were making for seemed as far off as ever, when two youths, absolutely nude and armed with long sticks, introduced themselves to us with loud laughter and much gesticulation. They made us understand that they would guide us to our destination, and we meekly followed at a much slower speed than they were evidently accustomed to; but this no doubt gave them greater opportunity than they would otherwise have had of explaining to all onlookers who they thought we were, and how nearly we were related to them since they were our guides.

They did not disappoint us, for after what seemed an interminable journey, we saw evidence of civilisation, and hurried with lighter hearts towards a distant umbrella. Imagine our disgust and disappointment to find that it covered an aspiring African escorted by a crowd of admirers, who were far more interested in this native parade than in the advent of two Europeans.

A few yards, however, brought us to the euphorbia fence of what was to be our home, and there we met the two English missionaries, the Rev. W. A. and Mrs. Crabtree, who, some time before, had come out from Uganda to have a holiday in this district, with the Uganda chief, Semei Kakungulu, and were so impressed with the needs and opportunities in this part of the world, that they did not go back to Uganda, but stayed on in Masaba, lived in the chief's house after he had left the place, made friends with the people, and generally prepared the way for us.

I found them both broken in health, and speedily got porters together to take them to rail-head at Kisumu, a distance of a hundred miles.

When Mr. Crabtree heard of our location to Masaba he got the natives to prepare quarters for us. A small, round hut which had served as *a small-pox hospital* was put in order for our boys, and a shed which had been erected to keep the sun off some visitor's tent was made into a house by the Masaba women filling in the sides and ends with wet mud. A hole was left to serve as window, and another as doorway, and these were covered at night-time, and when it rained—as the rainy season was on, it seemed to be always raining — by doors made of reeds.

I have never yet dared to ask my wife what she thought when on that first evening I led her into that shed and told her we should have to live there for some little time. My own feelings were somewhat intense, for what I had treated as a joke when I heard that an application had been sent to headquarters for 1 rupee (1s. 4d.), the cost of my house, I now realised was grim reality.

The walls were wet, the mud had not even begun to crack as a sign that it was drying; the floor was considerably lower than the outside earth, and a convenient ant-hill just outside the door turned all the water into the house. I was—well, I had better not say what I was!—and my feelings were not relieved when my wife complained of headache, and in spite of every precaution, eventually went down with a temperature of 103°.

We removed her to the Crabtrees' house, a

small mud and thatched affair, bequeathed to Mr. Crabtree by a native chief.

Infested though it was with rats and snakes, and responsible no doubt for the ill-health of our predecessors, it was incomparably better than the wet shed outside.

Our first care was to cut down the thick fence of euphorbia, which gave to the place the aspect of a fort.

The Bamasaba were delighted to think that we were not afraid of them, and were willing for them to come about us at all hours. They wondered what would be the next move; and I did not leave them long in doubt, for suspicious smells had been troubling us until we could stand them no longer, and having decided to follow one up, I soon found out the reason of all the others; the natives of Masaba do not as a rule bury their dead, and the long grass surrounding our house was a most convenient place in which to deposit the corpses.

The condition of the atmosphere immediately near us before that long grass was removed may be faintly imagined, yet would have been infinitely worse but for the work of human hyænas who leave very little for the four-legged animal.

The custom of throwing out the dead is

BAGISHU MARRIED WOMEN.

universal among all the clans of Bagishu, except in the case of the youngest child or the old grandfather or grandmother, for whom, like the child, a prolonged life on earth is desired.

As a general rule, it is believed that when the spirit leaves the body it goes to Makombe, the place of departed spirits, which is a very similar place to this earth, for there men meet all friends who have gone before, and come once more into possession, even if they have to fight for them, of all cattle that once belonged to them, but had died or been killed.

The hills of Makombe are beautiful, providing luxuriant and everlasting pasture, and death is quite unknown. It is sometimes said that Were (God) is the great ruling spirit of Makombe.

When it is desired to perpetuate on the earth the life of some old man or woman, or that of some young baby, the corpse is buried inside the house or just under the eaves, until another child is born to the nearest relation of the corpse. This child, male or female, takes the name of the corpse, and the Bagishu firmly believe that the spirit of the dead has passed into this new child and lives again on earth. The remains are then dug up and thrown out into the open.

The hyæna is the chief scavenger of Masaba, and is sacred in the eyes of the people. It is not classified in the language as other animals, but has received a name which puts it on a level with persons.

The work of clearing the ground for a mission station was a big task, but the people undertook it willingly when they realised that I meant to pay them for their work. Large crowds came each day, and if only they had really worked the whole place would have been cleared in a very short time. But different clans had to exchange compliments or epithets that were anything but complimentary, and it sometimes looked as if the mission station was about to be turned into common ground where long-standing clan disputes were to be settled by any and every means.

Expostulation by a European who could hardly make himself understood went for very little, but a threat to give no pay—the currency was small white beads—for that day generally induced them to do a little work.

On the whole the Bagishu worked regularly until a more serious interruption than usual took place, namely, the advent of the Roman Catholic Mission. They had built a small shed, a mile from our station, when the C.M.S. missionary Crabtree took up residence at

Masaba, but they had never permanently occupied it. Now, however, the bishop and
two priests came to inaugurate a more permanent settlement, one mile from my door,
on the land of the same clan; and that
although there was no other mission station
for a hundred miles to the south, some
hundreds of miles to the east, and thousands of miles to the north, all teeming with
population.

The priests had to do what they were told,
but undoubtedly they realised as I did the
sad pity of such a move, which tended to
degrade the mission of Christ's professed
disciples to the level of trade competition.

There was much to try us, for the natives
are cute enough to play one European off
against another, if possible; but we laid ourselves out to understand each other, and as
a result became fast friends.

In May, 1907, I journeyed from Masaba to
Uganda. I had been down with a slight attack
of blackwater fever early in the year, and got
out of bed to make the journey. Ill and
wretched, I called on the Roman Catholic priest,
Father Kirk, at Budaka, and he would fain
have had me stay with him until I felt better;
but I determined to push on, and was much
touched and grateful when later in the day a

messenger from Father Kirk came into my camp with some milk and a bottle of wine. I was not destined to see him again, but I wrote my thanks, and since coming to England have received a letter from the priests in "Bukedi," full of kindly sympathy at my being invalided and speaking much too generously of the work God enabled me to do in that land.

I know, too, how grateful my wife is to Father Spere, of Masaba, for his kind sympathy and help when I lay ill in Uganda, and my fellow-worker, Mr. Holden, was enjoying (!) a temperature of 104° at Masaba. The Roman Catholic priests and the strongly Evangelical yet Catholic C.M.S. missionaries at Masaba, and I am certain in other parts of Africa, live and work happily together because they realise that the true issues of life do not depend on minor shibboleths. Without trespassing on private judgment and opinions, we learn to know and respect each other's work for something like its true value.

Eventually a large clearing was made, roads laid out, and a mission station planned which would contain a church, schools, dispensary, teachers' houses, house for boarders, house for European in charge of district with accommodation for visitors, house for Euro-

NEW IDEAS IN BUILDING NEAR MOUNT ELGON.

pean ladies, and house for second European man.

All this entailed a feature quite novel to the life and custom of Masaba—persistent, consecutive work ; and I was repeatedly warned that to try and get the clans to work together was to attempt the impossible. However, I attempted it with the most gratifying results, for as soon as they realised that I was not there to force them to work, and would pay them for their labour, hundreds came with poles and wattles, fibre for thatching, to stamp mud for walls, to carry stones for foundations, to build a house in the hills, to go with me on the march whenever necessary ; and when the first brick house was built, some three hundred Bagishu went to Jinja, a distance of a hundred miles, with a native headman, and brought the corrugated iron for the roof.

All this time we were making friends with the people, and many evidences of friendship they gave us. I well remember how, on one occasion, when, because of a long drought, famine was sore in the land, and our native teachers and house-boys were wondering what they would eat, a native chief—head of his family—Wanyonyobolo by name, marched up to our house, followed by more than a hundred people, each one carrying a small basket filled with peas and beans, which they had treasured up from the last harvest for such a time of need.

This raw native, with true gentlemanly instincts, quietly asked a boy where they could deposit their present, and having been told, they took themselves off, without even so much as "how do you do?" to the European.

This kindness was repeated again and again by people who knew that I had made a rule to send away again with their gifts those who came with ulterior motives.

It is said that the ulterior motive is never far from the African; well, perhaps not, but the present condition of European social amenities, such, for instance, as the close connection between a wedding invitation and a wedding present, or the *quid pro quo* now being demanded with loud-mouthed threats by the brewers from the bishops, prevent our throwing anything that might expose to attack our own glass houses.

The Church Missionary Society sets its face dead against the "no blanketi no Hallelujah" type of Christian, and the Bagishu of Masaba did not come to us for what they could get.

For some time we gathered a few people

together daily in a small shed for instruction and worship, but this building was soon too small, and through the great kindness of our Bishop, Dr. Tucker, we erected a building to hold four hundred people.

The day appointed for the formal opening of this building was wet, cold, and dreary; but these wild, naked people crowded in from hill and dale, and must have presented a weird spectacle to their loving Bishop, who has always been much interested in Masaba, to the Venerable Archdeacon Walker, of Uganda, and to the Rev. T. R. Buckley, now Archdeacon of Usoga, who had cycled over to be with the Bishop and myself at the opening.

The building is so arranged that the men use one door and the women another. Two men are appointed as churchwardens, and they regulate the incoming and outgoing of the people. All spears, knives, sticks, and pipes are given up at the door and returned at the close of the service.

On the day of the opening the wardens refused to take responsibility for sticks, so great was the crowd, and I well remember the amazement of the Bishop at the pile of sticks outside the church door, and the wonderfully good-natured scramble for them at the close of the service. From that day a short service has been held each morning in the building, and daily morning and afternoon school at which reading, writing, arithmetic, singing, and sewing has been taught.

For nearly two years my wife and I were alone, but the demands of the school, dispensary, visiting, building, and language work became very heavy, and a European lady, Miss Pilgrim, a qualified nurse, sensible woman and true missionary, was sent to help us.

It is almost if not wholly impossible for people at home to realise the variety of work one may be called upon to perform at such a station. Imagine a clergyman at home being called upon at the close of the morning's service to perform an operation on a youth whose head had been terribly mauled by a leopard, summoned from lunch to amputate a finger, or hauled out of bed at night to stop a fight and dress the wounded !

The most interesting surgical cases are brought to one's notice in such a country, and I should like to mention one of special note. A man who joined with others in some attack was speared in the abdomen and carried home, presumably to die. After some days I was asked to visit him, and found that his bowel was pierced. I had him brought to the dispensary, where the wound was cleansed

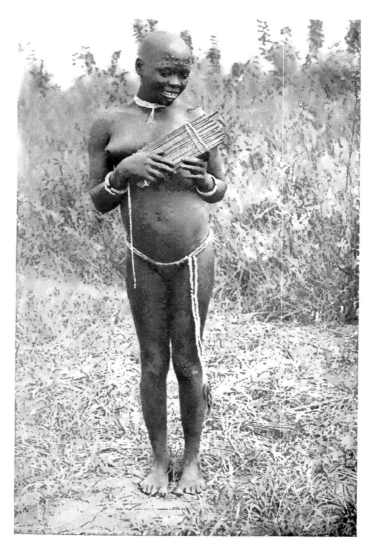

A MUGISHU GIRL HARPIST.

313

from what appeared to be a filthy application
of native herbs and cowdung; the nurse also
verified the diagnosis that the bowel was perforated, and the man said he knew it was so,
and was careful as to what he ate. The case
was hopeless from our point of view, and we
told him so, but expressed our willingness to
do all we could for him. He expressed his
gratitude, but said he would go on with the
native medicine, and we were positively amazed
to find that he got gradually better, and is now
quite well.

After seeing such a case, one is tempted to
ask, Why is it that we Westerns have been
civilised beyond such powers of natural healing?

The dispensary and school work continued
to grow, and two more missionaries were
added to our staff—a lady from Australia,
Miss McNamara, and Mr. Walter Holden, from
England.

My own time was now taken up with language work, building, and occasionally visiting
other parts of my district. A temporary
church, used also as a girls' school, a boys'
school a house for teachers and boarders, a
brick dispensary, a brick house with corrugated iron roof for the missionary in charge,
and a brick house for a second man were
completed. A brick house for ladies was built

to the top of the windows, a site prepared for the permanent brick church, a football ground cleared, and on Christmas Day, 1906, I had the unspeakable pleasure of baptizing the first Bagishu, and of receiving them into the visible Church of Christ.

CHAPTER XV

LANGUAGE DIFFICULTIES

Preliminary difficulties—Publication of the Lumasaba Grammar
—A primitive language—Legend about Victoria Nyanza
Bantu group—Comparative study advised—Bantu language
characteristics—Confusing similarity in Luganda—Perfect
grammatical construction — Rich vocabulary — How to
express abstract ideas—A faithful lad—A prayer- and hymn-
book—Idiomatic phrases—Politeness.

THERE were many difficulties to contend
with that at first sight seemed to me
insurmountable, and the greatest of them was
the language.

Mr. Crabtree, a recognised linguist, was
unable to help me as he would have desired,
but he placed at my disposal what little he
had done in Lugishu, and with this help I
was content to go on until a lull in building
operations, the advent of new missionaries,
and my own ear told me I must go deeper
into linguistic matters.

In the country of Uganda such a desire for knowledge has only to be expressed by the new-comer from Europe to receive every encouragement from the people. Careful, kindly, polite, and able, the Uganda man or woman will answer questions and guide one over pitfalls. How different in the country of Masaba! Almost every question was answered by a look of amazement, as much as to say, " What in the world is he after ? " or a loud guffaw of laughter, as if they much enjoyed my endeavour to be funny.

Yet they were not slow to protest most vigorously against the translations used. On one occasion an indignation meeting was held and a protest was sent to me against reading a certain word in church, and a plain intimation that if it continued the women would not attend.

I called the people together, told them how anxious I was to use correct words, but unless they helped me by answering questions whenever I asked for meanings, names, &c., I could not get on.

From that time I had less difficulty, and worked continuously at the compilation of a dictionary and the general construction of the language.

Any one will understand something of the difficulties one had to contend with in trying to master the details of grammar in a language not hitherto reduced; but every one conversant with the construction of Bantu languages will understand that since Lumasaba is a Bantu tongue, I had some general rules to go upon.

I completed the Lumasaba Grammar in Holy Week, 1907, and at the end of the same year the work was published by that great Missionary Society of the English Church known as the S.P.C.K. (Society for Promoting Christian Knowledge).

In the Introduction to that work I say, "There seems little doubt but that in the country of Masaba, *i.e.*, the land on and near Mount Elgon, we have the most primitive language of what might well be called the Victoria Nyanza Bantu group."

There is undoubtedly something more than legend in the story that long, long ago a vast body of people, probably Gallas,* led by two brothers, came from the east and settled for a time at Masaba. Here they discussed the direction of their further wanderings, and it was finally decided to go off north-east.

* A. H. Keane's " Ethnology," second edition.

At Bugondo, a large hill in the Teso country, overlooking Lake Kyoga, and from which can be seen the countries of Usoga, Unyoro, and Uganda, there are pits pointed out from which the natives declare these early wanderers quarried the ore with which to provide iron for their weapons.

After a stay at Bugondo it was agreed to separate. The elder brother, Lukidi, crossed Lake Kyoga and took possession of Unyoro, while Kintu crossed to Usoga, where he settled his nephew, and then went on to Uganda, where his name is still well known in connection with legends dealing with the beginning of things in that country.

Probably large numbers of the Negroid natives of Masaba joined the Hamitic invaders and went off with them westward, whilst other Bantu Negroids are said to have gone off independently toward the south, settling throughout Kavirondo and still farther on; and some few more daring spirits are accredited with having crossed the Lake Victoria to Uganda.

Certain it is, there seems a wonderful relationship, which can scarcely be wholly due to the similarity of construction that exists in all Bantu tongues, between Lumasaba, Lukavirondo, and Lusukuma towards the south, and between Lumasaba and Lugwere (old Lusoga), Lunyoro, and Luganda.

It remains but to compare the dialects spoken in the districts of Ketosh, Bunyuli, Bugwere, Bulamogi, and South-east Kyagwe, North Bulondaganyi, and the shores of Lake Kyoga, to find the stages of transition.

Such a comparative study would, I am certain, well repay the effort; but I can refer to it only incidentally, in order to make known a striking peculiarity in Lumasaba.

Learners are always reminded the "one characteristic of Bantu grammatical structure is that nouns have prefixes according to classes." As the languages of the Victoria Nyanza Bantu group are at present used, this is not strictly correct, for no learner can possibly differentiate by the class prefix the singular of Class I. from the singular of Class II., or the plural of Class III. from the singular of the same class, or the plural of Class VI. from the plural of Class III.; and it is not until the pronominal concords are known that nouns can be correctly classified.

This confusing similarity in substantival class forms, but clear differentiation of classes in pronominal agreements, is a real difficulty to one trying to learn Luganda, for the noun is often represented pronominally by a form quite foreign to the known substantival form, *e.g.* :—

Class.	Noun.	Poss. Pron. Form.	Pron. Form.
I.	S. omuntu, a man	wange (the man) of me	bamulese, they have brought him
	P. abantu, the men	bange, they of me	babalese, they have brought them
II.	S. omuti, a tree	gwange, mine or it of me	bagulese, they have brought it
	P. emiti, the trees	gyange, mine or they of me	bagilese, they have brought them
III.	S. ente, a cow	yange	bagilese, they have brought it
	P. ente, the cows	zange	bazilese, they have brought them
IV.	S. ekintu, a thing	kyange	bakilese, they have brought it
	P. ebintu, the things	byange	babilese, they have brought them
V.	S. ejinja, a stone	lyange	balilese, they have brought it
	P. amainja, the stones	gange	bagalese, they have brought them
VI.	S. olugoye, a cloth	lwange	balulese, they have brought it
	P. engoye, the cloths	zange	bazilese, they have brought them

So far as I am aware, no hint has ever been given as to why, to take one case only, the pronominal forms of Class II. should be "gu" and "gi"; and, bearing in mind the difficulty to account for the initial vowel, I have dared to think that the substantival class forms found in the Victoria Nyanza Bantu group are not

now in their original perfect forms; and, as
evidence in favour of this opinion, I most
respectfully ask the attention of all interested
in "Bantu" to the class forms used by these
primitive mountain people, the Bagishu, or
Bamasaba :—

Class	Noun	Poss. Pron. Form	Pron Form
I.	S. umundu, a man	wase	bamurerere
	P. babandu	base	babarerere
II	S kumubano, a knife	kwase	bakurerere
	P kimibano	kyase	kakirerere
III.	S ingafu, a cow	yase	bakirerere
	P. tsingafu	tsase	batsirerere
IV.	S kikindu, a thing	kyase	bakirerere
	P. bibindu	byase	babirerere
V.	S. libali, a stone	lyase	balirerere
	P kamabali	kase	bakarerere
VI.	S. lugoye, a piece of bark	lwase	balurerere
	P tsingoye	tsase	batsirerere

I have purposely chosen for comparison the first
six classes only, because the remaining classes
are subordinate; but these are sufficient to
show the enormous value to the Lumasaba
language of the prefixes, not found in this complete form, so far as I can find in any other
Bantu tongue.

The question as to whether the more perfect
class forms found at Masaba are more primitive
than those used by kindred peoples, is still an

open one; but to me it seems hardly likely that the Masaba language has developed whilst the customs, manners, and general surroundings of the people have remained stationary.

The perfectly regulated grammatical construction of the Lumasaba language was a revelation to me, as was also their comparatively rich vocabulary.

I have been able to compile a dictionary of some ten thousand words, and although with this number it is quite possible to understand and be understood, yet it forms but a portion of the native vocabulary.

There is an almost total lack of words which we Europeans use to express abstract ideas, and in missionary work this lack is very much felt. Such ideas as love, grace, faith, trust, holiness, &c., are quite unknown; and it is necessary to take other words, commonly used for the nearest equivalent meanings, and read and teach into them the fuller, deeper meanings.

If "love" exists, it is not expressed, and the Bagishu will only learn to express it by reading the deeper meaning into the word "Kugana" (want).

"Holiness" is quite unknown in reality or as an idea, but it is remarkable how quickly they grasp the idea of holiness, and the appropriateness of using the word " Kikosefu" (cleanness or whiteness) to express it.

"Faith " is expressed by the word " Kufu-kirira," which means "to agree to," whilst the deeper meanings of "grace" will be given to the word used to express " good-nature."

Many other words were equally difficult but more amusing to locate.

For months I was endeavouring to get the Lugishu equivalent for the English word *hypocrite*, and was met on nearly every hand with the statement that a person possessing such properties as we think go to make a hypocrite is a liar—a truth indeed!

The adjective *mad* conveys all the Bagishu wish to say about a person of constantly changeful mind; and in answer to the question of what they call a person who cannot come to a definite conclusion upon a subject, I was informed that they had no people of that kind in their country ; and I quite believe it.

Having solved some grammar rules, I was able, with the help of a Mugishu lad, Polo, who was afterwards baptized Andrew, to prepare a small reading-book which enjoys the title "Bimanyisa Kusoma " (the things which cause to know how to read). It opens with letters in Roman character, script and ordinary, small and capital;

figures, syllables, words, sentences, prayers, Creed, Commandments, texts of Scripture, the copy of a written letter, and a multiplication table.

Such a little book is of very great help in trying to teach these people, and it is not a little amusing to receive, most carefully folded, a piece of old newspaper, upon which is written an exact copy of the letter set at the end of the book :—

MASABA, *Julai* 20, 1907.

Ibaruwa ya Nayu.

Nakuchyesere lugalı mulebe wase: Wena? ugona oryena? Ne bimutsu barye? Ubambonere bosi, ni babolera ngana kubabona wangu. Byaweye.

Ise wakyo,
NAYU.

TRANSLATION.

The letter of What's-his-name

I salute you very much, my brother : How are you? How have you slept? And how are all in the house? See them all for me, and tell them I wish to see them soon. The (words) are finished.

I am yours,
WHAT'S-HIS-NAME.

The youngsters are fairly quick to learn, and quite a large number are now able to read

a small catechism called "Katabo Kanyoher-
wako," *i.e.*, the first book, which is used to
teach them elementary religious truths.

One has also been able to translate Morning
and Evening Prayer, The Litany, Baptism Service, Church Catechism, Confirmation Service,
and various hymns. From these the S.P.C.K.
have published what is called

KULOMBA
KWIKUMUTIKINYI NI KWIHANGOLOBE

NU

BAKIRI KUBATISIWA

NI MU

BANA BAKECHE

NE

KULOMBA KWIMUBIRO BIKALI BITWERA

NE

TSINYIMBO TSIKUBOLERESA WERE

MU

BABANDU BOSI

(Service Book, Hymns, and Occasional Prayers
in Lumasaba.)

In mission work of this kind there are many discouragements; but any man would feel more than repaid to know that a people who answer almost exactly to Dr. F. C. Shrubsall's description given in the *Lancet* for April, 1908, of the Bushmen Hottentots, "They are said to have greater powers than the average of twisting their bolas and to practise sitting down and shooting poisoned arrows at one another. . . . Their habitations were caverns, rock-shelters, or merely mats spread over branches. . . . They slept coiled up. . . . They wore little clothing, and adorned themselves with necklets of beads made from the shells of ostrich eggs," can meet together and evidently enjoy the using of prayers and the singing of hymns such as we in England know so well.

"Papa wefwe ali mu igulu, Lisinalyo likosewe. Bubwaka-bakabwo bwitse. Byogana babikole mu kyalo, nga nibabikola mu igulu. Ukuhe kya lero biryo byefwe bya kifuku, Ukuya-kire kukwonaga kwefwe, ngefwe bwekubayakira bakwonaga Ukakuhira mu bukongeresi, ne ukuhonese mu bubi. Kubanga bubwakabaka, ni bunyala, ni kitifwa, nibyo byowo, biro ni biro. Amina."

is the Lord's Prayer in Lumasaba, whilst the following are verses translated from well-known hymns:—

Onward, Christian Soldiers.

" Babana ba Yesu mwinyuke mwesi !
Mulole Yesu, uyu warangiye :
Mu basıku bosı Yesu ufura ;
Nakulanga Umwami ; kutsye naye.
Babana ba Yesu, mwınyuke mwesi,
Mulole Yesu, uyu warangiye."

For My Sake and the Gospel's.

" Kulwase nı Kalwenjiri
Mutsiye bana base :
Nibiramu " Hakutsiye ;
Kıtıfwa kıbe kyuli."
Itsa kufira babandu,
Papa we nga muruma :
Wamalaho bibi byefwe,
Iwe kufwa hukisına."

Rock of Ages.

" Lurale lwikale iwe
Lwıtıkira kulwase
Muchi mwenibisıra
Mafugike ichıkama.
Bibi byosi binduseko,
Mbonesa mu mani kabyo."

That the language is fairly rich in idiom may be gathered from the following examples of how the question " Why ? " may be asked :—

Kıkulobeye Kukwıtsa kina ?—Why dıd you refuse to come ?
Kina kigırire wala kwitsa ?—Why dıd you not come ?

Kina kɪgɪra ukatsya ?—Why have you not gone ?

Kɪna kigira akagobola ?—Why is he not returned ?

Kina kɪgɪrɪre balaɪre kugobola?—Why have they not returned?

Kɪna kyagira bala kugobola ?—Why did they not return ?

Kɪna kɪkukingiriye kukwitsa wangu ?—Why did you not come at once?

Kɪna kigɪra ukateka ?—Why do you refuse to cook ?

Kɪna kigɪrɪre walahakuteka ?—Why have you not cooked ?

Kina kɪkukolesere kiri ?—What causes you to act thus ?

Kɪkukolesere kiryo kina ?—Why did you do this or that ?

Ukolere kɪna oryo ?—Why have you done thus ?

Wakola kɪna oryo?—Why did you do thus ?

Kɪna kigɪra ukola oryo ? or Kɪgɪra ukola oryo kɪna ?—Why are you doing thus ?

Urerere kametsi ka ki ?—Why have you brought the water?

Kikurerere kɪna ?—Why have you come ? (Lɪt., What has brought you ?)

Loma kigirire ukola oryo ?—Give the reason why you act thus ?

The language reveals to us that even these primitive people know how to be polite, and a stranger will do fairly well among them if he learns nothing more than a few salutations. Certain of these are used irrespective of time, such as "Mulembe? or Mirembe?—Peace."

Ans. Mulembe—Peace.

Ques. Ulame ?—A very old form. Probably means "Are you there ? "

Ans. Ulame.

Ques. Wena? Are you well?
Ans. Wena? Are you well?

Morning Salutations.

Wagonere oryena?—How have you slept?
Nagonere bulahi? Njebewe?—I have slept well. Perhaps you? *i e.,* How about yourself?
Bengo baryena?—How are those at home?
Baliyo balwakire.—They are well. How are you?

Afternoon Salutations.

Wabuyire oryena?—How have you passed the day?
Nabuyire bulahi. Njebewe?—I have passed it well. Perhaps you?
If the person addressed is ill he uses the word *nindwala*—I am ill—instead of *bulahi.*

There is no exact equivalent for our *Goodbye.* The departing guest says *Nitsya*—I am going; to which is often added the wish *Nule,* or *Nule bulahi*—May I reach, or May I reach safely.

Nutsye wule bulahi.—Go, may you reach safely.
Nule bulahi.—May I reach safely.
Nutsye ugona bulahi.—May you go and sleep well.
Ngone bulahi.—May I sleep well.

My great hope was to translate the Scriptures, but such a work was not to be begun until the details and scope of the language had been mastered. With the Grammar and Dictionary completed, the way seemed open for the contemplation of the greater work; but evidently it had not to be, for doctor's orders are imperative, and one can only live in hope that another opportunity for this work will be given.

VISITORS TO THE YOUNG WHITE CHIEF.

CHAPTER XVI

LIGHT AND SHADE

Slow progress—Friendly and trustful natives—Spirit of independence—Indian hemp-smoking—Effect of evil practices
—Native dances—Drink and fighting—Wailing—Native
industry—Lighthearted geniality—Witchcraft—The power
of suggestion—Protection against witchcraft—No God of
love in Masaba—Evil spirits—Altars and offerings—
Sacrifices—Sacred groves—A liking for football—Ghoulish
practices—A low standard of civilisation—Compensations
—Native ability—Open doors.

WITH buildings, books, and additional staff
the work is more definitely organised,
hopeful, and interesting; but Masaba is one of
those mission fields where mental, moral, and
spiritual progress will be slow. The habits and
customs of past generations will not be lightly
cast off, and loving patience will be necessary to
hold the people until they understand, appre-
ciate, and accept the structure you are trying
to erect to some extent on the foundation of
belief already found among them.

17

One of the greatest pleasures of life at Masaba has been the perfectly friendly and trustful manner of the natives towards us at all times; and this attitude is one to be encouraged and reciprocated whether the people attend church and school or not, for it enables the missionary to get to the back of the native mind—to know something of their beliefs and unbeliefs, strength and weakness, likes and dislikes, hopes and fears. It will also enable him to do his work and limit his expectations according to the character of the people, rather than according to preconceived ideas gathered in a country such as Uganda, where the history of the people and the circumstances of life are totally different.

Here there is no king or feudal chief to influence his followers one way or the other. Every man, woman, and child claims to be independent, and we often see the effect of this independence on our school children.

Probably through some early Arab traveller, the Indian hemp plant has been introduced into Masaba, and is cultivated by almost every householder, then gathered, dried, and smoked through a very primitive hubble-bubble pipe, made from a hollowed gourd which contains the water.

As a rule the adults are temperate in the use of the weed: a man will even forbid his wife to smoke it on account of some evil effect it is said to have upon her or her child, should she be about to become a mother; but father and mother are quite careless about their children smoking it: for are not the children themselves responsible for their habits?

I have heard and seen the effect of this "bhang" smoking on porters from the coast, and thought it dangerous enough in the case of strong men, but when I saw its effect upon the Bagishu children I was appalled.

The brightest little boys and girls have attended our classes and made remarkable progress for a time; then suddenly lost their brightness, interest, health, and intelligence. At first this puzzled me; but there is little doubt but that it is due to the smoking of hemp, or, as the natives put it, to the *drinking* of "itsayi," since the act of smoking can only be described by the native as *drinking*.

Contributory causes to this dulness are sexual connection among the young and drinking the native strong drink, though the latter is not often indulged in by children.

It seems incomprehensible that a people so strict at certain times about the purity of their girls, that a girl pregnant before marriage is punished, and a girl suffering from specific disease becomes an outcast, should at other times encourage them in what they pronounce wrongdoing. Yet the heads of families actually do this by holding at certain seasons of the year what they call an "ingoma," *i.e.*, an all-night orgy, to which all young people of other clans are invited by the beating of a peculiar long drum known as an ingoma.

These festivals are generally held about the time of full moon, and sometimes go on night after night. Undoubtedly the idea is to pair off the young people and to fix up engagements.

The Bagishu are passionately fond of dancing, and crowd to these "ingomas" for the professedly innocent as well as the wrong sport to be obtained.

Dancing plays an important part in their lives, for at marriage and death, to mark sorrow and joy, they dance until they are ready to drop from fatigue.

Intoxicating drink, too, is a source of great evil in the country, for it is used to mark every event in life. Births, deaths, marriages, preparing the land and gathering the harvest, before a fight and after a fight, are all opportunities upon which recourse is had to one or other of the native drinks.

The drinks native to the country are "indali inyana," an unfermented drink made from sweet bananas only; a fermented drink, "indali indule," made from sweet bananas and fermented with millet seed; and another fermented drink, "busera," made from two kinds of millet seed.

I have said that dancing plays an important part in the lives of the Bagishu; well, even dancing loses its relish if drink is absent.

There are private drinks, clan drinks, cultivation drinks, wedding drinks—the people of Mabasa have not yet reached the stage so prevalent in England of serving out intoxicating liquors at funerals—circumcision drinks, and drinks indulged in to prepare the warriors for a fight; a real fight I mean, not a political election.

The candour with which the Bagishu announced their drinking proclivities was at first rather a shock, but after all was so unusual that it proved refreshing. Building operations had been going on for some time at the mission station, and I anticipated a successful and hasty conclusion, when some of the elders approached me and said they were going off for at least two weeks to *drink*, and I must get on as best I could without them. No humbug about them in that matter at any rate, and I found them much the same if an individual was missing from work, school, or church at any time. They did not say he had gone into the country, or had a sudden attack of illness; they said he was at home or elsewhere drinking.

The effect of hard drinking is as evident among the adults as that of hemp-smoking is among the young. Some of them are in a constant state of drivelling inebriation, whilst others become cantankerous and quarrelsome.

A foolish word of boasting or contempt spoken at a drinking party has led to many a quarrel with serious results; and one such termination happened soon after our arrival at Masaba. A company of men were drinking not far from our station, and one of the visitors had spoken disrespectfully of his hosts. He realised his mistake and made tracks for home as hard as he could go followed by about half a dozen young fellows each armed, like himself, with a long, business-like stick. They caught him as he passed our door, and but for our instant intervention he would undoubtedly have been killed. As it was I had to bind up his frightfully cut and bruised head and shoulders, his assailants looking on muchly interested but crestfallen.

On another occasion my wife and I were at the rest-house in the hills. The men of a neighbouring village had been up the mountain to a large drinking party, and on their return I had some conversation with them and found that some argument was being continued. This led to a quarrel when they reached home,

and we were not surprised to see some of the
houses of the village go up in flames. It was,
however, rather disconcerting to know that
the quarrel had become a general fight, and
it was something of a shock to me next morning, on my going down to see if any required
their wounds dressed, to find one fine young
fellow lying dead. In the heat of the argument
he had given his companion the lie, and the
other had promptly rammed a spear down his
throat.

As is always the case, the murderer had fled
with his nearest male relatives, and men and
women had gathered near the corpse to dance
the death dance—a weird sight and sound, for
the men as a rule dress in war attire and with
iron bells fastened just below the knee dance to
the rhythm of the sound, whilst the women with
their string dress hanging down loose behind,
dance near the men but not with them, and add
to the weirdness of the occasion by wailing at
regular intervals.

This ceremony is performed with the idea of
giving honour to the spirit as it enters
" Makombe," the spirit-world.

We must not run away with the idea that
the people of Masaba do nothing but drink
and fight, for one is amazed at the little harm
they do each other, and at the amount of

industry that might be turned into channels more profitable to the people and the country.

The native blacksmiths are men who work with the most elementary tools it is possible to conceive : a stone for an anvil, and another for a hammer, yet their work will certainly bear inspection.

The houses are better than the houses of Usoga, and indeed superior to the houses that have, until this last year or two, satisfied the peasant of Uganda

It is remarkable too that in Masaba the men help to cultivate; indeed, they are primarily responsible for the cultivation of all cereals whilst the women are responsible for the plantain groves.

There is a charming lightheartedness, breezy geniality, and kind good-nature about the Mugishu that reminds one of Ireland; and when prospects are darkest keep one hopeful.

The crowds that came from far and near to listen to the gramophone—or at other times to see and play with the little white boys until the baby or his father would produce a doll, when off they would scamper with shrieks of wonder and fear real and feigned—were always good-natured crowds, ready to do anything for the white babies or their mother.

These visits enabled us to get a little insight

BAGISHU BLACKSMITHS.

into their inmost thoughts, and showed us
something of their terribly strong belief in the
power of witchcraft and the evil eye, for not
only were the visitors themselves sometimes
frightened by the children's dolls or mechanical
toys, but men have again and again come to ask
for the loan of a doll with which they wished
to bewitch some opponent or other.

This belief in witchcraft is one of the greatest
and most dangerous powers in the land, and is
sometimes responsible for most terrible consequences.

One such case came under my notice not long
ago. My wife and I were visiting a native
village and saw a young woman of fine physique,
known to us, leaning listlessly against a grain
store. I suggested her doing some work, but her
answer was that she was seriously ill. I told
her she did not look ill, and that perhaps a little
work would put her right; but the chief and
other people came near and assured me that
she was seriously ill, having been bewitched.
I begged for an explanation, and they told me
that some little time before my visit the girl
and others were playing, when a man, well
known to them all, ran off with her beads,
kept them for some time, and then returned
them to the girl, who put them on and immediately believed herself bewitched. From that

moment she declared herself unable to work, and no amount of argument, ridicule, or expostulation availed to shake the foolish belief of herself and people. Her mind was fixed, her body gradually but somewhat rapidly gave way and she died, whereupon a solemn meeting of the clan was called to try the case : witnesses gave evidence against the man, who was declared guilty of witchcraft and straightway beaten to death.

There was no attempt on the part of the clan to shirk responsibility for his death. I understand the matter was reported to the Government officer, who sent for the man really responsible for this judicial murder, and he went immediately, declared his responsibility, as head of that portion of the clan, and justified his action by native custom.

I do not suppose that even so-called Christian Scientists can give us a more striking example of the effect of mind over matter than the one just quoted; and there are many such in Masaba.

The people are often charging each other with witchcraft and the practice of the evil eye, and great care is taken to detect such people.

Every house is built with little spy-holes through which watchers look at night for any

THE WONDER OF THE WILD MOUNTAINEERS.

347

enemy who may creep up and place a *kumusala*, that is, a piece of tree specially used by bewitchers, who place it outside the door of a house in such a way that a person coming out, unless very careful, is obliged to touch it. I need not say that the Bagishu are *very careful* as they come out of their houses in the early morning; and they are also careful to find out who travels about at night.

The fear of being charged with witchcraft is an effectual deterrent against late hours in Masaba, and the trial of culprits is indeed laughable were the consequences of an adverse verdict not so terrible.

Not long ago a clan met together to try A for witchcraft. He was not a favourite in the clan, and they were willing to grasp at any evidence against him. He was charged with being seen near a certain house late one night, and B, who was a great favourite, gave evidence that he saw A near the said house. When passing the assembled crowd I asked the reason for their being together, and the elders came and told me of A's guilt as proved by B. They looked very much surprised when I suggested that B should be charged with witchcraft, for, on his own confession, he was near the said house at a wrong hour. In his case there was no doubt about it, but in A's case there was some question.

I knew that B was safe, but my suggestion doubled him up and he made for home amid the loud laughter of the assembly, which immediately congratulated A on his innocence.

A recent letter from Masaba says : " Only the other day some of the Bagishu went up the hill to burn down a medicine-man's house, because he had promised them rain, had taken their cattle, and had sent them only a terrible wind, which blew down their *toki* (plantain-trees)."

It is to be expected that such beliefs interfere very considerably with missionary effort, for although the Bagishu believe in *Were*, the Creator of all things, the Great Spirit, they think of Him as one to be greatly feared on account of His ability to do them harm; and almost their chief thought in life is how to appease *Were* and the many evil spirits known as *Kimisambwa*.

An altar is erected inside every house to the spirit responsible for the safe-keeping of houses; and upon it is placed food and drink offerings. Then just outside the door may be seen little altars built in the form of tiny houses, erected to the honour of various spirits responsible for health, weather, &c.

When examining these shrines I have often reminded the people that they cannot think highly of the wisdom of these spirits when they dare to eat the inside out of an egg and then place the shell in such a position that a casual onlooker might think it full.

There is no such thing as worship among the Bagishu of Masaba such as we understand it; but in times of sickness, famine, war, and pestilence sacrifices of goats and oxen are made to *Were*, and presents offered through the witch-doctors to the evil spirits.

In the case of sickness, the nearest relative of the sick person provides the offering, which is brought to the door of the house in which the sick person lies. This relative places his hand on the head of the offering and professedly gives it to *Were*. If the goat or ox micturates, the offering has been accepted, and there is great joy and hope; but if not, it is said that *Were* refuses the offering, and it is killed in gloom and despair.

The offering is cut up and distributed to the onlookers in the hope that any who may have bewitched the sick person will withdraw the evil influence. God and man, they hope, is thus appeased.

It behoves every member of the clan to attend these offerings, and also the dance performed after the death of a person, in order to remove any suspicion of having been concerned by witchcraft in the sickness or death.

There are also periodic processions to the sacred groves found on the land of each clan, when offerings are made by the witch-doctors to the evil spirits, much drink consumed, and licentious practices indulged in.

It may be difficult to credit that these men are good companions on the march, and delightful in the football field; yet such they are, and nothing appeals to them more than a good game of "Association," and even the little chaps will leave their imitation fights with bows, arrows, spears, and shields to learn all about "off-side," "corner," "throw in," &c. In fact, their appetite for football is greater than we can satisfy, for the outer cases of footballs rot very quickly in the severe sun.

Europeans are always astonished at the way these "All blacks" can kick off the toe of a naked foot, and also at the sportsmanlike way in which they take a "charge" or a beating.

I have already referred to the custom of throwing out the dead practised at Masaba; and possibly this is responsible for, and not because of, the more loathsome custom of cannibalism.

No Mugishu will own that he is guilty of such a practice, but every one says that some one else does it.

Without doubt it is done and in a ghoulish

manner; for the dead are not always left to the hyænas. The natives suggest that it is only done in the case of bitter enemies at war with each other; but the more horrible practice of eating the corpse of a dead friend was once brought to my knowledge, and the only redeeming feature about it was that, when known, it caused bitter shame.

Sir H. H. Johnston was surely right—so far as some things are concerned—regarding their low standard of civilisation. A glimpse at some of the faces is enough to satisfy on that point, but the pleasure and satisfaction of helping them upward is all the greater; and to see a naked, wild, uncouth youth grow reasonable, kindly, thoughtful, and manly is worth a good deal more than a " go " of blackwater fever. This has been the case again and again in various parts of the Uganda Protectorate, due to the influence of the Gospel of Jesus Christ: and I have reason to think it has been so, in a small measure, at Masaba, where the lad Polo, not beautiful to look at, but one of the best wrestlers in the country, stuck to me day after day and helped me with the language until I was invalided. He with others was baptized more than a year ago, and to-day he is a teacher in the boys' school at our central station in Masaba, and, if I mistake not, has with the help of a European, been endeavouring to translate the Gospels.

On every hand there is evidence that a mission station has been a peace-factor and blessing to the district, for drinking and fighting went decidedly out of fashion ; and my collection of curios prove that weapons of warfare have been given up for instruments of agriculture, one hoe for a spear, two for a knife, and from three to five for a shield.

Old beliefs and customs die hard, and no one outside Masaba can conceive what it means to have a hundred of these people under daily instruction, or a congregation of over two hundred at the central station on Sundays.

If one of these attenders fall sick, the outsiders tell him that we have bewitched him, or that *Were* has punished him for presuming to speak to Him as we do in our prayers.

Some of the Bagishu even come near the church to see what will happen to such audacious people as those who join us at worship ; and some of the parents are so nervous that when the school drum sounds they drive their children into the bush to prevent their attending. A glimpse at some of the pictures will show, however, that this fear is not universal, for the tiniest little mites come and squat down at our door or in the school ;

DOORS THAT ARE BEING OPENED.

and for every childish ailment the help of the European is now sought and gladly given.

In the more distant fortified villages the doors have been opened to the missionary ; and nearer home we organise sports as well as offer work to counteract the dangerous tendencies of a decidedly energetic people.

CHAPTER XVII

NATIONALISING AND DENATIONALISING THE NATIVE

The unsettling of the native mind—Bringing them into line—A bad inheritance—Painful memories—The evils of armed agents and punitive expeditions—Improvements—Possibilities.

ONE of the greatest difficulties that we have had to contend with in the work at Masaba was the unsettling of the native mind and mode of life by the incoming of Government administration.

In 1903 the actual work of dealing with the natives was done by the Muganda chief, Semei Kakungulu, who is now in Usoga. He had placed his agents in various parts of the country to rule it on lines similar to the feudal system of Uganda, and he was answerable for the general condition of the district to the British official at Budaka, situate some twenty miles from Masaba.

It was the express wish of the then Commissioner of Uganda that the raw natives in this eastern portion of his district should be "brought into line," as the expression goes, very gradually; and probably to make sure that the Muganda chief and his men played square with the native and the Government the official post was moved from Budaka to Mbale, a Uganda colony situate at the western side of the Elgon foothills, brought into existence by the dogged perseverance and hard work of the chief Kakungulu and his people.

New assistant collectors were appointed from time to time, and gradually a new order of things was evolved which brought the Baganda in outlying places directly under the control of the Government officer.

I am convinced that this step was taken for the good of the Bagishu; but after some four years' residence in the district I am bound to say, having earnestly and carefully weighed the seriousness of the statement, that during the years of my residence which mark the introduction of law into Masaba there seems to me to have been less peace, less security of property, and more, very much more, bloodshed than during the period I lived there without direct British administration. The method of collecting hut-tax inherited by each assistant collector —in every case a kindly man and a gentleman —was no doubt responsible to a great extent for the unsatisfactory condition of things; and the introduction of punitive expeditions as a means of meting out punishment did not tend to idealise British rule in the minds of the natives.

My memories of the troubles between the Administration and the people of Masaba are altogether painful, for in almost every instance my sympathies are with the native, as I am sure would be those of any man who had been asked by the men of a clan to beg back the women who had been taken prisoners; to console the relatives and friends of a dead woman whom they deposited at my door, and said to have been one of four, besides men, shot that day by the native police; and obliged to turn the vestry into a hospital for the wounded, shot by native hut-tax collectors and their men without any provocation whatever.

These armed Baganda hut-tax collectors, many of them of the very worst type, distributed throughout the district and working on the percentage system, could be no other than a menace to peace and prosperity; and I am firmly convinced that they and their methods were responsible for at least two of the troubles for which the natives were punished by the expensive and deplorable method of a punitive —I had almost written *primitive*—expedition. The punitive expedition is one method of dealing with an uncivilised people, but I believe too much in British common sense to think that the general verdict will be that it is the only or even a commendable method. A hundred pounds' worth of rubber-trees sent to an erring clan, with a sensible man who could teach them how to plant and rear them, would do far more good to them and us than all the punitive expeditions in the world.

The system of hut-tax collection has been altered by the Administration, and for that we are deeply grateful, but hope the use of the gun will be absolutely forbidden except in cases of direst necessity for self-defence. The darkness of such a people as the Bagishu of Masaba, Mount Elgon "savage and uncivilised," as they have been called, is great indeed, but they are capable of responding to gentle methods, and the dawn, though slight, is visible and hopeful. Shall we not encourage and strengthen the gentle methods, though slow and tedious, remembering the Luganda proverb quoted once before, "Akwata mpola atuka wala"

("He who goes slowly reaches far"), rather than seek by harsher methods to make haste in a direction the end of which can be none other than moral and physical desolation ?

INDEX

The Gresham Press,
UNWIN BROTHERS, LIMITED,
WOKING AND LONDON.

A

CLASSIFIED CATALOGUE

OF

T. FISHER UNWIN'S

PUBLICATIONS.

CONTENTS.

Book Buyers are requested to order any volumes they may require from their bookseller. On receipt of a post-card, Mr Fisher Unwin will be pleased to furnish the address of the nearest local bookseller where the works detailed in this list may be inspected

Should any difficulty arise, the Publisher will be happy to forward any book in the list to any country in the Postal Union, on receipt of the price marked and a sufficient sum to cover postage, together with full Postal Address. Any amount forwarded in excess will be returned to the sender

Remittances may be made by Cheque, draft on London, Money Orders, or Stamps

After reading this Catalogue, kindly pass it on to some book-buying friend, or send an address to which this or

INDEX of AUTHORS, some ILLUSTRATORS, and EDITORS.

INDEX in order of Titles.

LITERARY HISTORY.

ABRAHAMS. A Short History of Jewish Literature, from the Fall of the Temple (70 C.E.) to the Era of Emancipation (1706 C.E.) By Israel Abrahams, M.A., Reader in Rabbinic Literature in the University of Cambridge. Cr. 8vo, cloth.   net   2/6

BAILEY. The Novels of George Meredith. By E. E. J. Bailey. Cr. 8vo, cloth.   net   5/-

BEERS. A Short History of American Literature. By Henry A. Beers. Large cr. 8vo, cloth.   net   3/6

BRERETON (Austin). The Literary History of the Adelphi and its Neighbourhood. See under "History."

BROWNE. A Literary History of Persia. Vol. 1. From the Earliest Times until Firdawsi. By Edward G. Browne, M.A , M.B., Fellow of Pembroke College. With Photogravure Frontispiece. (Library of Literary History.) Demy 8vo, cloth.   net   12/6

—— A Literary History of Persia. Vol. 2. From Firdawsi until Sa'di (A.D. 1000—1290). By Edward G. Browne. With Photogravure Frontispiece. (Library of Literary History.)   Demy 8vo, cloth.   net   12/6

BRÜCKNER. A Literary History of Russia. By Professor A. Brückner, of Berlin. Edited by Ellis H. Minns, M.A. Translated by H. Havelock, M.A. With Photogravure Frontispiece. (Library of Literary History.) Demy 8vo, cloth.   net   12/6

BRUNETIÈRE. Essays in French Literature. A Selection, translated by D. Nichol Smith, with a Preface by the Author specially written for this, the authorised English translation. Large cr. 8vo, cloth.   7/6

—— Manual of the History of French Literature. By Ferdinand Brunetière. Demy 8vo., cloth.   12/-

CANNING. Shakespeare Studied in Eight Plays. By the Hon. Albert S. G. Canning. Demy 8vo, cloth.   net   16/-

—— Shakespeare Studied in Six Plays. By the Hon. Albert S. G. Canning. Demy 8vo, cloth.   net   16/-

—— Shakespeare Studied in Three Plays. By the Hon. Albert S. G. Canning. Demy 8vo, cloth.   net   7/6

—— Literary Influence in British History. By the Hon. Albert S. G. Canning. Demy 8vo, cloth.   net   7/6

—— History in Scott's Novels. By the Hon. Albert S. G. Canning. Demy 8vo, cloth.   net   10/6

—— British Writers on Classic Lands. By the Hon. Albert S. G. Canning. Demy 8vo, cloth.   net   7/6

DUFF. A Literary History of Rome. From the Origins to the Close of the Golden Age. By J. Wight Duff, M.A. With Photogravure Frontispiece. (Library of Literary History.) Demy 8vo, cloth.   net   12/6

FAGUET. A Literary History of France. By Emile Faguet, Member of the French Academy. With Photogravure Frontispiece. (Library of Literary History.)   net   12/6

FRAZER. A Literary History of India. By R. W. Frazer, LL.B., I.C.S. Frontispiece. (Library of Literary History.) Demy 8vo, cloth. net   12/6

HORRWITZ. A Short History of Indian Literature. By Ernest Horrwitz. With an Introduction by Professor T. W Rhys Davids. Cr. 8vo, cloth.   net   2/6

HYDE. A Literary History of Ireland. By Douglas Hyde, LL.D. With Photogravure Frontispiece. (Library of Literary History.) Demy 8vo, cloth. net 12/6

—— The Story of Early Gaelic Literature. By Douglas Hyde, LL.D. (New Irish Library. Vol. 6.) Sm. cr. 8vo, paper covers, 1/- ; cloth 2/-

JONES. Dafydd ap Gwilym : A Welsh Poet of the Fourteenth Century. By W. Lewis Jones, M.A., Professor of English Language and Literature, University College of North Wales. Large cr. 8vo, cloth. [In Preparation.] net 7/6

JUSSERAND. The English Novel in the Time of Shakespeare. By J. J. Jusserand, Conseiller d'Ambassade. Translated by Elizabeth Lee. Second Edition. Revised and enlarged by the Author. Illustrated. Large cr. 8vo, cloth. 7/6

—— A Literary History of the English People. Vol. 1. From the Origins to the Renaissance. By J. J. Jusserand. With Photogravure Frontispiece. Demy 8vo, cloth. net 12/6

—— A Literary History of the English People. Vol. 2. From the Renaissance to the Civil War. 1. By J. J. Jusserand. Wi h Photogravure Frontispiece. Demy 8vo, cloth. net 12/6

—— A Literary History of the English People. Vol. 3. From the Renaissance to the Civil War II. By J. J Jusserand. With Photogravure Frontispiece. Demy 8vo, cloth. net 12/6

—— Shakespeare in France. By J. J. Jusserand. Illustrated. Demy 8vo, cloth. 21/-

LANGLAND'S (William) Vision of Piers Plowman. Edited by Kate Warren. Second Edition, revised. Cloth. 3/6

LIBRARY OF LITERARY HISTORY, THE. Each with Photogravure Frontispiece. Demy 8vo, cloth. each, net 12 0

[*For full Titles see under Authors' names.*]

Published :—

(1) India. By Professor R. W. Frazer.

(2) Ireland. By Dr. Douglas Hyde.

(3) America. By Professor Barrett Wendell.

(4) Persia. Vol. 1. From the Earliest Times until Firdawsi By Professor E. G. Browne.

(5) Scotland. By J. H. Millar.

(6) Persia. Vol. 2. From Firdawsi until Sa'di By Professor E. G. Browne.

(7) The Arabs. By R. A. Nicholson.

(8) France. By Emile Faguet.

(9) Russia. By Professor A. Brückner.

In Preparation :—

Rome. By J. Wight Duff.

The Jews. By Israel Abrahams, M.A.

MARBLE Heralds of American Literature. By Annie Russell Marble. Illustrated. Cr. 8vo, cloth. net 6/6

MILLAR. A Literary History of Scotland. By J. H. Millar, Balliol College, Oxford. With Photogravure Frontispiece. (Library of Literary History.) Demy 8vo, cloth gilt. net 12/6

Also a *Fine Edition*, limited to 25 copies, on hand-made paper. net 42/-

—— A Short History of Scottish Literature. By J H. Millar. Cr. 8vo, cloth. [In Preparation.] net 2/6

MILLS. The Secret of Petrarch. By E. J. Mills. With 13 Photogravure Plates, one in colour. Demy 8vo, cloth. net 12/-

MOTTRAM. The True Story of George Eliot in relation to "Adam Bede." By William Mottram. Illustrated. Demy 8vo, cloth. net 7/6

NICHOLSON. A Literary History of the Arabs. By R. A. Nicholson, M.A., Lecturer in Persian in the University of Cambridge. With Coloured Frontispiece. (Library of Literary History.) Demy 8vo, cloth.   net 12/6
REA. Schiller's Dramas and Poems in England. By Thomas Rea, M.A., Lecturer in German and Teutonic Philology, University College of North Wales. Cr. 8vo, cloth.   net   3/6
SMITH. Shakespeare the Man : An Attempt to Find Traces of the Dramatist's Personal Character in his Dramas. By Professor Goldwin Smith. 8vo, cloth gilt.   net   2/6
WENDELL. A Literary History of America. By Barrett Wendell, Professor of English at Harvard College. With Frontispiece. (Library of Literary History.) Demy 8vo, cloth.   net 12/6
    [For reference see also under " Biography."]

POETRY and the DRAMA.

ADAMS The Lonely Way, and Other Poems. By W. A. Adams, M.A. Demy 12mo, cloth.   3/6
—— **Rus Divinum. (Poems.)** By Auguste Smada. (W. A. Adams.) Demy 12mo, parchment binding.   3/6
Bards of the Gael and Gall. See under "Sigerson."
BLIND. The Complete Poems of Mathilde Blind. Edited by Arthur Symons. With an Introduction by Dr. Garnett. Cr. 8vo, cloth gilt.   7/6
—— **A Selection from the Poems of Mathilde Blind.** Edited by Arthur Symons. Portrait. Fcap. 8vo, parchment gilt.   7/6
    Edition de Luxe, in Japan paper, in vellum.   net 10/6
BURNS. The Love Songs of Robert Burns. Selected and Edited, with Introduction, by Sir George Douglas, Bart. With Frontispiece Portrait. (Cameo Series. Vol. 11.) Demy 12mo, half-bound, paper boards.   3/6
CAMEO SERIES, THE. Demy 12mo, with Frontispiece, half-bound. Paper boards, 3/6 each ; vols. 14-20, each, **net**   3/6
    Also an Edition de Luxe, limited to 30 copies, printed on Japan paper.
                    Prices on Application.
          [*For full Titles see under Authors' names.*]

(1) **The Lady from the Sea.** By Henrik Ibsen.
(2) **Iphigenia in Delphi.** By Richard Garnett.
(3) **A London Plane Tree.** By Amy Levy.
(4) **Wordsworth's Grave.** By William Watson.
(5) **Miréio.** By Frederic Mistral.
(6) **Lyrics.** Selected from the Works of A. Mary F. Robinson.
(7) **A Minor Poet.** By Amy Levy.
(8) **Concerning Cats.**
(9) **A Chaplet from the Greek Anthology.** By Richard Garnett.
(10) **The Countess Kathleen.** By W. B. Yeats.
(11) **The Love Songs of Robert Burns.**
(12) **Love Songs of Ireland.** Collected by K. Tynan.
(13) **Retrospect.** By A. Mary F. Robinson.
(14) **Brand.** By Henrik Ibsen.
(15) **The Son of Don Juan.** By Don José Echegaray.
(16) **Mariana.** By Don José Echegaray.
(17) **Flamma Vestalis.** By Eugene Mason.
(18) **The Soul's Departure.** By E. Willmore.
(19) **The Unpublished and Uncollected Poems of William Cowper.**
(20) **Ultima Verba.** By Alfred de Kantzow.

CAPES. Amaranthus. A Book of Little Songs. By Bernard Capes. Small cr. 8vo, cloth. net 3/6

CARDUCCI. Poems by Giosuè Carducci. Selected and Translated, and with an Introduction by Maud Holland. Cr. 8vo, half-parchment. net 5/-

Concerning Cats. A Book of Verses by many Authors. Edited by Graham R. Tomson. Illustrated. (Cameo Series. Vol. 8.) Demy 12mo, half-bound, paper boards. 3/6

COWPER. The Unpublished and Uncollected Poems of William Cowper. Edited by Thomas Wright. Frontispiece. (Cameo Series. Vol. 19.) Demy 12mo, paper boards, half-bound. net 3/6

CRUSO. Sir Walter Raleigh. A Drama in Five Acts. By H. A. A. Cruso. Cr. 8vo, cloth. net 5/-

DYER. The Poems of John Dyer. Edited by Edward Thomas. With Portrait of J. D. (Welsh Library. Vol. 4.) Fcap. 8vo.
Paper covers, 1/- ; cloth 2/-

ECHEGARAY. Mariana. An Original Drama in 3 Acts and an Epilogue. By Don José Echegaray. Translated into English by James Graham. With a Photogravure of a recent Portrait of the Author. (Cameo Series. Vol. 16.) Demy 12mo, half-bound, paper boards. net 3/6

—— The Son of Don Juan. An Original Drama in 3 Acts. By Don José Echegaray. Translated into English, with Biographical Introduction by James Graham. With Etched Portrait of the Author by Don B. Maura. (Cameo Series. Vol. 15.) Demy 12mo, half-bound, paper boards. net 3/6

FIELD. Wild Honey from Various Thyme. By Michael Field. Cr. 8vo, cloth. net 5/-

GARNETT. A Chaplet from the Greek Anthology. By Richard Garnett, LL.D. (Cameo Series. Vol. 9.) Demy 12mo, half-bound, paper boards. 3/6

—— Iphigenia in Delphi. A Dramatic Poem. With Homer's "Shield of Achilles" and other Translations from the Greek. By Richard Garnett, LL.D. Frontispiece. (Cameo Series. Vol. 2.) Demy 12mo, half-bound, paper boards. 3/6

GOETHE'S Werke. Mit Goethe's Leben Bildnis and Faksimile, Einleitungen und Anmerkungen. Unter Mitwirkung mehrerer Fachgelehrter herausgegeben von Professor Dr. K. Heinemann. 15 vols., large cr. 8vo cloth. net 30/-

GRAVES. The Irish Poems of Alfred Perceval Graves. In two volumes. Cloth, each, net 2/- ; leather, each, net 3/-

HALL. God's Scourge. A Drama in Four Acts. By Moreton Hall. Cr. 8vo, cloth. net 3/6

HEINRICH HEINE'S Samtliche Werke. Herausgegeben von Professor Dr. Ernst Elster. Kritisch durchgesehene und erläuterte Ausgabe. With Frontispiece and Facsimile. 7 vols., large cr. 8vo, cloth, net 16/-

HERBERT. The Temple. By George Herbert. Sacred Poems. Facsimile Reprint of the First Edition, 1633. With an Introduction by J. H. Shorthouse. Sixth Edition. Fcap. 8vo, cloth. net 3/6

HILL. Alfred the Great. A Play in Three Acts, wrought in Blank Verse. By Edmund L. Hill. Demy 12mo, cloth. net 2/6

HOBBES. The Ambassador : A Comedy in 4 Acts. By John Oliver Hobbes. With Frontispiece. Cr. 8vo, paper, net 2/- ; cloth, net 3/6

—— The Wisdom of the Wise : A Comedy in 3 Acts. By John Oliver Hobbes. Cr. 8vo. Paper covers, net 2/- ; cloth, net 3/6

HYDE. **The Religious Songs of Connacht.** By Douglas Hyde. LL.D., M.R.I.A. Author of "A Literary History of Ireland." "Love Songs of Connacht," &c. 2 vols., cloth.   net   10/-

IBSEN. **Brand:** A Dramatic Poem. By Henrik Ibsen. Translated by F. Edmund Garrett. With Frontispiece. (Cameo Series. Vol. 14.) Demy 12mo, half-bound, paper boards.   net   3 6

—— **The Lady from the Sea.** By Henrik Ibsen. Translated by Eleanor Marx-Aveling. With Critical Introduction by Edmund Gosse. Third Edition. Portrait. (Cameo Series. Vol. 1.) Demy 12mo, half-bound, paper boards.   3/6

LAW. **Songs of the Uplands.** By Alice Law.   Cr 8vo, cloth, net   3/6

LEVY. **A London Plane Tree.** By Amy Levy. Illustrated by Bernard Partridge. (Cameo Series. Vol. 3.) Demy 12mo, half-bound, paper boards.   3/6

—— **A Minor Poet.** By Amy Levy. With Frontispiece. Second Edition. (Cameo Series. Vol. 7.) Demy 12mo, half-bound, paper boards.   3/6

LYTTELTON. **Warp and Woof.** A Play. By Edith Lyttelton. Cr. 8vo, cloth.   net   3/6

MACDONALD. **A Wanderer, and Other Poems.** By Leila Macdonald. Cr. 8vo, white cloth, gilt.   net   3/6

MASON. **Flamma Vestalis, and Other Poems.** By Eugene Mason. Frontispiece after Sir Edward Burne-Jones. (Cameo Series. Vol. 17.) Demy 12mo, half-bound, paper boards.   net   3/6

MERMAID SERIES (THE): The Best Plays of the Old Dramatists. Literal Reproductions of the Old Text. With Photogravure Frontispieces. The volumes may now be obtained bound in the following styles :

1. Cr. 8vo, uncut. Brown paper boards, with label.	3/6
2. Cr. 8vo, uncut. Green cloth, with gilt lettering on ink panel.	3/6
3. Cr. 8vo, uncut top. Brown cloth, with gilt lettering and decorative design in brown.	3 6
4. Cr. 8vo. Full vellum, with gilt lettering and gilt top. net	6/-

The Thin Paper Edition is also obtainable in cloth at 2/6 net ; and in leather, at   net   3/6

	No :
Beaumont. The Best Plays of Beaumont and Fletcher. Introduction and Notes by J. St. Loe Strachey. 2 vols.	
Chapman. The Best Plays of George Chapman. Edited by William Lyon Phelps, Instructor in English Literature at Yale College.	9, 10
Congreve. The Complete Plays of William Congreve. Edited by Alex. C. Ewald.	21
Dekker. The Best Plays of Thomas Dekker. Notes by Ernest Rhys.	11
Dryden. The Best Plays of John Dryden. Edited by George Saintsbury. 2 vols.	16
Farquhar. The Best Plays of George Farquhar. Edited, and with an Introduction, by William Archer.	24, 25
Fletcher. See Beaumont.	26
Ford. The Best Plays of John Ford. Edited by Havelock Ellis	
Greene. The Complete Plays of Robert Greene. Edited with Introduction and Notes by Thomas H. Dickinson.	3 27
Heywood. The Best Plays of Thomas Heywood. Edited by A W. Verity. With Introduction by J. A. Symonds.	6

MERMAID SERIES, THE—*continued.*

	No :
Jonson. The Best Plays of Ben Jonson. Edited, with Introduction and Notes, by Brinsley Nicholson and C. H. Herford. 3 vols.	17, 19, 20
Marlowe. The Best Plays of Christopher Marlowe. Edited, with Critical Memoir and Notes, by Havelock Ellis ; and containing a General Introduction to the Series by John Addington Symonds.	1
Massinger. The Best Plays of Philip Massinger. With Critical and Biographical Essay and Notes by Arthur Symons. 2 vols.	4, 5
Middleton. The Best Plays of Thomas Middleton. With an Introduction by Algernon Charles Swinburne. 2 vols.	13, 14
Nero, and Other Plays. Edited by H. P. Horne, Arthur Symons, A. W. Verity, and H. Ellis.	8
Otway. The Best Plays of Thomas Otway. Introduction and Notes by the Hon. Roden Noel.	2
Shadwell. The Best Plays of Thomas Shadwell. Edited by George Saintsbury.	23
Shirley. The Best Plays of James Shirley. With Introduction by Edmund Gosse.	15
Steele. The Complete Plays of Richard Steele. Edited, with Introduction and Notes, by G. A. Aitken.	18
Tourneur. See Webster.	
Vanbrugh. The Select Plays of Sir John Vanbrugh. Edited, with an Introduction and Notes, by A. E. H. Swain.	22
Webster. The Best Plays of Webster and Tourneur. With an Introduction and Notes by John Addington Symonds.	12
Wycherley. The Complete Plays of William Wycherley. Edited, with Introduction and Notes, by W. C. Ward.	7

MILLER. The Tragedies of Seneca. By Frank Justus Miller. Large cr. 8vo, cloth. net 12/6

MISTRAL. Miréio : A Provençal Poem. By Frederic Mistral. Translated by H. W. Preston. Frontispiece by Joseph Pennell. (Cameo Series. Vol. 5.) Demy 12mo, half-bound, paper boards. 3/6

MOORE. The Bending of the Bough. (Drama.) By George Moore. Cr. 8vo, cloth. net 3/6

MYRON. Of Una, and other African Memories. (Poems.) By A. Kiel Myron. Cr. 8vo, cloth. 2/6

NICHOLSON (F. C.). Old German Love Songs. Translated from the Minnesingers of the 12th—14th centuries. By F. C. Nicholson, M.A. Large cr. 8vo, cloth. 6/-

—— **(L.).** Vagrant Songs. By L. Nicholson. Crown 8vo, cloth. net 3/6

PRESLAND. The Marionettes. A Puppet Show in Two Acts. With other Poems. By John Presland. Cr. 8vo, half-parchment. net 5/-

RICHARDSON. Artist Songs. By E. Richardson, LL.A., Author of "Sun, Moon, and Stars," and "Songs of Near and Far Away." Illustrated. Fcap. 8vo, cloth. net 3/6

ROBINSON. The Collected Poems of Mary F. Robinson. Cr. 8vo, cloth. 7/6

—— **Lyrics.** Selected from the Works of A. Mary F. Robinson. (Cameo Series. Vol. 6.) 3/6

—— **The New Arcadia.** (Poems.) By A. Mary F. Robinson (Mme. James Darmesteter). Cr. 8vo, paper covers. 3/6

—— **Retrospect, and Other Poems.** By A. Mary F. Robinson. (Cameo Series. Vol. 13.) Demy 12mo, half-bound, paper boards. 3/6

SANTAYANA. A Hermit of Carmel, and other Poems. By George Santayana, Author of " The Life of Reason," &c. Cr. 8vo, cloth. **net** 3/6

SCHILLER'S Werke. Herausgegeben von Ludwig Bellermann. Kritisch durchgesehene und erläuterte Ausgabe. With frontispiece and facsimile. 8 vols., cr. 8vo, cloth. **net** 16/-

SCHULLER. Within Four Walls, and Children at Play. Two Plays. By Leo Sarkadi Schuller. Cr. 8vo, cloth. **net** 5/-

SERVICE. Songs of a Sourdough. By Robert W. Service. Small cr. 8vo, cloth. **net** 2/6

SHAKESPEARE. The "First Folio" Shakespeare. The Complete Works of William Shakespeare, reprinted from the First Folio. Edited, with an Introduction to each play, Complete Glossaries, and Variant Readings, by C. Porter and H. A. Clark, and with a General Introduction by John Churton Collins, M.A., D.Litt. In 13 volumes (sold in sets only). Cr. 8vo. the set, **net** 42/-

SIGERSON. Bards of the Gael and Gall : Examples of the Poetic Literature of Erinn, done into English after the Metres and Modes of the Gael. By George Sigerson, M.D., F.R.U.I. Second Edition, Revised and Enlarged. Large cr. 8vo, cloth. **net** 6/1

TUNISON. Dramatic Traditions of the Dark Ages. By Joseph S. Tunison. Large cr. 8vo, cloth. **net** 5/6

TYNAN. Love Songs of Ireland. Collected and Edited by Katherine Tynan. (Cameo Series. Vol. 12.) Demy 12mo, half-bound, paper boards. 3/6

WALSH. Shakespeare's Complete Sonnets. A new arrangement. With Introduction and notes by C. M. Walsh. Cr. 8vo, cloth. **net** 5/-

WATSON. Wordsworth's Grave, and Other Poems. By William Watson. (Cameo Series. Vol. 4.) Demy 12mo, half-bound, paper boards. 3/6

WHITAKER, L'Avocat Patelin. A Comedy in Three Acts. Adapted by the Abbé Brueys, from the Famous Farce of the Fifteenth Century. Translated by Samuel F. G. Whitaker. Cr. 8vo, imitation parchment wrapper. **net** 2/-

WILLMORE. The Soul's Departure, and Other Poems. By E. Willmore. With Frontispiece. (Cameo Series. Vol. 18.) Demy 12mo, paper boards. **net** 3/6

YEATS. The Countess Kathleen. A Dramatic Poem. By W. B. Yeats. With Frontispiece by J. T. Nettleship. (Cameo Series. Vol. 10.) Demy 12mo, half-bound, paper boards. 3/6

—— **Poems.** By W. B. Yeats. A New Edition entirely revised and reset. Large cr. 8vo, cloth. 7/6

—— **Poems.** 1899—1905. By W. B. Yeats. Large cr. 8vo. **net** 6/-

—— **The Secret Rose.** By W. B. Yeats. Large cr. 8vo. **net** 6/-

—— **The Celtic Twilight.** By W. B. Yeats. Large cr. 8vo. 6/-

—— **Ideas of Good and Evil.** By W. B. Yeats. Large cr. 8vo. 6/-

—— **The Shadowy Waters.** (1st Version). By W. B. Yeats. Large cr. 8vo. 3/6

—— **Where There is Nothing.** By W. B. Yeats. Large cr. 8vo. **net** 3/6

—— **Shorter Plays.** By W. B. Yeats. Large cr. 8vo. **net** 3/6

—— **The King's Threshold, and On Baile's Strand.** By W. B. Yeats. Large cr. 8vo. **net** 3/6

—— **Deirdre.** By W. B. Yeats. Large cr. 8vo. **net** 3.6

—— **The Hour Glass.** Acting version, in paper covers. 6d.

—— **The Shadowy Waters.** Acting version, in paper covers. 6d.

—— **On Baile's Strand.** Acting version, in paper covers. 6d.

NOVELS, HUMOROUS WORKS, SHORT STORIES, &c.

ADAMS. Tussock Land. By Arthur H. Adams. (First Novel
    Library.) Cr. 8vo, cloth.   6/-
THE ADELPHI LIBRARY. Standard Fiction. Cr. 8vo, cloth, each vol.   3/6
    (1) **Through Sorrow's Gates.** By Halliwell Sutcliffe.
    (2) **The Canon in Residence.** By Victor L. Whitechurch.
    (3) **Evelyn Innes.** By George Moore.
    (4) **The Portent, and Other Stories.** By George Macdonald.
    (5) **The Beetle.** By Richard Marsh.
In Preparation :—
    Sister Teresa. By George   **Tales of Unrest** By Joseph
      Moore.   Conrad.
    The Haunts of Men. By R. W.   **The Tales of John Oliver**
      Chambers.   **Hobbes.**
    Willowdene Will. By Halliwell   **The Shulamite.** By Alice and
      Sutcliffe.   Claude Askew.
AHO (Juhani). Squire Hellman. See Pseudonym Library. No. 25.
ALEXANDER. Brown, V.C. By Mrs. Alexander. (Unwin's Green
    Cloth Library.) Cr. 8vo, cloth.   6/-
    Popular Series for Boys and Girls. Illustrated, cloth.   3/6
    Also (Popular Copyright Novels), cr. 8vo, cloth.   2/6
—— **Kitty Costello.** By Mrs. Alexander. With a Memorial Note
    by Isa Duffus Hardy. (Unwin's Red Cloth Library.) Cr. 8vo, cloth.   6/-
    Popular Series for Boys and Girls. Cloth.   3/6
—— **Stronger than Love.** By Mrs. Alexander. (Unwin's Red Cloth
    Library.) Cr. 8vo, cloth.   6/-
    Also (Popular Copyright Novels), cr. 8vo, cloth.   2/6
—— **Through Fire to Fortune.** By Mrs. Alexander. (Unwin's Green
    Cloth Library.) Cr. 8vo, cloth.   6/-
    Also (Popular Copyright Novels), cloth.   2/6
—— **A Winning Hazard.** By Mrs. Alexander. (Popular Copyright
    Novels.) Cr. 8vo, cloth.   2/6
—— **The Yellow Fiend.** By Mrs. Alexander. (Unwin's Green Cloth
    Library.) Cr. 8vo, cloth.   6/-
ALIEN. The Devil's Half Acre. By "Alien." (Unwin's Green Cloth
    Library.) Cr. 8vo, cloth.   6/-
AMBER. Wistons. A Story in Three Parts. By Miles Amber. (First
    Novel Library.) Crown 8vo, cloth.   6/-
ANDREIEF. The Red Laugh. By Leonidas Andreief. Translated by
    A. Linden. With Portrait of the Author. Cr. 8vo, paper cover. net   1/-
ANDREWS. Stephen Kyrle. By Katherine Andrews. Cr. 8vo, cloth.   6/-
ARCHER. A Bush Honeymoon, and Other Australian Stories. By
    Laura M. Palmer Archer. (Unwin's Red Cloth Library.) Cr. 8vo,
    cloth.   6/-
ARMSTRONG. Passports. See under "Little Novels." No. 9.
ASKEW. The Shulamite. By Alice and Claude Askew. Illustrated.
    Crown 8vo. (Green Cloth Library.)   6/-
    Also (The Adelphi Library), cloth.   3/6
    Also in picture wrapper.   net   1/-
—— **The Tempting of Paul Chester.** By Alice and Claude Askew.
    Cr. 8vo, cloth.   6/-

AUTONYM LIBRARY, THE. Uniform in style and price with "The Pseudonym Library."   Paper covers, each, 1/6 , cloth, each   2/-

(1) The Upper Berth. By F Marion Crawford

(2) Mad Sir Uchtred of the Hills By S R Crockett.

(3) By Reef and Palm By Louis Becke

(4) The Play Actress. By S R Crockett.

(5) A Bachelor Maid. By Mrs Burton Harrison

(6) Miserrima By G. W. T Omond

(7) The Two Strangers. By Mrs Oliphant

(8) Another Wicked Woman. By S De Pentheny

(9) The Spectre of Strathannan. By W E Norris.

(10) Kafir Stories By W C Scully

(11) Molly Darling. By Mrs Hungerford

(12) A Game of Consequences By Albert Kinross

(13) Sleeping Fires. By George Gissing

(14) The Red Star By L. McManus

(15) A Marriage by Capture. By Robert Buchanan

(16) Leaves from the Life of an Eminent Fossil. By W Dutton Burrard.

(17) An Impossible Person. By Constance Cotterell

(18) Which is Absurd. By Cosmo Hamilton

BACHELLER. Eben Holden. By Irving Bacheller. Cr 8vo, cloth, net   2/6
Also paper covers   6d

—— Silas Strong By Irving Bacheller. Cr. 8vo, cloth (Unwin's Green Cloth Library)   6/-

BAILLIE-SAUNDERS. London Lovers By Margaret Baillie-Saunders, Author of the Prize Novel, " Saints in Society " Cr. 8vo, cloth Decorative binding   6/-

—— Saints in Society By Margaret Baillie-Saunders. £100 prize novel Cr. 8vo, cloth. (First Novel Library)   8/-
Also paper covers   6d.

BAKER (H B) Margaret Grey. See under "Little Novels " No 4.

BAKER (J.) A Double Choice By James Baker (Unwin's Green Cloth Library) Cr 8vo, cloth   6/-

BARLOW By Beach and Bogland. By Jane Barlow, Author of " Irish Idylls," &c With Frontispiece Cr 8vo cloth (Unwin's Green Cloth Library)   6/-

BARR (A E.) The Black Shilling By Amelia E Barr. (Unwin's Red Cloth Library.) Cr. 8vo, cloth.   6/-

—— Cecilia's Lover By Amelia E Barr Cr 8vo, cloth (Unwin's Red Cloth Library)   6/-

—— I, Thou, and the Other One. By Amelia E Barr. (Unwin's Green Cloth Library) Cr 8vo, cloth   6/-
Also (Popular Copyright Novels), cloth   2/6

—— The Lion's Whelp. By Amelia E Barr (Unwin's Green Cloth Library) Cr 8vo, cloth   6/-

—— The Maid of Maiden Lane. By Amelia E. Barr Fully Illustrated (Unwin's Green Cloth Library) Cr 8vo, cloth.   6/-

—— Prisoners of Conscience. By Amelia E. Barr Cr 8vo, cloth   6/-
Popular Series for Boys and Girls Illustrated, cloth   3/6
Also (Popular Copyright Novels), cloth   2/6

—— A Song of a Single Note By Amelia E Barr (Unwin's Red Cloth Library) Cr 8vo, cloth.   6/-

—— Souls of Passage By Amelia E Barr (Unwin's Green Cloth Library) Cr 8vo, cloth   6/-

BARR (A E.) Thyra Varrick By Amelia E Barr (Unwin's Red Cloth Library) Cr 8vo, cloth — 6/-

—— Trinity Bells A Tale of Old New York By Amelia E Barr Fully Illustrated in handsome decorated cover Cr 8vo, cloth gilt — 6/-

—— Was it Right to Forgive? A Domestic Romance By Amelia E Barr (Unwin's Green Cloth Library) Cr 8vo, cloth. — 6/-
Also (Popular Copyright Novels), cloth — 2/6

BARR (W). Shacklett The Evolution of a Statesman. By Walter Barr Large cr 8vo, cloth. — 6/-

BARRY. Arden Massiter. By William Barry (Unwin's Green Cloth Library) Cr 8vo, cloth — 6/-

—— The Dayspring—A Romance By William Barry, D D (Unwin's Red Cloth Library.) Cr 8vo — 6/-

—— The Two Standards By William Barry, D D (Unwin's Green Cloth Library) Cr 8vo, cloth. — 6/-

—— The Wizard's Knot. By William Barry. (Unwin's Green Cloth Library.) Cr. 8vo, cloth — 6/-

BARTRAM People of Clopton By George Bartram (Unwin's Green Cloth Library.) Cr 8vo, cloth — 6/-

—— The White-headed Boy By George Bartram (Unwin's Green Cloth Library) Cr 8vo, cloth — 6/-

BEALBY A Daughter of the Fen. By J T Bealby (Unwin's Green Cloth Library) Cr. 8vo, cloth — 6/-

BECKE The Adventures of a Supercargo. By Louis Becke. (Unwin's Red Cloth Library) Cr 8vo, cloth — 6/-

—— Breachley Black Sheep. By Louis Becke (Unwin's Red Cloth Library) Cr 8vo, cloth. — 6/-

—— By Reef and Palm, See Autonym Library Vol 3

—— By Reef and Palm, and Other Stories. By Louis Becke. (Popular Copyright Novels) Cr 8vo, cloth. — 2/6

—— By Rock and Pool By Louis Becke (Unwin's Green Cloth Library) Cr 8vo, cloth — 6/-

—— Chinkie's Flat, and Other Stories. By Louis Becke (Unwin's Red Cloth Library) Cr 8vo, cloth. — 6/-

—— The Ebbing of the Tide By Louis Becke (Unwin's Green Cloth Library) Cr 8vo, cloth — 6/-

—— Edward Barry South Sea Pearler By Louis Becke (Unwin's Green Cloth Library) Cr 8vo, cloth — 6/-

—— Helen Adair By Louis Becke. (Unwin's Red Cloth Library) Cr 8vo, cloth — 6/-

—— His Native Wife By Louis Becke. (Century Library No. 4) Paper covers, 1/6; cloth — 2/-
Also paper covers. — 8d.

—— Old Convict Days. Edited by Louis Becke Cr 8vo, cloth — 6/-

—— Pacific Tales By Louis Becke Frontispiece Portrait of the Author (Unwin's Green Cloth Library.) Cr 8vo, cloth — 6/-

—— Ridan the Devil, and Other Stories By Louis Becke. (Unwin's Green Cloth Library) Large cr 8vo, cloth — 6/-

—— Rodman the Boatsteerer. By Louis Becke. (Unwin's Green Cloth Library) Cr. 8vo, cloth — 6/-

—— The Strange Adventure of James Shervington, and Other Stories By Louis Becke (Unwin's Red Cloth Library) Cr 8vo, cloth. — 6/-
Also (Popular Copyright Novels), cloth. — 2/6

BECKE. Tessa, and the Trader's Wife. By Louis Becke. (Popular
Copyright Novels.) Cr. 8vo, cloth.   2/6

—— Tom Gerrard. By Louis Becke. (Unwin's Red Cloth Library.)
Cr. 8vo, cloth.   6/-

—— **Under Tropic Skies.** By Louis Becke. (Unwin's Red Cloth
Library.) Cr. 8vo, cloth.   6/-

—— Wild Life in the Southern Seas. By Louis Becke. Cr. 8vo, cloth.   5/-

—— Yorke the Adventurer, and Other Tales. By Louis Becke.
(Unwin's Green Cloth Library.) Cr. 8vo, cloth gilt.   6/-

BECKE and JEFFERY. A First Fleet Family. By Louis Becke and
Walter Jeffery. (Unwin's Green Cloth Library.) Cr. 8vo, cloth.   6/-

—— The Mutineer. By Louis Becke and Walter Jeffery. (Unwin's
Green Cloth Library.) Cr. 8vo, cloth.   6/-

—— **The Mystery of Laughlin Islands.** By Louis Becke and Walter
Jeffery. (Yellow Library. Vol. 3.)   Paper covers, 1/- ; cloth   2/-

BLAKE (Bass). A Lady's Honour. By Bass Blake. (First Novel
Library.) Cr. 8vo, cloth.   6/-

BLAKE (B. C.) The Peculiar History of Mary Ann Susan.
By Bernard C Blake. Cr. 8vo, cloth.   3/6

BLOUNT. Sylvia in Society. By Mrs. George Blount ("Mrs. George
Norman"). With a Frontispiece. Sm. demy 8vo, cloth.   net   3/6

BODKIN. The Quests of Paul Beck. By M. McDonnell Bodkin,
K.C. With 8 Illustrations. Cr. 8vo, cloth.   6/-

—— The Capture of Paul Beck. By W. McDonnell Bodkin, K.C.
Cr. 8vo, cloth.   6/-

BOLT (Ben). Anthony Jasper. See Pseudonym Library. No. 52.

BOURGET. The Disciple. A Novel. By Paul Bourget. Cr. 8vo, cloth.   6/-

—— Divorce. By Paul Bourget. Cr. 8vo. (Red Cloth Library.)   6/-

BOWEN-ROWLANDS. The Passion of Mahael. By Lilian Bowen-
Rowlands. Cr. 8vo, cloth.   6/-

BRAINERD. In Vanity Fair. A Tale of Frocks and Femininity. By
Eleanor Hoyt Brainerd. Cr. 8vo, cloth.   6/-

BREDA. From One Man's Hand to Another. By G. H. Breda.
(First Novel Library.) Cr. 8vo, cloth.   6/-

BROOKE (Magdalene). Eleanor Lambert. See Pseudonym
Library. No. 2.

BUCHANAN (A.). She Loved Much. By Alfred Buchanan, Author
of "The Real Australia," "Bubble Reputation," &c. Cr. 8vo, cloth.   6/-

BUCHANAN. Diana's Hunting. By Robert Buchanan. Demy 12mo.   2/6

—— Effie Hetherington. By Robert Buchanan. (Popular Copyright
Novels.) Cr. 8vo, cloth. 2/6.   Also paper covers   6d.

—— A Marriage by Capture. By Robert Buchanan. (The Autonym
Library.)   Paper covers, 1/6 ; cloth   2/-

BULLEN Cut Off from the World. By Frank T. Bullen. Cr. 8vo,
cloth.   6/-

BURRARD (W. Dutton.) Leaves from the Life of an Eminent
Fossil. See Autonym Library. Vol. 16.

By Creek and Gully. Edited by Lala Fisher. Cr. 8vo, cloth.   6/-

BYRDE. The Searchers. A Story in Four Books. By Margaretta
Byrde. (First Novel Library.) Cr. 8vo, cloth.   6/-

—— The Interpreters. By Margaretta Byrde. Cr. 8vo, cloth.   6/-

CAMPBELL The Problem of Prejudice. See "Little Novels" No. 3

CAREY. The Motor Cracksman By Charles Carey Cr 8vo, cloth 6/-
Also paper covers. 6d.

CARTWRIGHT. A Slight Indiscretion. See "Little Novels." No 7.

CARYL (Valentine). Ne'er-Do-Weel See Pseudonym Library No 54

CENTURY LIBRARY, THE. With specially designed covers, printed in colours, by William Hyde. Paper covers, 1/6, cloth 2/-
    (1) Toxin. By Ouida Illust   (4) His Native Wife. By Louis
    (2) Moff By John Tweeddale   Becke   Frontispiece by
    (3) Monsieur Paulot. By Sir   Leslie Brooke
       Hubert Jerningham.

CERVANTES. Don Quixote. By Miguel de Cervantes With 260 Drawings by Daniel Vierge. 4 volumes, super royal 8vo, cloth, with leather label and gilt lettering Edition limited to 155 copies
net £15

    Fine Edition (limited to 10 copies) on Imperial Japan paper, with 2 additional Illustrations and a duplicate set of the full-page plates (proofs after letters). Full vellum with gilt back. net £30

CHAMBERS. The Haunts of Men. By R W. Chambers. (The Adelphi Library) Cr 8vo, cloth 3/6

CHESSON. Father Felix's Chronicles. By Nora Chesson With a new portrait of the Author, reproduced in Photogravure, and an Introduction by W. H Chesson Cr. 8vo, cloth 6/-

CHOMLEY. The Wisdom of Esau. By C H. Chomley and R L Outhwaite (Unwin's Green Cloth Library) Cr. 8vo, cloth 6/-

CLARE Court Cards. By Austin Clare (Unwin's Red Cloth Library.) Cr 8vo, cloth. 6/-

CLEEVE. Anglo-Americans. By Lucas Cleeve. (Unwin's Red Cloth Library) Cr 8vo, cloth 6/-

—— Blue Lilies. By Lucas Cleeve. (Unwin's Green Cloth Library) Cr. 8vo, cloth. 6/-

—— The Children of Endurance By Lucas Cleeve (Unwin's Red Cloth Library) Cr 8vo, cloth 6/-

—— Counsels of the Night. By Lucas Cleeve. (Unwin's Red Cloth Library) Cr. 8vo. 6/-

—— A Double Marriage. By Lucas Cleeve. Cr. 8vo, cloth (Unwin's Red Cloth Library) 6/-

—— The Fool-killer. By Lucas Cleeve. (Unwin's Red Cloth Library) Cr. 8vo, cloth. 6/-

—— The Fool's Tax. By Lucas Cleeve. Cr 8vo, cloth. 6/-

—— The Man in the Street By Lucas Cleeve (Unwin's Red Cloth Library) Cr 8vo, cloth 6/-

—— An Old Man's Darling. By Lucas Cleeve. Cr. 8vo, cloth 6/-

—— The Progress of Priscilla. By Lucas Cleeve (Unwin's Red Cloth Library) Cr 8vo. 6/-

—— The Rose Geranium. By Lucas Cleeve. Cr 8vo, cloth 6/-

—— Seven Nights in a Gondola. By Lucas Cleeve (Unwin's Red Cloth Library) Cr 8vo 6/-

—— Stolen Waters. By Lucas Cleeve (Unwin's Red Cloth Library) Cr. 8vo, cloth 6/-
    Also paper covers. 6d.

CLIFFORD. Mrs. Keith's Crime. By Mrs. W. K. Clifford. (Unwin's
Green Cloth Library.) Cr. 8vo, cloth   6/-

CLYDE. A Pagan's Love. By Constance Clyde. (Unwin's First
Novel Library.) Cr. 8vo, cloth.   6/-

COBBLEIGH (Tom). Gentleman Upcott's Daughter. See Pseudonym
Library. No. 19.

—— Young Sam. See Pseudonym Library. No. 40.

CONRAD. Almayer's Folly : A Romance of an Eastern River. By
Joseph Conrad. (Unwin's Green Cloth Library.) Cr. 8vo, cloth.   6/-

—— An Outcast of the Islands. By Joseph Conrad. (Unwin's Green
Cloth Library.) Cr. 8vo, cloth.   6/-

—— Tales of Unrest. By Joseph Conrad. (Unwin's Green Cloth
Library.) Cr. 8vo, cloth.   6/-
Also (The Adelphi Library). Cloth.   3/6

CORKRAN. Lucie and I. By Henriette Corkran. Cr. 8vo, cloth   6/-

COSTELLOE. The World at Eighteen. By Ray Costelloe. Cr.
8vo, cloth.   3/6

COTTERELL. An Impossible Person. By Constance Cotterell.
(The Autonym Library.)   Paper covers, 1/6 ; cloth   2/-

—— Love is Not so Light. By Constance Cotterell. (Unwin's Green
Cloth Library.) Cr. 8vo, cloth.   6/-

COURLANDER. Eve's Apple. By Alphonse Courlander. With
Frontispiece. Cr. 8vo, cloth.   6/-

—— The Sacrifice. By Alphonse Courlander. With a coloured Frontispiece. (Green Cloth Library.) Cr. 8vo.   6/-

CRAMPTON. The Story of an Estancia. By George Crampton.
Cr. 8vo, cloth.   3/6

CRAWFORD (F. Marion.) The Upper Berth. See Autonym Library.
Vol. 1.

CRESPIGNY. From Behind the Arras. By Mrs. Philip Champion
de Crespigny. (First Novel Library.) Cr. 8vo, cloth.   6/-

—— The Mischief of a Glove. By Mrs. Philip Champion de Crespigny.
(Unwin's Red Cloth Library.) Cr. 8vo, cloth.   6/-
Also paper covers   6d.

Cricket on the Brain. By M. C. C. Illustrated by "Gil." Fcap. 4to,
paper covers.   net   11d.

CROCKETT. Cinderella. By S. R. Crockett. (Unwin's Green Cloth
Library.) With 8 Illustrations. Cr. 8vo, cloth.   6/-

—— The Grey Man. By S. R. Crockett. (Unwin's Green Cloth Library.)
Cr. 8vo, cloth, gilt tops.   6/-
Also an Edition de Luxe, cr. 4to, cloth gilt.   net 21/-

—— Kit Kennedy : Country Boy. By S. R. Crockett. (Unwin's Green
Cloth Library. Cr. 8vo, cloth gilt.   6/-

—— The Lilac Sunbonnet. By S. R. Crockett. (Unwin's Green Cloth
Library.) Cr. 8vo, cloth, gilt tops.   6/-

—— Mad Sir Uchtred of the Hills. See Autonym Library. Vol. 2.

—— Me and Myn. By S. R. Crockett. (Unwin's Green Cloth Library.)
Cr. 8vo.   6/-

—— The Play Actress. See Autonym Library. Vol. 4.

—— The Play Actress and Mad Sir Uchtred. By S. R. Crockett.
With a new Preface. (Popular Copyright Novels.) Cr. 8vo, cloth.   2/6

—— The Raiders. By S. R. Crockett. (Unwin's Green Cloth Library.)
Cr. 8vo, cloth, gilt tops.   6/-

CROCKETT The Stickit Minister By S R Crockett. (Unwin's
Green Cloth Library) Crown 8vo, cloth, gilt tops 6/-
    Cheap Edition (Popular Copyright Novels) Cloth 2/6
    Also cr 8vo, cloth 1/- net   Paper covers 6d.

CROTTIE The Lost Land By Julia M. Crottie (Unwin's Green
Cloth Library). Cr 8vo, cloth. 6/-
—— Neighbours Being Annals of a Dull Town By Julia M. Crottie.
Cr 8vo, cloth. 6/-

DALIN (Talmage) European Relations See Pseudonym Library
No 9

DALTON Olive in Italy By Moray Dalton Cr 8vo, cloth 6/-

DALZIEL In the First Watch, and Other Engine-Room Stories.
By James Dalziel. Cr 8vo, cloth 6/-
—— High Life in the Far East. By James Dalziel Cr 8vo, cloth.

DAVIDSON The Confessions of a Match-making Mother. By
Lillias Campbell Davidson. (Idle Hour Series. No. 6)
    Paper covers, 1/-, cloth 2/-

DEAN (Mrs Andrew) Splendid Cousin See Pseudonym Library
No 20.
—— Lesser's Daughter. See Pseudonym Library No. 43.

von DEGEN. Mystery of the Campagna See Pseudonym Library.
No 3

DEW-SMITH. Diary of a Dreamer. By Mrs Dew-Smith. Cr. 8vo,
cloth gilt 6/-

DICKESON. Tychiades. A Tale of the Ptolemies Written in the
Third Century, B C., by Ornithovius, and now faithfully translated
out of the Original by Alfred Dickeson Cr 8vo, cloth 6/-

DRACHMANN (Holger). Cruise of the "Wild Duck" See
Pseudonym Library No 24

DROSINES (Georgios). Amaryllis. See Pseudonym Library. No 5.
—— Herb of Love. See Pseudonym Library No 16

DUMILLO (Alice). On the Gogmagogs. See "Little Novels" No 10.

DUNDAS The Journeys of Antonia By Christian Dundas
(Unwin's Red Cloth Library.) Cr 8vo 6/-

DUTT. The Lake of Palms. By Romesh Dutt, C I E With Frontispiece Cr. 8vo, cloth 6/-

DYKE. As Others See Us By Watson Dyke (Unwin's Green Cloth
Library) Cr 8vo 6/-

von EBNER-ESCHENBACH (Marie). Two Countesses See
Pseudonym Library No. 27

van EEDEN. The Deeps of Deliverance. By F. Van Eeden.
(Unwin's Red Cloth Library) Cr 8vo, cloth 6/-

FALCONER (Lanoe) Mademoise'le Ixe See Pseudonym Library
No 1
—— Hotel d'Angleterre. See Pseudonym Library No 6
—— Mademoiselle Ixe, The Hotel d'Angleterre, and Other
Stories By Lanoe Falconer Popular Ed Cr 8vo, cloth 1/-

FARRER. The Great Noodleshire Election A Comedy of Political
Life By J A Farrer Cr 8vo, cloth 3/6

FERGUSON. Lays of the Red Branch. By Sir Samuel Ferguson
(New Irish Library) Small cr. 8vo   Paper covers, 1/-, cloth 2/-

FIRST NOVEL LIBRARY, THE. First Novels of New Authors.
Cr. 8vo, cloth.   each   6/-

(1) **Wistons.** By Miles Amber.
(2) **The Searchers.** By Margaretta Byrde.
(3) **A Lady's Honour.** By Bass Blake.
(4) **From Behind the Arras.** By Mrs. Philip Champion de Crespigny.
(5) **The Flame and the Flood.** By Rosamond Langbridge.
(6) **A Drama of Sunshine.** By Mrs. Aubrey Richardson.
(7) **Rosemonde.** By Beatrice Stott.
(8) **The Cardinal's Pawn.** By K. L. Montgomery.
(9) **Tussock Land.** By Arthur H. Adams.
(10) **The Kingdom of Twilight.** By Forrest Reid.
(11) **A Pagan's Love.** By Constance Clyde.
(12) **Saints in Society.** By Margaret Baillie-Saunders.
(13) **At the Sign of the Peacock.** By K. C. Ryves.
(14) **From One Man's Hand to Another.** By G. H. Breda.
(15) **Woman and the Sword.** By Rupert Lorraine.

FITZGERALD.   Josephine's Troubles. A Story of the Franco-German War. By Percy Fitzgerald. Illustrated. Cr. 8vo, cloth.   **5/-**

FLETCHER.   Grand Relations. By J. S. Fletcher. Author of " The Arcadians." (Unwin's Red Cloth Library.) Cr. 8vo, cloth.   **6/-**
Also paper covers.   **6d.**

—— **Paradise Court.** By J. S. Fletcher. Cr. 8vo, cloth.   **6/-**

—— **The Queen of a Day.** By J. S. Fletcher. (Unwin's Red Cloth Library.) Cr. 8vo.   **6/-**

—— **The Threshing Floor.** By J. S. Fletcher. Cr. 8vo, cloth.   **6/-**

FLOWERDEW.   The Ways of Men. By Herbert Flowerdew. Cr. 8vo, cloth.   **6/-**

FOGAZZARO.   The Woman (Malombra). By Antonio Fogazzaro. Translated by F. Thorold Dickson. Cr. 8vo, cloth.   **6/-**

FORREST.   The Bond of Blood. See under " Little Novels." No. 6.

FRAPAN (Ilse).   Heavy Laden. See Pseudonym Library. No. 13.

—— **God's Will.** See Pseudonym Library. No. 31.

FRASER.   Death, the Showman. By John Fraser. (Unwin's Green Cloth Library.) Cr. 8vo.   **6/-**

FREDERIC.   Marsena. By Harold Frederic. (Yellow Library. Vol. 2.)   Paper covers, 1/- ; cloth   **2/-**

FRENCH.   Desmonde, M.D. By Henry Willard French. (Popular Copyright Novels.) Cr. 8vo, cloth.   **2/6**

FURNESS.   The Melpomene Papers. By Annette Furness. Cr. 8vo, cloth.   **3/6**

GISSING (George).   Sleeping Fires. See Autonym Library. Vol. 13.

GORKY.   Foma Gordyeeff. By Maxim Gorky. Illustrated and unabridged. (Unwin's Green Cloth Library.) Cr. 8vo, cloth.   **6/-**

—— **The Man who was Afraid (Foma Gordyeeff).** By Maxim Gorky. Popular Edition. Cr. 8vo, cloth.   net   **1/-**

—— **The Outcasts, and Other Stories.** By Maxim Gorky. Cr. 8vo, cloth.   **3/6**
Contents :—The Outcasts, and Waiting for the Ferry. Translated by Dora B. Montefiore. The Affair of the Clasps. Translated by Vera Volkhovsky.
New Popular Edition. Cr. 8vo, cloth.   net   **1/-**

—— **Three of Them.** By Maxim Gorky. Cr. 8vo, cloth.   **2/6**
New Popular Edition. Cr. 8vo, cloth.   net   **1/-**

Grandmother's Advice to Elizabeth. See under " Trowbridge."

GREEN. The Filigree Ball. By Anna Katherine Green, Author of " The Leavenworth Case." (Unwin's Red Cloth Library.) Cr. 8vo, cloth. 6/-
Also paper covers. 6d.

GREEN CLOTH LIBRARY. See Unwin's Green Cloth Library.

GRIFFITHS (Arthur). A Royal Rascal. By Major Arthur Griffiths. Cr. 8vo (Unwin's Red Cloth Library). 6/-
Also paper covers. 6d.

GRIFFITHS (D.R.) Elgiva, Daughter of the Thegn. By D. R. Griffiths. Cr. 8vo, cloth gilt. 6/-

GUEST (Lady Charlotte). See under " Mabinogion."

GYP. Ginette's Happiness. By Gyp. Translated by Ralph Derechef. (Popular Copyright Novels.) Cr. 8vo, cloth. 2/6

HALES. A Lindsay o' the Dale. By A. G. Hales. With a Frontispiece by Stanley L. Wood. Crown 8vo, cloth. 6/-
——— **Marozia.** By A. G. Hales. Cr. 8vo, cloth. 6/-
——— **The Watcher on the Tower.** By A. G. Hales. (Unwin's Red Cloth Library.) Cr. 8vo, cloth. 6/-
Also paper covers. 6d.

HAMILTON (Cosmo). Which is Absurd. See Autonym Library. Vol. 18.

HAMILTON (E.). The Mawkin of the Flow. By Lord Ernest Hamilton. (Unwin's Green Cloth Library.) Cr. 8vo, cloth. 6/-
——— **Outlaws of the Marches.** By Lord Ernest Hamilton. (Unwin's Green Cloth Library) Cr. 8vo, cloth. 6/-
——— **The Perils of Josephine.** By Lord Ernest Hamilton. (Unwin's Green Cloth Library.) Cr. 8vo, cloth. 6/-

HARDING. The Woman Who Vowed (The Demetrian). By Ellison Harding. Cr. 8vo, cloth. 6/-

HARDY. Pen Portraits of the British Soldier. By the Rev. E. J. Hardy. Illustrated. Demy 12mo, cloth, decorated cover. 1/-
——— **Mr. Thomas Atkins.** A study in Red, Blue, Green and Khaki. By the Rev. E. J. Hardy, M.A. 6/-
Also decorative paper covers. net 1/-

HARRISON (B.). Latter-day Sweethearts. By Mrs. Burton Harrison, Cr 8vo, cloth. 6/-
——— **Transplanted Daughters.** By Mrs. Burton Harrison. Cr. 8vo, cloth. 6 -
——— **A Triple Entanglement.** By Burton Harrison. Cr. 8vo, cloth. 6/-
——— **A Bachelor Maid.** See Autonym Library. Vol. 5.

HARRISON (D.). Master Passions. By Mrs. Darent Harrison. Cr. 8vo, cloth. 6/-

HAY. Herridge of Reality Swamp. By William Hay. Cr. 8vo, cloth. 6/-

HENSHAW. Why Not, Sweetheart ? By Julia W. Henshaw. Cr. 8vo, cloth. 6/-

HENTY. The Lost Heir. By G. A. Henty. Cr. 8vo, cloth. 6/-
Also Popular Series for Boys and Girls. Illustrated, cloth. 3/6

HERTZ-GARTEN (Theodor). Red-Litten Windows. See Pseudonym Library. No. 11.

HINKSON   Father Alphonsus   By H A Hinkson.   Cr. 8vo, cloth.   6/-

HOBBES   A Bundle of Life   See Pseudonym Library, No 34.

—— The Dream and the Business.   By John Oliver Hobbes
With a cover design by Aubrey Beardsley   Cr 8vo, cloth   6/-

—— The Flute of Pan   By John Oliver Hobbes.   (Unwin's
Red Cloth Library)   Cr 8vo, cloth   6/-

—— The Gods, Some Mortals, and Lord Wickenham   By John
Oliver Hobbes   (Unwin's Green Cloth Library)   Cr 8vo, cloth   6/-
Also (Idle Hour Series.   No 3)   Paper covers, 1/- , cloth   2/-
Also paper covers   6d

—— The Herb-Moon   By John Oliver Hobbes   (Unwin's Green Cloth
Library.)   Large cr. 8vo, cloth   6/-
Also (Popular Copyright Novels).   2/8

—— Love and the Soul Hunters   By John Oliver Hobbes.   (Unwin's
Red Cloth Library)   Cr 8vo, cloth   6/-
Popular Edition.   Cr 8vo.   Paper covers, net, 6d. , cloth, net   1/-

—— Robert Orange . A Sequel to "The School for Saints"   (Unwin's
Green Cloth Library.)   Cr. 8vo, cloth.   6/-
Also paper covers.   6d.

—— The School for Saints.   By John Oliver Hobbes.   (Unwin's Green
Cloth Library)   Large cr 8vo, cloth   6/-
Also paper covers.   6d

—— The Sinner's Comedy.   See Pseudonym Library, No 28

—— Some Emotions and a Moral, and The Sinner's Comedy
By John Oliver Hobbes   Cr. 8vo, cloth   net   1/-

—— Some Emotions and a Moral   See Pseudonym Library, No. 8.
Also paper covers.   6d

—— A Study in Temptations, and A Bundle of Life   By John Oliver
Hobbes   Cr. 8vo   Paper covers, net, 6d , cloth, net   1/-

—— A Study in Temptations.   See Pseudonym Library, No. 23.

—— Tales about Temperaments.   By John Oliver Hobbes   Cr 8vo,
cloth gilt.   net   2/6

—— The Tales of John Oliver Hobbes.   Portrait of the Author
(Unwin's Green Cloth Library)   Large cr 8vo, cloth
Contents :—Some Emotions and a Moral   A Bundle of Life   6/-
A Study in Temptations   The Sinner's Comedy.
Also (The Adelphi Library), cloth.   3/6

—— The Vineyard   By John Oliver Hobbes   (Unwin's Red Cloth
Library.)   With Six Illustrations   Cr. 8vo, cloth.   6/-
Also paper covers.   6d

—— Life and To-morrow   Selections from the Writings of John
Oliver Hobbes   Edited by Zoe Procter   Cr 8vo, cloth   6/-

HOCKING.   Meadowsweet and Rue   By Silas K Hocking   (Unwin's
Red Cloth Library)   Cr. 8vo, cloth.   6/-

HOLDSWORTH   The Iron Gates   By Annie E. Holdsworth
(Unwin's Green Cloth Library)   Cr 8vo, cloth   6/-

HORNIMAN. **That Fast Miss Blount.** A Novel. By Roy Horniman. (Unwin's Red Cloth Library.) Cr. 8vo, cloth.   6/-
Also paper covers.   6d.

—— **The Living Buddha.** By Roy Horniman. (Unwin's Red Cloth Library.) Cr. 8vo, cloth.   6/-

HUDSON. **A Crystal Age.** By W. H. Hudson. Cr. 8vo, cloth, decorative binding.   6/-

HUMPHREY (Frank Pope). **New England Cactus.** See Pseudonym Library, No. 15.

HUMPHREY (Mrs.) **Beauty Adorned.** By Mrs. Humphrey. Long 8vo, cloth, decorated cover.   1/-

HUNGERFORD (Mrs.) **Molly Darling.** See Autonym Library. Vol. 11.

IDLE HOUR SERIES, THE. Cr. 8vo.   Paper covers, 1/- ; cloth   2/-
- (1) **Another Englishwoman's Love Letters.** By Barry Pain.
- (2) **The Letters of Her Mother to Elizabeth.** By W. R. H. Trowbridge.
- (3) **The Gods, Some Mortals, and Lord Wickenham.** By John Oliver Hobbes (Mrs. Craigie).
- (4) **De Omnibus.** By the Conductor (Barry Pain).
- (5) **Certain Personal Matters.** By H. G. Wells.
- (6) **The Confessions of a Match-making Mother.** By Lillias C. Davidson.
- (7) **The Grandmother's Advice to Elizabeth.** By W. R. H. Trowbridge.
- (8) **Hookey.** By A. Neil Lyons.
- (9) **The Adventures of Prince Aga Mirza.** By Aquila Kempster.

IRVING. **Six Girls.** By Fanny Belle Irving. Illustrated. (Unwin's Popular Series for Boys and Girls.) Cloth.   8/6

IRWIN. **With Sword and Pen.** A Story of India in the Fifties. By H. C. Irwin. (Unwin's Red Cloth Library.) Cr. 8vo, cloth.   6/-

JEFFERY (Walter). See "Becke (Louis)."

JENNINGS **Under the Pompadour.** A Romance. By Edward W. Jennings. Cr. 8vo, cloth.   6/-

JEPSON. **The Lady Noggs, Peeress.** By Edgar Jepson. With 8 Illustrations. Cr. 8vo, cloth.   6/-
Also decorative paper covers, 1/- net.   Also paper covers.   6d.

—— **The Four Philanthropists.** By Edgar Jepson. Crown 8vo, cloth.   6/-

JERNINGHAM. **Monsieur Paulot.** By Sir Hubert Jerningham. (Century Library. No. 3.)   Paper covers, 1/6 ; cloth   2/-

JESSOPP. **Frivola, and Simon Ryan the Peterite.** By Augustus Jessopp, D.D. New Edition, Revised and Expanded. With portrait. Cr. 8vo, limp cloth, silk sewn.   3/6

—— **Simon Ryan the Peterite.** By Augustus Jessopp, D.D. (Yellow Library. Vol. 1.)   Paper covers, 1/- ; cloth   2/-

KEARY. **High Policy.** By C. F. Keary. (Unwin's Red Cloth Library.) Cr. 8vo, cloth.   6/-

—— **A Mariage de Convenance.** By C. F. Keary. (Unwin's Green Cloth Library.) Cr. 8vo, cloth.   6/-

KELLER (Gottfried). **A Selection of his Tales.** Translated, with a Memoir, by Kate Freiligrath Kroeker. With Portrait. Cr. 8vo. cloth.   6/-

KEMPSTER. **The Adventures of Prince Aga Mirza.** By Aquila Kempster. (Idle Hour Series. No. 9).   Paper covers, 1/- ; cloth   2/-

KETTLE (Rosa Mackenzie), **THE WORKS OF.**

Cr. 8vo, cloth.   each   6/-

Highland Sister's Promise.   The Old Hall Among the
Magic of the Pine Woods.   Water Meadows.
Rose, Shamrock and Thistle.

Cr. 8vo, cloth.   each   5/-

Earl's Cedars.   Smugglers and Foresters.
Fabian's Tower.   My Home in the Shires.
Hillesdon on the Moor.   The Ranger's Lodge.
Carding Mill Valley.

Cr. 8vo, cloth.   each   4/-

Lewell Pastures.   Lord Maskelyne's Daughter.
La Belle Marie.   On Leithay's Banks.
The Falls of the Loder.   By Sea and Moor.
Last Mackenzie of Redcastle.   The Wreckers.
The Tenants of Beldornie.   Sir Frederick Derwent.
Autumn Leaves.   The Memoirs of Charles
Summer Shade and Winter   Boner (2 vols.).
   Sunshine Poets.

Cr. 8vo, cloth.   each   3/6

The Mistress of Langdale Hall   Under the Grand Old Hills.
Sisters of Ombersleigh.   Furze Blossoms.

Cr. 8vo, cloth.   2/6

Christmas Berries and Summer Roses.

KILDARE. Up from the Slums. By Owen Kildare. Large cr. 8vo,
cloth.   net   6/-

KINROSS (Albert). A Game of Consequences. See Autonym Library.
Vol. 12.

KOROLENKO (V). Makar's Dream. See Pseudonym Library. No. 14.

—— Saghalien Convict. See Pseudonym Library. No. 18.

LAMBE. By Command of the Prince. By J. Lawrence Lambe.
Cr. 8vo, cloth.   6/-

LANDON. Mid Pleasures and Palaces. By Mary Landon. With 16
Illustrations. Cr. 8vo, cloth.   6/-

LANGBRIDGE. The Flame and the Flood. By Rosamond
Langbridge. (First Novel Library.) Cr. 8vo, cloth.   6/-

—— The Third Experiment. By Rosamond Langbridge. (Unwin's
Red Cloth Library.) Cr. 8vo, cloth.   6/-

LANYON. "Sarah P. G." A Novel. By H. Saint Martin-Lanyon.
Cr. 8vo, cloth gilt.   6/-

LAVERTON. The Romance of a Hill Station. And Other Stories.
By Mrs. H. S. Laverton (Valete). Illustrated. Crown 8vo, cloth.   2/6

LEE (Vernon). Ottilie. See Pseudonym Library. No. 22.

—— Penelope Brandling. See Pseudonym Library. No. 55.

LEE-HAMILTON. The Romance of the Fountain. By Eugene
Lee-Hamilton. Cr. 8vo, cloth.   6/-

LELAND. Hans Breitmann in Germany—Tyrol. By Charles
Godfrey Leland. Frontispiece and Decorated Title-page. Fcap.
8vo, cloth.   3/6

—— The Hundred Riddles of the Fairy Bellaria. By Charles Godfrey
Leland ("Hans Breitmann").   Paper covers, 1/- ; cloth   2/-
Also a *Fine Edition.*   net   7/6

Letters of Her Mother to Elizabeth. See under Trowbridge.

LEWIS. A Modern Monarch. By Frank C. Lewis. Cr. 8vo, cloth. 6/-

LITTA. The Soul of a Priest. By the Duke Litta. Cr. 8vo, cloth. 6/-

LITTLE. A Millionaire's Courtship. By Mrs. Archibald Little. Cr. 8vo, cloth. (Red Cloth Library.) 6/-

LITTLE NOVELS. Demy 8vo, printed in bold type.

Paper covers, 6d. ; cloth 1/-

(1) **The World is Round.** By Louise Mack.

(2) **No Place for Repentance.** By Ellen F. Pinsent.

(3) **The Problem of Prejudice.** By Mrs. Vere Campbell.

(4) **Margaret Grey.** By H. Barton Baker.

(5) **A Painter's Honeymoon.** By Mildred Shenstone.

(6) **The Bond of Blood.** By R. E. Forrest.

(7) **A Slight Indiscretion.** By Mrs. Edward Cartwright.

(8) **A Comedy of Three.** By Newton Sanders.

(9) **Passports.** By I. J. Armstrong

(10) **On the Gogmagogs.** By Alice Dumillo.

(11) **A Noble Haul.** By W. Clark Russell.

LLOYD. Bergen Worth. By Wallace Lloyd. Cr. 8vo, cloth. 6/-

LOCKE. The Stem of the Crimson Dahlia. By James Locke. With a Coloured Frontispiece. Cr. 8vo, cloth. 6/-

LORRAINE. The Woman and the Sword. By Rupert Lorraine. (First Novel Library. Vol. 15.) Cr. 8vo, cloth. 6/-

LYNCH. A Parish Providence. By E. M. Lynch. (New Irish Library.) Small cr. 8vo. Paper covers, 1/- ; cloth 2/-

LYONS (A. E.). Mister Bill : A Man. By Albert E. Lyons. Cr. 8vo, cloth. 3/6

LYONS. Hookey. By A. Neil Lyons. (Idle Hour Series. No. 8.) Cr. 8vo Paper covers, 1/- ; cloth 2/-

MABINOGION, THE. Translated from the Red Book of Hergest by Lady Charlotte Guest. 3 vols. (Welsh Library. Vols. 1-3.) Fcap. 8vo. Paper covers, 1/- ; cloth, each 2/-

Popular One-Volume Edition, cloth. net 2/-

McAULAY. Black Mary. By Allan McAulay. (Unwin's Green Cloth Library.) Cr. 8vo, cloth. 6/-

—— The Rhymer. By Allan McAulay. (Unwin's Green Cloth Library.) Cr. 8vo, cloth. 6/-

MAC BRIDE. Wonderfu' Weans : Sketches from Living Models. By Mac Kenzie Mac Bride. With a cover designed by John Duncan. Cr. 8vo. net 1/-

MACDONALD. The Portent and Other Stories. By George Macdonald. (Adelphi Library.) Cr. 8vo, cloth. 3/6

MACMANUS (J.). The Humours of Donegal By James MacManus ("Mac"). Cr. 8vo. Paper covers, 1/- ; cloth 2/-

—— Through the Turf Smoke. By Seumas MacManus ("Mac"). Cr. 8vo. Paper covers, 1/- ; cloth 2/-

McMANUS (L.). Lally of the Brigade. By L. McManus. (Popular Copyright Novels.) Cr. 8vo. Paper covers, 1/- ; cloth gilt 2/6

—— The Red Star. By L. McManus. (The Autonym Library.) Paper covers, 1/6 ; cloth 2/-

—— Silk of the Kine. By L. McManus (C. MacGuire) Cr. 8vo, cloth. 3/6

MAGNAY. The Amazing Duke. By Sir William Magnay, Bart. Cr. 8vo, cloth. 6/-

MANN. Among the Syringas. By Mary E. Mann. (Unwin's Green Cloth Library.) Cr. 8vo.   6/-

—— **In Summer Shade.** By Mary E. Mann. Cr. 8vo, cloth.   6/-
Also in decorative paper covers.   net   1/-

—— **The Mating of a Dove.** By Mary E. Mann. (Unwin's Green Cloth Library.) Cr. 8vo, cloth.   6/-

—— **Moonlight.** By Mary E. Mann. (Unwin's Green Cloth Library.) Cr. 8vo.   6/-

—— **The Patten Experiment.** By Mary E. Mann. (Unwin's Green Cloth Library.) Cr. 8vo, cloth.   6/-

—— **Susannah.** By Mary E. Mann. (Unwin's Green Cloth Library.) Cr. 8vo, cloth.   6/-

MARQUIS. Marguerite de Roberval. By T. G. Marquis. Cr. 8vo, cloth.   6/-

MARSH. The Beetle. A Mystery. By Richard Marsh. With Illustrations by John Williamson. Cr. 8vo, cloth.   6/-
Also (The Adelphi Library), cloth.   3/6

MARTYN. The Tale of a Town and an Enchanted Sea. By Edward Martyn. Cr. 8vo, cloth.   5/-

MAUGHAM. 'Liza of Lambeth. By W. Somerset Maugham. Cr. 8vo. cloth.   3/6
Also paper covers.   6d.

—— **The Making of a Saint.** By W. Somerset Maugham. (Unwin's Green Cloth Library.) Cr. 8vo, cloth.   6/-

—— **Orientations, and Other Stories.** By W. Somerset Maugham. Cr. 8vo, cloth.   6/-

MAYNE. The Clearer Vision. By Ethel Colburn Mayne. Cr. 8vo, cloth gilt.   5/-

MEADE. Love Triumphant. By Mrs. L. T. Meade. (Unwin's Red Cloth Library.) Cr. 8vo, cloth.   6/-
Also Popular Series for Boys and Girls. Illustrated, cloth.   3/6

MEIRION (Ellinor). Cause and Effect. See Pseudonym Library. No. 49.

MIKOULITCH (V.). Mimi's Marriage. See Pseudonym Library. No. 35.

MILNE. The Epistles of Atkins. By James Milne. With 12 Illustrations from War Sketches. Cr. 8vo, cloth.   6/-

MITCHELL. Hugh Wynne. By S. Weir Mitchell. (Unwin's Green Cloth Library.) Cr. 8vo.   6/-

—— **Far in the Forest.** By S. Weir Mitchell. Cr. 8vo, cloth.   6/-

MONTAGU. Naomi's Exodus. By Lily H. Montagu. Cr. 8vo, cloth.   3/6

MONTGOMERY. The Cardinal's Pawn. By K. L. Montgomery. (First Novel Library. No. 8.) Cr. 8vo, cloth.   6/-
Also paper covers.   6d.

—— **Love in the Lists.** By K. L. Montgomery. Cr. 8vo, cloth.   6/-

—— **Major Weir.** By K. L. Montgomery. With 8 Illustrations. (Unwin's Red Cloth Library.) Cr. 8vo, cloth.   6/-

MOORE. Evelyn Innes. By George Moore. (Unwin's Green Cloth Library.) Cr. 8vo, cloth.   6/-
Also (The Adelphi Library), cloth.   3/6
Also paper covers.   6d.

MOORE. **Sister Teresa.** A Novel. By George Moore. (Unwin's
Green Cloth Library.) Cr. 8vo, cloth.   6/-
Also (The Adelphi Library). Cloth.   3/6
Paper covers.   6d.

—— **The Untilled Field.** By George Moore. (Unwin's Red Cloth
Library.) Cr. 8vo, cloth.   6/-

MUIR. **The Mystery of Muncraig.** By Robert James Muir. Cr. 8vo,
cloth gilt.   6/-

MURRAY. **He that had Received the Five Talents.** By J. Clark
Murray. (Unwin's Red Cloth Library.) Cr. 8vo, cloth.   6/-

NELSON (Jane). **The Rousing of Mrs. Potter.** See Pseudonym
Library. No. 36.

NESBIT. **Man and Maid.** By E. Nesbit. Cr. 8vo, cloth.   6/-

NESBIT'S **Children's Stories.** See under "Books for Children."

NORMYX. **Unprofessional Tales.** By Normyx. Cr. 8vo, cloth.   6/-

NORRIS (W. E.). **The Spectre of Strathannan.** See Autonym
Library. Vol. 9.

O'GRADY. **The Bog of Stars, and Other Stories of Elizabethan
Ireland.** By Standish O'Grady. (New Irish Library. No. 2.)
Small cr. 8vo.   Paper covers, 1/- ; cloth   2/-

OLIPHANT (Mrs.). **The Two Strangers.** See Autonym Library.
Vol. 7.

OMOND (G. W. T.). **Miserrima.** See Autonym Library. Vol. 6.

ORCZY. **The Case of Miss Elliott.** By the Baroness Orczy, Author
of "The Scarlet Pimpernel," &c. With 16 Illustrations. Cr. 8vo,
cloth.   6/-

OUIDA. **A Rainy June and Don Gesualdo.** By Ouida. (Popular
Copyright Novels.) Cr. 8vo, cloth.   2/6

—— **The Silver Christ, and Other Stories.** By Ouida. (Unwin's
Green Cloth Library.) Cr. 8vo, cloth.   6/-
See also Pseudonym Library. No. 41.

—— **Toxin.** See Century Library. No. 1.

OWEN. **Captain Sheen.** By Charles Owen. Cr. 8vo, cloth.   6/-

PAIN. **Another Englishwoman's Love Letters.** By Barry Pain.
(Idle Hour Series. No. 1.)   Paper covers, 1/- ; cloth   2/-
—— **Curiosities.** By Barry Pain. Paper covers.   1/-
—— **De Omnibus.** By The Conductor (Barry Pain). Paper covers, 1/-
Cloth.   2/-
—— **De Omnibus and Another Englishwoman's Love Letters.** By
Barry Pain. Paper covers   6d.
—— **Little Entertainments.** By Barry Pain. Cr. 8vo. Paper covers, 1/-
Cloth.   2/-
—— **The Memoirs of Constantine Dix.** By Barry Pain. Cr. 8vo, cloth   3/6
Also in decorative paper covers. 1/- net.   Also paper covers   6d.

de PENTHENY (S.) **Another Wicked Woman.** See Autonym
Library. Vol. 8.

PIDGIN. **Quincy Adams Sawyer.** By Charles F. Pidgin. Cr. 8vo, cloth.   6/-

PINSENT. **No Place for Repentance.** See under Little Novels. No. 2.

PLAYNE. **The Romance of a Lonely Woman.** By C. E. Playne.
Cr. 8vo, cloth.   6/-
—— **The Terror of the Macdurghotts.** By C. E. Playne. Cr. 8vo, cloth   6/-

de POLEN. Clairice : The Story of a Crystal Heart. By Narcisse Lucien de Polen. Cr. 8vo, cloth.   3/6

POPULAR COPYRIGHT NOVELS. Cheap re-issue. In cr. 8vo, cloth gilt.   each 2/6

ALEXANDER (MRS.).
  Brown, V.C.
  Stronger than Love.
  Through Fire to Fortune.
  A Winning Hazard.
BARR (AMELIA E.).
  I, Thou, & the Other One.
  Prisoners of Conscience.
  Was it Right to Forgive?
BECKE (LOUIS).
  By Reef & Palm.
  The Strange Adventures
    of James Shervington.
  Tessa and The Trader's
    Wife.
BUCHANAN (ROBERT).
  Effie Hetherington.
CROCKETT (S. R.).
  The Play Actress and
    Mad Sir Uchtred.
  The Stickit Minister.
CROMMELIN (MAY).
  Half Round the World for
    a Husband.

FRENCH (H. W.).
  Desmonde, M.D.
GYP.
  Ginette's Happiness.
HOBBES (JOHN OLIVER).
  The Herb-Moon.
McMANUS (L.).
  Lally of the Brigade.
OUIDA.
  A Rainy June.
RITA.
  The Ending of My Day.
  Vanity! The Confessions
    of a Court Modiste.
RUSSELL (W. CLARK).
  The Romance of a Mid-
    shipman.
SALA (GEORGE AUGUS-
  TUS).
  Margaret Forster.
SCHREINER (OLIVE).
  Trooper Peter Halket.

POTAPENKO (J.). Russian Priest. See Pseudonym Library. No. 7.

—— **General's Daughter.** See Pseudonym Library. No. 17.

—— **Father of Six.** See Pseudonym Library. No. 26.

PRAED. The Insane Root. By Mrs. Campbell Praed. (Unwin's Green Cloth Library.) Cr. 8vo, cloth.   6/-

—— **Nyria.** By Mrs. Campbell Praed. (Unwin's Red Cloth Library.) Cr. 8vo, cloth.   6/-

PRICHARD. The New Chronicles of Don Q. By K. and Hesketh Prichard. Illustrated. Cr. 8vo, cloth.   6/-

PRYCE. John Jones, Curate. By G. Pryce. (Unwin's Green Cloth Library.) Cr. 8vo, cloth.   6/-

—— **A Son of Arvon.** A Welsh Novel. By Gwendolen Pryce. (Unwin's Green Cloth Library.) Cr. 8vo.   6/-

PSEUDONYM LIBRARY, THE. 24mo. Paper covers, 1/6 ; cloth, each 2/-

(1) Mademoiselle Ixe. By Lanoe Falconer.
(2) The Story of Eleanor Lambert. By Magdalene Brooke.
(3) A Mystery of the Campagna. By von Degen.
(4) The School of Art. By Isabel Snow.
(5) Amaryllis. By Georgios Drosines.
(6) The Hotel d'Angleterre. By Lanoe Falconer.
(7) A Russian Priest. By J. Potapenko. Translated by W. Gaussen.
(8) Some Emotions and a Moral. By John Oliver Hobbes.
(9) European Relations. A Tirolese Sketch. By Talmage Dalin.

PSEUDONYM LIBRARY, THE.—*continued.*

(10) **John Sherman, & Dhoya.** By Ganconagh (W.B. Yeats).

(11) **Through the Red-Litten Windows.** By Theodor Hertz-Garten.

(12) **Green Tea.** A Love Story. By V. Schallenberger.

(13) **Heavy Laden, and Old Fashioned Folk.** By Ilse Frapan. Translated by Helen A. Macdonell.

(14) **Makar's Dream, and Other Russian Stories.** By V. Korolenko, and Others.

(15) **A New England Cactus.** By Frank Pope Humphrey.

(16) **The Herb of Love.** By Georgios Drosines. Translated by Eliz. M. Edmonds.

(17) **The General's Daughter.** By J. Potapenko. Translated by W. Gaussen.

(18) **The Saghalien Convict, and Other Russian Stories.** By V. Korolenko, and Others.

(19) **Gentleman Upcott's Daughter.** By Tom Cobbleigh.

(20) **A Splendid Cousin.** By Mrs. Andrew Dean.

(21) **Colette.** By Philippe St. Hilaire.

(22) **Ottilie.** By Vernon Lee.

(23) **A Study in Temptations.** By John Oliver Hobbes.

(24) **The Cruise of the "Wild Duck."** By Holger Drachmann.

(25) **Squire Hellman, and Other Finnish Stories.** By Juhani Aho. Translated by R. Nisbert Bain.

(26) **A Father of Six, and An Occasional Holiday.** By J. Potapenko. Translated by W. Gaussen.

(27) **The Two Countesses.** By Marie von Ebner-Eschenbach. Translated by Mrs. Waugh.

(28) **The Sinner's Comedy.** By John Oliver Hobbes.

(29) **Cavalleria Rusticana, and Other Tales of Sicilian Peasant Life.** By Giovanni Verga. Translated by Alma Strettell.

(30) **The Passing of a Mood, and Other Stories.** By V. O. C. S.

(31) **God's Will, and Other Stories.** By Ilse Frapan. Translated by Helen A. Macdonell.

(32) **Dream Life and Real Life.** By Ralph Iron (Olive Schreiner).

(33) **The Home of the Dragon.** A Tonquinese Idyll. By Anna Catharina.

(34) **A Bundle of Life.** By John Oliver Hobbes.

(35) **Mimi's Marriage.** By V. Mikoulitch.

(36) **The Rousing of Mrs. Potter, and Other Stories.** By Jane Nelson.

(37) **A Study in Colour.** By Alice Spinner.

(38) **The Hon. Stanbury.** By Two.

(39) **The Shen's Pigtail, and Other Stories of Anglo-China Life.** By Mr. M—.

(40) **Young Sam and Sabina.** By Tom Cobbleigh.

(41) **The Silver Christ, and a Lemon Tree.** By Ouida.

(42) **A Husband of No Importance.** By Rita.

(43) **Lesser's Daughter.** By Mrs. Andrew Dean.

(44) **Helen.** By Oswald Valentine.

(45) **Cliff Days.** By Brian Rosegarth.

(46) **Old Brown's Cottages.** By John Smith.

(47) **Under the Chilterns.** By Rosemary.

(48) **Every Day's News.** By R. E. Francis.

(49) **Cause and Effect.** By Eilinor Meirion.

(50) **A White Umbrella, and Other Stories.** By Sarnia.

(51) **When Wheat is Green.** By Jos. Wilton.

(52) **Anthony Jasper.** By Ben Bolt.

(53) **As a Tree Falls.** By L. Parry Truscott.

(54) **A Ne'er-Do-Weel.** By Valentine Caryl.

(55) **Penelope Brandling.** By Vernon Lee.

RED CLOTH LIBRARY. See Unwin's Red Cloth Library.

REETH. Legions of the Dawn   By Allan Reeth   Cr. 8vo, cloth.   6/-

REID. The Kingdom of Twilight. By Forrest Reid. (First Novel Library) Cr 8vo, cloth   6/-

RICHARDSON. A Drama of Sunshine—Played in Homburg   By Mrs Aubrey Richardson   (First Novel Library) Cr 8vo, cloth.   6/-

—— They Twain. By Mrs Aubrey Richardson   (Unwin's Red Cloth Library) Cr 8vo, cloth.   6/-

RICHINGS In Chaucer's Maytime. By Emily Richings. (Unwin's Red Cloth Library)   C . 8vo, cloth gilt   6/-

RITA   The Ending of My Day   By Rita   (Popular Copyright Novels) Cr 8vo, cloth gilt.   2/6

—— A Husband of No Importance. See Pseudonym Library. No 42

—— A Jilt's Journal. (Unwin's Green Cloth Library) Cr 8vo, cloth.   6/-

—— Vanity : The Confessions of a Court Modiste   By Rita. Cr. 8vo, cloth   6/-

Also (Popular Copyright Novels), cloth   2/6

ROOSEVELT   The Siren's Net   By Florence Roosevelt. (Unwin's Red Cloth Library) Cr 8vo, cloth.   6/-

ROSEGARTH (Brian). Cliff Days. See Pseudonym Library. No 45

ROSEGGER   The Light Eternal   By Peter Rosegger. Cr. 8vo, cloth.   6, -

ROWBOTHAM   Tales from Plutarch. By F Jameson Rowbotham   Fully illustrated   Cr. 8vo, cloth.   5/-

ROWLANDS. The Passion of Mahael   See under " Bowen-Rowlands."

RUSSELL. The Honour of the Flag. By W Clark Russell   Demy 12mo, cloth.   2/6

—— A Noble Haul. See under " Little Novels " No 11.

—— The Romance of a Midshipman. By W. Clark Russell (Popular Copyright Novels) Cr 8vo, cloth.   2/6

- —— The Yarn of Old Harbour Town. A Sea Romance   By W. Clark Russell (Unwin's Red Cloth Library) Cr 8vo, cloth   6/-

RUTHERFORD. The Autobiography of Mark Rutherford. Edited by Reuben Shapcott. Cr 8vo, cloth   3/6

—— Catherine Furze: A Novel by Mark Rutherford   Cr 8vo, cloth.   3/6

—— Clara Hopgood. By Mark Rutherford. Cr. 8vo, cloth.   3/6

—— Mark Rutherford's Deliverance. Cr 8vo, cloth.   3/6

—— Miriam's Schooling, and Other Papers. By Mark Rutherford. With Frontispiece by Walter Crane. Cr 8vo, cloth.   3/6

—— The Revolution in Tanner's Lane. Cr 8vo, cloth.   3/6

—— Pages from a Journal. By Mark Rutherford. Cr 8vo, cloth.   6/-

—— A New Popular Edition. Each vol. cr 8vo, cloth gilt, each, net   1/-

LIST OF VOLUMES.

(1) The Autobiography of Mark Rutherford.

(2) Mark Rutherford's De- l.verance.

(3) The Revolution in Tanner's Lane.

(4) Miriam's Schooling.

(5) Catherine Furze.

(6) Clara Hopgood.

RYVES. At the Sign of the Peacock. By K. C. Ryves. (First Novel Library.) Cr. 8vo, cloth.　　6,-

ST. HILAIRE (Philippe). Colette. See Pseudonym Library. No. 21.

SALA. Margaret Forster: A Novel. By George Augustus Sala. (Popular Copyright Novels.) Cr. 8vo, cloth gilt.　　2/6

SANDERS. A Comedy of Three. See under "Little Novels." No. 8.

SARNIA. White Umbrella. See Pseudonym Library. No. 50.

SCHALLENBERGER (V.). Green Tea. See Pseudonym Library. No. 12.

von SCHLICHT. Life in a Crack Regiment (Erstklassige Menschen). A Novel of German Military Manners and Morals. By Baron von Schlicht. Translated by F. B. Low. Cr. 8vo, cloth.　6/-
Also paper covers.　　6d.

SCHREINER. Dream Life and Real Life. By Olive Schreiner. Cloth.　　2/-

—— **(RALPH IRON).** Dream Life and Real Life. See Pseudonym Library. No. 32.

—— **Dreams.** By Olive Schreiner. Demy 12mo, cloth.　　2/6

—— **Trooper Peter Halket of Mashonaland.** By Olive Schreiner. Frontispiece. (Popular Copyright Novels.) Cr. 8vo, cloth gilt.　2/6
Cheap Edition, cr. 8vo, cloth.　　net　1/-

SCOTT (Sir Walter). The "Century" Scott. In 25 vols. Fcap. 8vo (6 by 4). Each with Collotype Frontispiece, and with book plate, title-pages, binding, and devices in two colours by James Allen Duncan.　　Decorative cloth, 1/- ; green leather　2/6

LIST OF VOLUMES.

Ivanhoe.	The Bride of Lammermoor.
Waverley.	The Fortunes of Nigel.
Guy Mannering.	Quentin Durward.
Old Mortality.	St. Ronan's Well.
Rob Roy.	Redgauntlet.
The Antiquary.	The Betrothed and Highland
The Heart of Midlothian.	Widow, &c.
The Monastery.	The Talisman.
The Abbot.	Woodstock.
Kenilworth.	The Fair Maid of Perth.
The Pirate.	Anne of Geierstein.
Peveril of the Peak.	The Surgeon's Daughter and
The Legend of Montrose and	Castle Dangerous.
Black Dwarf.	Count Robert of Paris.

SCULLY (W. C.). Kafir Stories. See Autonym Library. Vol. 10.

—— **By Veldt and Kopje.** By W. C. Scully. Cr. 8vo, cloth.　6/-

SHEEHAN. A Spoiled Priest, and Other Stories. By the very Rev. P. A. Sheehan, D.D. Illustrated. Cr. 8vo, cloth.　　5/-

SHENSTONE. A Painter's Honeymoon. See under "Little Novels."

SHERWOOD. Tongues of Gossip. By A. Curtis Sherwood. Cr. 8vo　6/-

SHOLL. The Greater Love. By Anna McClure Sholl. Cr. 8vo, cloth　6/-

SMITH (F. C.). A Daughter of Patricians. By F. Clifford Smith. Illustrated. Cr. 8vo, cloth.　　6/-

SMITH (I.). The Minister's Guest. By Isabella Smith. (Unwin's Green Cloth Library.) Cr. 8vo, cloth.　　6/-

SMITH (John). Old Brown's Cottages. See Pseudonym Library, 46.

SNOW (Isabel). School of Art. See Pseudonym Library. No. 4.

SPINNER (Alice). Study in Colour. See Pseudonym Library, 37.

STACPOOLE. The Bourgeois. By H. de Vere Stacpoole. (Unwin's Green Cloth Library.) Cr. 8vo, cloth.   6/-

—— **The Blue Lagoon** A Romance. By H. de Vere Stacpoole. Cr. 8vo, cloth.   6/-
Also in decorative paper covers.   net   1/-

—— **The Crimson Azaleas.** By H. de Vere Stacpoole. Cr. 8vo, cloth.   6/-
Also paper covers.   6d.

—— **The Doctor.** By H. de Vere Stacpoole. (Unwin's Green Cloth Library.) Cr. 8vo, cloth gilt.   6/-

—— **Fanny Lambert.** By H. de Vere Stacpoole. (Unwin's Red Cloth Library.) Cr. 8vo, cloth.   6/-
Also Paper covers.   6d.

—— **The Lady Killer.** By H. de Vere Stacpoole. (Unwin's Red Cloth Library.) Cr. 8vo.   6/-

—— **Patsy.** By H. de Vere Stacpoole. With Frontispiece. Cr. 8vo, cloth   6/-

—— **The Vulture's Prey.** By H. de Vere Stacpoole. Cr. 8vo, cloth   6/-

STEVENS. The Perils of Sympathy. By Nina Stevens. (Unwin's Red Cloth Library.) Cr. 8vo, cloth.   6/-

STOTT. Rosemonde. By Beatrice Stott. (First Novel Library.) Cr. 8vo, cloth.   6/-

STRAIN. Laura's Legacy. By E. H. Strain. (Unwin's Red Cloth Library.) Cr. 8vo, cloth.   6/-

SUMMERS. Renunciation. By Dorothy Summers. Cr. 8vo, cloth.   6/-

—— **A Man's Love.** By Dorothy Summers. Cr. 8vo, cloth.   6/-

SUTCLIFFE. A Bachelor in Arcady. By Halliwell Sutcliffe. With Frontispiece. (Unwin's Green Cloth Library.) Cr. 8vo, cloth.   6/-
Also a Presentation Edition.   net   6/-

—— **By Moor and Fell :** Landscape and Lang-Settle Talk in West Yorkshire. By Halliwell Sutcliffe. Cr. 8vo, cloth.   6/-

—— **Mistress Barbara Cunliffe.** By Halliwell Sutcliffe. (Unwin's Green Cloth Library.) Cr. 8vo, cloth.   6/-

—— **Ricroft of Withens.** By Halliwell Sutcliffe. (Unwin's Green Cloth Library.) Cr. 8vo, cloth.   6/-
Paper covers.   6d.

—— **Shameless Wayne.** By Halliwell Sutcliffe. (Unwin's Green Cloth Library.) Cr. 8vo.   6/-

—— **Through Sorrow's Gates. A Tale of the Wintry Heath.** By Halliwell Sutcliffe. (Unwin's Green Cloth Library.) Cr. 8vo, cloth   6/-
Also (The Adelphi Library), cloth.   3/6

—— **Willowdene Will.** By Halliwell Sutcliffe. (Adelphi Library.) Cloth   3/6

SWIFT. The Destroyer. By Benjamin Swift. (Unwin's Green Cloth Library.) Cr. 8vo, cloth.   6/-

—— **Nancy Noon.** By Benjamin Swift. (Unwin's Green Cloth Library.) Cr. 8vo, cloth.   6/-

—— **The Tormentor.** By Benjamin Swift. (Unwin's Green Cloth Library.) Cr. 8vo, cloth.   6/-

SYNGE. The Coming of Sonia. By Mrs. Hamilton Synge. Cr. 8vo, cloth.   6/-

—— **A Supreme Moment.** By Mrs. Hamilton Synge. (Unwin's Green Cloth Library.) Cr. 8vo, cloth.   6/-

TAYLER. The Long Vigil. By F. Jenner Tayler. (Unwin's Red
Cloth Library.) Cr. 8vo, cloth.   6/-

TAYLOR. A Thousand Pities. By Ellen Taylor. Cr. 8vo, cloth.   2/6

THYNNE. Facing the Future; or, the Parting of the Ways. By
R. Thynne. Cr. 8vo, cloth.   6/-

TREHERNE. A Love Cure. By Philip Treherne. Cr. 8vo, cloth.   3/6

TROUBRIDGE. The Millionaire. By Lady Troubridge. Cr. 8vo, cloth.   6/-

—— **The Woman Thou Gavest.** By Lady Troubridge. Cr. 8vo, cloth.   6/-
Also paper covers.   6d.

TROWBRIDGE. A Girl of the Multitude. By W. R. H. Trowbridge.
Cr. 8vo, cloth.   6/-

—— **A Dazzling Reprobate.** By W. R. H. Trowbridge. (Unwin's
Red Cloth Library.) Cr. 8vo.   6/-

—— **The Grandmother's Advice to Elizabeth.** A companion
volume to "The Letters of Her Mother to Elizabeth." (Idle Hour
Series. No. 7.)   Paper covers, 1/- ; cloth   2/-

—— **The Letters of Her Mother to Elizabeth.** A Series of Smart
Letters for Admirers of "The Visits of Elizabeth." (Idle Hour
Series. No. 2.)   Paper covers, 1/- ; cloth   2/-
Also an Edition in paper covers.   6d.

—— **The Situations of Lady Patricia:** A Satire for Idle People. By
W. R. H. Trowbridge. (Unwin's Red Cloth Library.) Cr. 8vo,
cloth.   6/-

TRUSCOTT. As a Tree Falls. See Pseudonym Library. No. 53.

—— **The Mother of Pauline.** By L. Parry Truscott. Paper covers.   6d.

—— **Motherhood.** By L. Parry Truscott. (Unwin's Red Cloth Library.)
Cr. 8vo, cloth.   6/-

—— **The Poet and Penelope.** By L. Parry Truscott. Cr. 8vo, cloth.   6/-

—— **Stars of Destiny.** By L. Parry Truscott. (Unwin's Red Cloth
Library.) Cr. 8vo, cloth.   6/-

TURNER. That Girl. By Ethel Turner (Mrs. Curlewis). With 25
Illustrations by Frances Ewan. Large cr. 8vo, cloth.   6/-

TWEEDDALE. Moff. By John Tweeddale. (Century Library. No. 2.)
Paper covers, 1/6 ; cloth   2/-

UNWIN'S GREEN CLOTH LIBRARY. In uniform green cloth, gilt
tops.   each   6/-

ALEXANDER (MRS.).
    The Yellow Fiend.
    Through Fire to Fortune.
"ALIEN."
    The Devil's Half-Acre.
ASKEW (ALICE and MAUDE).
    The Shulamite.
BACHELLER (IRVING).
    Silas Strong.
BAKER (JAMES).
    A Double Choice.
BARLOW (JANE).
    By Beach and Bogland.

BARR (AMELIA E.).
    Was It Right to Forgive?
    I, Thou, and the Other
    One.
    Souls of Passage.
    The Maid of Maiden Lane
    The Lion's Whelp.
BARRY (WILLIAM).
    Arden Massiter.
    The Two Standards.
    The Wizard's Knot.
BARTRAM (GEORGE).
    The People of Clopton.
    The White-Headed Boy.

UNWIN'S RED CLOTH LIBRARY. Cr. 8vo, cloth. each 6/-

ALEXANDER (Mrs).
  Kitty Costello.
  Stronger than Love.
ARCHER (L. M. PALMER).
  A Bush Honeymoon.
BARR (AMELIA E.).
  The Black Shilling.
  A Song of a Single Note.
  Thyra Varrick.
  Cecilia's Lovers.
BARRY (WILLIAM).
  The Dayspring.
BECKE (LOUIS).
  Breachley, Black Sheep.
  Chinkie's Flat.
  Adventures of a Supercargo.
  Helen Adair.
  The Strange Adventure of James Shervington.
  Tom Gerrard.
  Under Tropic Skies.
BOURGET (PAUL).
  Divorce.
CLARE (AUSTIN).
  Court Cards.
CLEEVE (LUCAS).
  Anglo-Americans.
  Children of Endurance.
  Counsels of the Night.
  Progress of Priscilla.
  Stolen Waters.
  The Fool-killer.
  The Man in the Street.
  A Double Marriage.
  Seven Nights in a Gondola
DE CRESPIGNY (Mrs. P. CHAMPION).
  The Mischief of a Glove.
DUNDAS (CHRISTIAN).
  Journeys of Antonia.
VAN EEDEN (F.)
  The Deeps of Deliverance.
FLETCHER (J. S.)
  Grand Relations.
  The Queen of a Day.
GREEN (A. KATHERINE).
  The Filigree Ball.
GRIFFITHS (MAJ. ARTHUR.)
  A Royal Rascal.
HALES (A. G.).
  The Watcher on the Tower.
HOBBES (JOHN OLIVER).
  The Flute of Pan.
  Love and the Soul Hunters.
  The Princess of Bene-
  The Vineyard.   [vento.

HOCKING (SILAS K.).
  Meadow-sweet and Rue.
HORNIMAN (ROY).
  That Fast Miss Blount.
  The Living Buddha.
IRWIN (H. C.).
  With Sword and Pen.
KEARY (C. F.).
  High Policy.
LANGBRIDGE (ROSAMOND).
  The Third Experiment.
LITTLE (Mrs. ARCHIBALD).
  A Millionaire's Courtship.
MACK (LOUISE).
  An Australian Girl in London.
MEADE (L. T.).
  Love Triumphant.
MONTGOMERY (K. L.).
  Major Weir.
MOORE (GEORGE).
  The Untilled Field.
MURRAY (J. CLARK).
  Five Talents.
PRAED (Mrs. CAMPBELL).
  Nyria.
RICHARDSON (Mrs. AUBREY).
  They Twain.
RICHINGS (EMILY).
  In Chaucer's Maytime.
ROOSEVELT (FLORENCE).
  The Siren's Net.
RUSSELL (W. CLARK).
  Yarn of Old Harbour Town.
STACPOOLE (H. DE VERE).
  Fanny Lambert.
  The Lady Killer.
STEVENS (NINA).
  The Perils of Sympathy.
STRAIN (E. H.).
  Laura's Legacy.
TAYLER (F. JENNER).
  The Long Vigil.
TROWBRIDGE (W. R. H.).
  A Dazzling Reprobate.
  The Situations of Lady Patricia.
TRUSCOTT (L. PARRY).
  Motherhood.
  Stars of Destiny.
VIELE (HERMAN K.).
  Myra of the Pines.
WHITECHURCH.
  The Canon in Residence.
YEIGH (KATE WESTLAKE).
  A Specimen Spinster.
YSTRIDDE (G.).
  Three Dukes.

UNWIN'S SHILLING REPRINTS OF STANDARD NOVELS.

Cr. 8vo, cloth.   each, **net**   **1/-**

CROCKETT (S. R.).
    The Stickit Minister.
FALCONER (LANOE).
    Mademoiselle Ixe, and
    the Hotel d'Angleterre.
GORKY (MAXIM).
    Three of Them.
    The Outcasts, and other
    Stories.
    The Man who was afraid
    (Foma Gordyeeff).
HOBBES (JOHN OLIVER).
    Love and the Soul
    Hunters.
    Some Emotions and a
    Moral, and The Sin-
    ner's Comedy.

HOBBES (JOHN OLIVER).
    A Study in Temptations, and
    A Bundle of Life.

RUTHERFORD (MARK).
    The Autobiography of Mark
    Rutherford.
    Mark Rutherford's Deliverance.
    The Revolution in Tanner's
    Lane.
    Miriam's Schooling.
    Catherine Furze.
    Clara Hopgood.
SCHREINER (OLIVE).
    Trooper Peter Halket of
    Mashonaland.

UNWIN'S SIXPENNY EDITIONS.

In paper covers.   each   **6d.**

Canon in Residence, The. By
    Victor L. Whitechurch.
Cardinal's Pawn, The. By K.
    L. Montgomery.
Crimson Azaleas, The. By
    H. de Vere Stacpoole.
De Omnibus and Another
    Englishwoman's Love Let-
    ters. By Barry Pain.
Eben Holden. By Irving
    Bacheller. 393rd Thousand.
Evelyn Innes. By Geo. Moore.
Fanny Lambert. By H. de
    Vere Stacpoole.
Filigree Ball, The. By Anna
    Katherine Green.
Gods, Some Mortals, and
    Lord Wickenham, The. By
    John Oliver Hobbes (Mrs.
    Craigie).
Grand Relations. By J. S.
    Fletcher.
His Native Wife. By Louis
    Becke.
House by the River, The. By
    Florence Warden.
How to be Happy though
    Married. By E. J. Hardy.
Lady Mary of the Dark House.
    By Mrs. C. N. Williamson.
Lady Noggs, The. By Edgar
    Jepson.
Letters of Her Mother to
    Elizabeth. 63rd Thousand.
Life in a Crack Regiment.
    By Baron Von Schlicht.

Liza of Lambeth. By W.
    Somerset Maugham. Revised
    Edition.
Memoirs of Constantine Dix,
    The. By Barry Pain.
Mischief of a Glove, The. By
    Mrs. Philip Champion de
    Crespigny.
Mother of Pauline, The. By
    L. Parry Truscott.
Motor Cracksman, The. By
    Charles Carey.
Ricroft of Withens. By Halli-
    well Sutcliffe.
Robert Orange. By John
    Oliver Hobbes.
Royal Rascal, A. By Major
    Arthur Griffiths.
Saints in Society. By Margaret
    Baillie-Saunders.
School for Saints, The. By
    John Oliver Hobbes.
Sister Teresa. By George
    Moore. Revised Edition.
Some Emotions and a Moral.
    By John Oliver Hobbes.
Stickit Minister, The. By
    S. R. Crockett.
Stolen Waters. By Lucas
    Cleeve.
That Fast Miss Blount. By
    Roy Horniman.
Vineyard, The. By John Oliver
    Hobbes.
Watcher on the Tower, The.
    By A. G. Hales.
Woman Thou Gavest, The.
    By Lady Troubridge.

UNWIN'S SHILLING NOVELS. A new series of high-class Novels by popular writers. In paper covers (see page 87). Each net   1/-

VALENTINE. The Red Sphinx. By E. U. Valentine and S. Eccleston Harper. Cr. 8vo, cloth.   6/-

VERGA (Giovanni). Cavalleria Rusticana. See Pseudonym Library. No. 29.

VIELE. Myra of the Pines. By Herman K. Viele. (Unwin's Red Cloth Library.) Cr. 8vo, cloth.   6/-

WARDEN. The Dazzling Miss Davison. By Florence Warden. Cr. 8vo, cloth.   6/-

—— **The House by the River.** By Florence Warden. Cr. 8vo, cloth.   6/-
Also paper covers.   6d.

—— **The Mis-Rule of Three.** By Florence Warden. Cr. 8vo, cloth.   6/

WARRY. The Sentinel of Wessex. By C. King Warry. Cr. 8vo, cloth   6/-

WATSON (M.). Driven! By Margaret Watson. (Unwin's Green Cloth Library.) Cr. 8vo.   6/-

WATSON (J. R.). In a Man's Mind. By John Reay Watson. (Unwin's Green Cloth Library.) Cr. 8vo, cloth.   6/-

WELLS. Certain Personal Matters. By H. G. Wells. (Idle Hour Series. No. 5.)   Paper covers, 1/- ; cloth   2/-

WHITE. Uncle Jem. By Hester White. Cr. 8vo, cloth.   6/-

WHITECHURCH. The Canon in Residence. By Victor L. Whitechurch. (Unwin's Red Cloth Library.) Cr. 8vo, cloth.   6/-
Also (The Adelphi Library), cloth.   3/6
Also decorative paper covers.   1/- net.   Also paper covers   6d.

—— **Concerning Himself.** By Victor L. Whitechurch. Cr. 8vo, cloth   6/-

—— **The Locum Tenens.** By Victor L. Whitechurch. Cr. 8vo, cloth   6/-

WILKINS. Doctor Gordon. By Mary E. Wilkins. Cr. 8vo, cloth.   6/-

WILLIAMSON. Lady Mary of the Dark House. By Mrs. C. N. Williamson. Cr. 8vo, cloth.   6/-
Also decorative paper covers.   1/- net.   Also paper covers   6d.

WILLIAMSON (W. H.). The Traitor's Wife. By W. H. Williamson. Cr. 8vo, cloth.   6/-

—— **The Prince's Marriage.** By W. H. Williamson. Cr. 8vo, cloth.   6/-

WILTON (Jos.). When Wheat Is Green. See Pseudonym Library. 51.

WITT. Innocent of a Crime. By Captain Paul Witt. Cr. 8vo, cloth gilt.   6/-

WYLWYNNE. The Dream Woman. By Kythe Wylwynne. Cr. 8vo, cloth.   6/-

YEATS, (W. B.). John Sherman and Dhoya. See Pseudonym Library, No. 10.

YEIGH. A Specimen Spinster. By Kate Westlake Yeigh. (Unwin's Red Cloth Library.) Cr. 8vo, cloth.   6/-

YELLOW LIBRARY. A bijou series printed on yellow paper (6¾ by 3¾ inches).   Paper covers, 1/- ; cloth   2/-

(1) **Simon Ryan the Peterite.** By Canon Augustus Jessopp, D.D.

(2) **Marsena.** By Harold Frederic.

(3) **The Mystery of the Laughlin Islands.** By Louis Becke and Walter Jeffery.

YSTRIDDE. Three Dukes. By G. Ystridde. (Unwin's Red Cloth Library.) Cr. 8vo, cloth.   6/-

ESSAYS, CRITICISM, PHILOSOPHY, &c.

BIGELOW. The Mystery of Sleep. By John Bigelow, LL.D.   Cr. 8vo,
  cloth.   net   6/-
BOUTMY. The English People : A Study of their Political Psychology.
  By Emile Boutmy, Membre de l'Institut.   Translated by E. English.
  With an Introduction by J. E. C. Bodley.   Demy 8vo, cloth gilt.   16/-
**BROOKE. The Need and Use of getting Irish Literature into the
  English Tongue.** By the Rev. Stopford A. Brooke.   1/- ; cloth   2/-
CHRISTY. Proverbs, Maxims, and Phrases of all Ages.   Classified
  subjectively and arranged alphabetically.   By Robert Christy.   One
  vol.   Cr. 8vo, cloth.   7/6
CRIMINOLOGY SERIES, THE. Large cr. 8vo, cloth.   each   6/-
  (1) **The Female Offender.** By   (3) **Juvenile Offenders.**   By
        Professor Lombroso.   W. Douglas Morrison.
  (2) **Criminal Sociology.** By   (4) **Political Crime**.   By Louis
        Professor Enrico Ferri.   Proal.
                  [For full Titles see under Authors' names.]
DETHRIDGE. The "Lucas Malet" Birthday Book. By G. Olivia
  Dethridge.   Large cr. 12mo, cloth.   net   4/-
DUFFY. The Revival of Irish Literature. A Series of Addresses by
  Sir Chas. Gavan Duffy, and others.   Paper covers, 1/- ; cloth   2/-
FERRI. Criminal Sociology. By Professor Enrico Ferri.   With Pre-
  face by W. Douglas Morrison. M.A.   (Criminology Series.   Vol. 2.)
  Large cr. 8vo, cloth.   6/-
Good Reading About Many Books.   Nos. 1, 2, and 3.   By their
  Authors.   With Portraits and Facsimile Autographs.   Demy 12mo.
                 Paper covers, 1/- each net ; cloth, each net   2/-
GORDON. The Social Ideals of Alfred Tennyson. By William
  Clark Gordon.   Large cr. 8vo, cloth.   net   6/6
HORNBY. Great Minds at One. A Year's Parallels in Prose and Verse.
  Compiled by F. M. Hornby.   Fcap. 8vo, cloth.   3/6
JESSOPP. Frivola. By Augustus Jessopp, D.D. See also " The Yellow
  Library."   Cr. 8vo, cloth.   3/6
——— **Frivola, Simon Ryan, and other Papers.** By Augustus Jessopp,
  D.D.   Cr. 8vo, limp cloth.   3/6
JUSSERAND. English Essays from a French Pen. By J. J. Jusserand.
  Photogravure Frontispiece and 4 other full-page Illustrations.
  Large cr. 8vo, cloth.   7/6
LE BON. The Crowd : A Study of the Popular Mind.   By Gustave
  Le Bon.   Cr. 8vo, cloth.   6/-
  Also in " Reformer's Bookshelf."   Large cr. 8vo, cloth.   3/6
LEE. Baldwin : Being Dialogues on Views and Aspirations.   By Vernon
  Lee.   Demy 8vo, cloth.   12/-
——— **Belcaro :** Being Essays on Sundry Æsthetical Questions. By Vernon
  Lee.   Cr. 8vo, cloth.   5/-
——— **Euphorion :** Studies of the Antique and the Mediæval in the
  Renaissance.   By Vernon Lee.   Fourth Impression. Cheap Edition.
  Demy 8vo, cloth.   7/6
——— **Gospels of Anarchy,** and other Contemporary Studies.   By Vernon
  Lee.   Demy 8vo, cloth.   net   10/6
——— **Juvenilia.** Essays on Sundry Æsthetical Questions.   By Vernon
  Lee.   Two vols., leather.   14/-

ART and MUSIC.

BLACKER. Chats on Oriental China. By J. F. Blacker. With a Coloured Frontispiece and about 70 other Illustrations. (Unwin's "Chats" Series. Large cr. 8vo, cloth. net 5/-

BLOOM. Shakespeare's Church, Otherwise the Collegiate Church of the Holy Trinity of Stratford-on-Avon. An Architectural and Ecclesiastical History of the Fabric and its Ornaments. By J. Harvey Bloom, M.A. Illustrated from photographs by L. C. Keighley-Peach. Large cr. 8vo, cloth. net 7/6

CARROLL. The Lewis Carroll Picture Book. Edited by Stuart Dodgson Collingwood. Profusely illustrated. Large cr. 8vo, cloth. 6/-

THE "CHATS" SERIES. Practical Guides for Collectors. Each volume fully Illustrated. Large cr. 8vo, cloth. net 5/-
- (1) Chats on English China. By Arthur Hayden.
- (2) Chats on Old Furniture. By Arthur Hayden.
- (3) Chats on Old Prints. By Arthur Hayden.
- (4) Chats on Costume. A Practical Guide to Historic Dress. By G. Woolliscroft Rhead.
- (5) Chats on Old Miniatures. By J. J. Foster, F.S.A.
- (6) Chats on Old Lace and Needlework. By Mrs. Lowes.
- (7) Chats on Oriental China. By J. F. Blacker.

In Preparation:—

    Chats on Book-Plates. By H. K. Wright.
    Chats on Earthenware. By Arthur Hayden.

DITTRICH. The Horse : A Guide to its Anatomy for Artists. 110 Drawings (reproduced by Photo Lithography) by Hermann Dittrich, with Explanatory Notes by Prof. Ellenberger and Prof. Baum. In portfolio, quarto. net 30/-

van DYKE. Modern French Masters. A series of Biographical and Critical Reviews. By American Artists. With 37 Wood Engravings by Timothy Cole and others, and 28 Half-Tone Illustrations. Edited by John C. van Dyke. Royal 8vo, elegantly bound in cloth gilt. 42/-

—— Old Dutch and Flemish Masters. The Text by John C. van Dyke, and the Notes on the Pictures by Timothy Cole. Imp. 8vo, cloth elegant. 42/-

ERSKINE. Lady Diana Beauclerk: Her Life and Work. By Mrs. Steuart Erskine. Illustrated with Coloured Plates, and many reproductions in half tone. Royal 4to. net 42/-
Also a *Fine Edition.* net 126/-

FISHER. The Harrison Fisher Book. A Collection of Drawings in Colours and Black and White. With an Introduction by James B. Carrington. Quarto. net 10/6

FITZGERALD. Robert Adam, Artist and Architect : His Works and his System. By Percy Fitzgerald, M.A., F.S.A. With collotype plates, and many other illustrations. Cr. 4to, cloth. net 10/6

FOSTER. Chats on Old Miniatures. By J. J. Foster, F.S.A. Copiously illustrated with examples from celebrated collections. (Unwin's "Chats" Series.) Large cr. 8vo, cloth. net 5/-
    Special Large Paper Edition. Medium 8vo. With 8 Illustrations in Coloured Collotype and about 100 reproductions in Black and White. net 10/6

FURNISS. Harry Furniss at Home. By Himself. With over 120 Illustrations. Medium 8vo, cloth gilt.   net 16/-

—— **The Confessions of a Caricaturist.** Being the Reminiscences of Harry Furniss. Illustrated with over 300 Illustrations, many made specially for the volume. In 2 vols. Super royal 8vo.   32/-
New and Cheap Edition in 1 vol., medium 8vo, cloth.   net 10/6

GRAVES. The Irish Song Book, with Original Irish Airs. Edited by Alfred Perceval Graves. Eighth Impression. (New Irish Library.)   Paper covers, 1/- ; cloth   2/-

GWYNN. Memorials of an Eighteenth Century Painter (James Northcote). By Stephen Gwynn. Fully Illustrated with Photogravures, &c. Demy 8vo, cloth gilt.   12/-

HARRISON. Introductory Studies in Greek Art. By Jane E. Harrison. Fourth Edition. Map and 10 Illustrations. Large cr. 8vo, cloth.   7/6

HAYDEN. Chats on English China. By Arthur Hayden. Illustrated with over 100 Specimens of Old China, and with over 150 China Marks. Three-colour Frontispiece. (Unwin's "Chats" Series.) Large cr. 8vo, cloth gilt.   net 5/-

—— **Chats on Old Furniture.** By Arthur Hayden. With 106 illustrations. (Unwin's "Chats" Series.) Large cr. 8vo, cloth.   net 5/-

—— **Chats on Earthenware.** [In Preparation.]

—— **Chats on Old Prints.** By Arthur Hayden. With a Coloured Frontispiece and 70 full-page Plates. (Unwin's "Chats" Series.) Large cr. 8vo, cloth.   net 5/-

LA FARGE. An Artist's Letters from Japan. See under "Geography."

LAWTON. The Life and Work of Auguste Rodin. By Frederick Lawton. With many Illustrations. Demy 8vo, cloth.   net 15/-

LEGGE. Some Ancient Greek Sculptors. By H. Edith Legge. With a Preface by Professor Percy Gardner, and illustrated by about 40 Plates. Cr. 8vo, cloth.   6/-

LOWES. Chats on Old Lace and Needlework. By Mrs. Lowes. With a Coloured Frontispiece and about 70 other Illustrations. (Unwin's "Chats" Series.) Large cr. 8vo, cloth.   net 5/-

MOSCHELES. In Bohemia with Du Maurier. By Felix Moscheles. Illustrated with 63 Original Drawings by G. Du Maurier. Third Edition. Demy 8vo, cloth.   10/6

MOSSO. The Palaces of Crete and their Builders. By Angelo Mosso, Author of "The Life of Man on the High Alps." With 187 Illustrations and 2 Plans. Royal 8vo, cloth.   21/-

NORDAU. On Art and Artists. By Max Nordau. With a Portrait Frontispiece. Large cr. 8vo, cloth.   net 7/6

PENNELL. The Illustration of Books: A Manual for the use of Students. By Joseph Pennell, Lecturer on Illustration at the Slade School, University College. With Diagrams. Cr. 8vo, cloth.   2/6

—— **Lithography and Lithographers:** Some Chapters on the History of the Art. With Technical Remarks and Suggestions by Joseph and Elizabeth Robins Pennell. Lithographic Frontispiece Portrait of Mr. Pennell by J. McNeill Whistler, and numerous Illustrations and Plates. Large royal 4to.   net 73/6
Also a *Fine Edition*, on Japan paper.   net 315/-

PENNELL The Work of Charles Keene. Introduction and Notes by Joseph Pennell, many pictures illustrative of the artist's method and vein of humour, and Bibliographical Notes by W. H. Chesson. Large royal 4to.   net 73/6

Fine Edition.   net 315/-

de QUEVEDO. Pablo de Segovia. By Francisco de Quevedo. Illustrated by Daniel Vierge. Introduction by Joseph Pennell. Super royal 4to, cloth.   net 73/6

van RENSSELAER. English Cathedrals. Described by Mrs. van Rensselaer, and Illustrated by Charles Pennell. Royal 8vo, cloth elegant.   25/-

—— Hand-Book of English Cathedrals. By Mrs. van Rensselaer. Fully Illustrated. Cr. 8vo, cloth.   10/6

RHEAD. Chats on Costume : A Practical Guide to Historic Dress. By G. Woolliscroft Rhead, R.E., A.R.C.A., Lond. With a Coloured Frontispiece and many Illustrations. (Unwin's "Chats" Series.) Large cr. 8vo, cloth.   net 5/-

SCOTSON-CLARK. The "Halls." A Collection of Portraits of eminent Music Hall Performers, Drawn in 3 Colours by Scotson-Clark. Introduction by George Gamble. Imperial 8vo, decorated title, &c., buckram, gilt.   net 6/-

SEYMOUR. Siena and Her Artists. By Frederick H. A. Seymour, Author of "Saunterings in Spain." With 16 Illustrations. Large cr. 8vo, cloth.   6/-

STILLMAN. Old Italian Masters. By W. J. Stillman. Engravings and Notes by T. Cole. Royal 8vo, cloth elegant.   42/-

STUART and PARKE. The Variety Stage. By C. Douglas Stuart and A. J. Parke. Cr. 8vo, cloth.   3/6

STURGIS. The Arts of Design. By Russell Sturgis, M.A., Ph.D., Fellow of the National Sculpture Society, &c. With 107 Illustrations. Royal 8vo, cloth.   net 7/6

VELDHEER. Old Dutch Towns and Villages of the Zuiderzee. By J. G. Veldheer. With Illustrations by J. G. Veldheer, W. J. Tuin, and W. O. J. Nieuwenkamp, and with Decorative Initials. Imperial cloth.   21/-

VIERGE, Don Quixote. By Miguel de Cervantes. With 260 Drawings by Daniel Vierge. 4 vols. Super royal 8vo. Edition limited to 155 copies.   net £15

Fine Edition (limited to 10 copies) on Imperial Japan paper, with extra set of full-page Plates.   net £30

—— The Nun-Ensign. Translated from the Original Spanish with an Introduction and Notes by James Fitzmaurice-Kelly, Fellow of the British Academy. Also La Monja Alferez, a Play in the Original Spanish by D. Juan Perez de Montalban. With Illustrations by Daniel Vierge, Illustrator of "Pablo de Segovia" and "Don Quixote." Large cr. 8vo, cloth.   net 7/6

VILLARI. Giovanni Segantini : His Life and Work. Edited by Luigi Villari. With upwards of 80 Illustrations reproduced direct from the original paintings. In one volume. With Photogravure Frontispiece. Imperial 8vo, with specially designed cover, and boxed, net 21/-

The Westminster Cathedral. A Free Criticism. By an Architectural Student. With 9 Plates. Quarto, cloth.   net 6/-

BIOGRAPHY, MEMOIRS, CORRESPONDENCE, &c.

ADAM. My Literary Life. By Madame Edmond Adam. (Juliette Lamber). 8vo, cloth, gilt top, with Portraits. net **8/6**
—— **Robert Adam, Artist and Architect.** By Percy Fitzgerald. See under "Art."

ADVENTURE SERIES, The. See at the end of this Section.

AUSTIN (Mrs. Sarah). See Ross, "Three Generations."

BAMFORD'S Passages in the Life of a Radical. See under "Politics."

BEACONSFIELD. Lord Beaconsfield. By T. P. O'Connor. Popular Edition. With Frontispiece. Large cr. 8vo, cloth. net **2/6**

BEARNE (Mrs.) Works. See under "History."

BEAUCLERK (Lady Diana). By Mrs. Steuart Erskine. See under "Art."

BELGIOJOSO. A Revolutionary Princess : Christina Belgiojoso-Trivulzio. Her Life and Times (1808-1871). By H. Remsen Whitehouse. With Photogravure Frontispiece and many other Illustrations. Demy 8vo, cloth. net **10/6**

BERNARD. Claude Bernard. By Sir Michael Foster. With Photogravure Frontispiece. (Masters of Medicine. Vol. 6.) Large cr. 8vo, cloth. **3/6**

BESANT. Annie Besant: An Autobiography. New Edition, with a new Preface. Illustrated. Large cr. 8vo, cloth. net **5/-**

BRADLAUGH. Charles Bradlaugh : A Record of His Life and Work. By His Daughter, Hypatia Bradlaugh Bonner. 2 vols. (Reformer's Bookshelf.) Large cr. 8vo, cloth. **7/-**
Also in Unwin's Half-Crown Standard Library. 1 vol. Cloth. net **2/6**

BRIGHTWEN. The Life and Thoughts of a Naturalist. Mrs. Brightwen. Edited by W. H. Chesson. With Portrait and Illustrations, and an Introduction by Edmund Gosse. Large cr. 8vo, cloth. net **5/-**

BRODIE. Sir Benjamin Brodie. By Timothy Holmes. With Photogravure Frontispiece. (Masters of Medicine. Vol. 5.) Large cr. 8vo, cloth. **3/6**

BROOKE. Rajah Brooke : The Englishman as Ruler of an Eastern State. By Sir Spencer St. John, G.C.M.G. With Frontispiece and Maps. (Builders of Greater Britain. Vol. 7.) Large cr. 8vo, cloth. **5/-**

BROWN. Captain John Brown of Harper's Ferry. By John Newton. Fully Illustrated. Cr. 8vo, cloth. **6/-**
"John Brown's body lies a 'mould'ring in the grave
But his soul's marching on."
Also (Lives Worth Living Series). **3/6**

BUCHANAN. Robert Buchanan : Some Account of His Life, His Life's Work, and His Literary Friendships. By Harriett Jay. Illustrated with Portraits and from other sources. Demy 8vo, cloth. net **10/6**

BUILDERS OF GREATER BRITAIN. Edited by H. F. Wilson. A Set of 8 volumes, with Photogravure Frontispiece and Maps to each. Large cr. 8vo, cloth. each **5/-**
[For full titles see under:]

(1) Sir Walter Ralegh.   (5) Lord Clive.
(2) Sir Thomas Maitland.   (6) Admiral Phillip.
(3) John and Sebastian Cabot.   (7) Rajah Brooke.
(4) Edward Gibbon Wakefield.   (8) Sir Stamford Raffles.

BURTON. The Real Sir Richard Burton. By Walter Phelps Dodge. With a Frontispiece. Large cloth.   net   6/-

CABOT. John and Sebastian Cabot; the Discovery of North America. By C. Raymond Beazley, M.A. With Frontispiece and Maps. (Builders of Greater Britain. Vol. 3.) Large cr. 8vo, cloth.   5/-

CARLYLE. The Story of Thomas Carlyle. By A. S. Arnold. With 6 Illustrations. (Lives Worth Living Series. Vol. 11.) Cr. 8vo, cloth.   3/6

CARROLL. The Life and Letters of Lewis Carroll (G. L. Dodgson). By S. D. Collingwood. With about 100 Illustrations. Large cr. 8vo, cloth.   3/6

CESARESCO. Italian Characters in the Epoch of Unification. By Countess Martinengo Cesaresco. Cheap Edition. Demy 8vo, cloth.   7/6

CHEVALIER. Before I Forget. Being the Autobiography of a Chevalier d'Industrie. Written by Albert Chevalier. Very fully Illustrated. Demy 8vo.   net 16/-

CLIVE. Lord Clive: The Foundation of British Rule in India. By Sir A. J. Arbuthnot, K.C.S.I., C.I.E. With Frontispiece and Maps. (Builders of Greater Britain. Vol. 5.) Large cr. 8vo, cloth.   5/-

COBDEN. The Life of Richard Cobden. By the Right Hon. John Morley, M.A. (Oxford), Hon. LL.D. With Photogravure Portrait from the Original Drawing by Lowes Dickinson. Jubilee Edition. (Reformer's Bookshelf.) 2 vols. Large cr. 8vo, cloth.   7/-

New Binding. Demy 8vo, cloth.   3/6

New Popular Unabridged Edition in 1 vol. Large cr. 8vo, cloth. net   2/6

The "Free Trade" Edition. Popular Re-issue, abridged. Demy 4to. Paper covers.   8d.

Special Edition, in 5 Parts. Demy 8vo, paper covers.   Each, net   6d.

—— Cobden as a Citizen. A Chapter in Manchester History. Containing a facsimile of Cobden's pamphlet, "Incorporate Your Borough!" with an Introduction and a complete Cobden Bibliography, by William E. A. Axon. With 7 Photogravure Plates and 3 other Illustrations. Demy 8vo, full vellum or buckram.   net 21/-

—— Richard Cobden and the Jubilee of Free Trade. See under "Politics."

—— Cobden's Work and Opinions. By Welby and Mallet. See under "Politics."

—— The Political Writings of Richard Cobden. See under "Politics."

COILLARD. Coillard of the Zambesi. The Lives of François and Christina Coillard, of the Paris Missionary Society (1834-1904). By C. W. Mackintosh. With a Photogravure Frontispiece, a Map, and 64 other Illustrations. Demy 8vo, cloth.   net 15/-

COLERIDGE. The Story of a Devonshire House. By Lord Coleridge, K.C. Illustrated. Demy 8vo, cloth.   net 15/-

CREMER. Life of W. Randal. See page 42.

CROMWELL. Oliver Cromwell and His Times. By G. Holden Pike. Cr. 8vo, cloth. Illustrated.   6/-
Also "Lives Worth Living" Series.   3/6

DAVIDSON. Memorials of Thomas Davidson the Wandering Scholar. Collected and Edited by William Knight, LL.D., formerly Professor of Moral Philosophy in the University of St. Andrews. With a Portrait.   net   7/6

DAVIS. A Short Life of Thomas Davis. By Sir Charles Gavan Duffy. (New Irish Library. Vol. 10.) Small cr. 8vo.
                                             Paper covers, 1/- ; cloth   2/-

DAVITT. Michael Davitt: Revolutionary, Agitator, and Labour Leader. See "Sheehy-Skeffington."

DE LA REY. A Woman's Wanderings and Trials During the Anglo-Boer War. By Mrs. (General) De La Rey. Illustrated. 2nd Edition. Cr. 8vo, cloth.   2/6

DOYLE. Bishop Doyle. By Michael MacDonagh. (New Irish Library. Vol. 11.) Small cr. 8vo.   Paper covers, 1/- ; cloth   2/-

DUFFY. My Life in Two Hemispheres. By Sir Charles Gavan Duffy, K.C.M.G. Two vols. demy 8vo, cloth.   32/-
   Cheap Edition. 2 vols. (Reformer's Bookshelf.) Large cr. 8vo, cloth.   7/-

DU MAURIER. By Felix Moscheles. See under "Art."

ELIZABETH. The Correspondence of Princess Elizabeth of England, Landgravine of Hesse-Homburg, for the most part with Miss Louisa Swinburne. With Portraits, and Edited with Preface by Philip C. Yorke, M.A., Oxon. With a Photogravure and other Illustrations. Demy 8vo, cloth.   12/-

EVANS. The Memoirs of Dr. Thomas W. Evans. Recollections of the Second French Empire. Edited by Edward A. Crane, M.D. Illustrated. 2 vols. Demy 8vo, cloth.   net 21/-

FITCH. Ralph Fitch: England's Pioneer to India and Burma. His Companions and Contemporaries. By J. Horton Ryley, Member of the Hakluyt Society. With 16 full-page and 3 smaller Illustrations. Large cr. 8vo, cloth.   net 10/6

FITZMAURICE-KELLY. The Nun-Ensign. Translated from the Original Spanish with an Introduction and Notes by James Fitzmaurice-Kelly, Fellow of the British Academy. Also La Monja Alferez, a Play in the Original Spanish by D. Juan Perez de Montalban. With Illustrations by Daniel Vierge, Illustrator of "Pablo de Segovia" and "Don Quixote." Large cr. 8vo, cloth. net   7/6

FULLER. The Love-Letters of Margaret Fuller (1845-1846). With an Introduction by Julia Ward Howe. To which are added the Reminiscences of Ralph Waldo Emerson, Horace Greeley, and Charles T. Congdon. With Portrait. 12mo, cloth, gilt top.   net   5/-

FURNISS (Harry). Confessions of a Caricaturist. See under "Art."

—— At Home. See under "Art."

GAMBIER. Links in My Life on Land and Sea. By Commander J. W. Gambier, R.N. With Frontispiece and 7 other Illustrations. Demy 8vo, cloth.   net 15/-
   Cheap Edition, with Frontispiece. (Modern Travel Series.) Large cr. 8vo, cloth.   5/-

GLADSTONE. My Memory of Gladstone. By Goldwin Smith. With Portrait. Cr. 8vo, cloth   net   2/6

GORDON. The Life of General Gordon. By Demetrius C. Boulger. Illustrated. New and Cheaper Edition. Demy 8vo, cloth.   6/-

—— (Lady Duff). See Ross, "Three Generations."

GOETHE. Life of Goethe. By Heinrich Düntzer. Translated by Thomas W. Lyster, Assistant Librarian, National Library of Ireland. With Authentic Illustrations and Facsimiles. (Unwin's Half-Crown Standard Library.) Large cr. 8vo, cloth.   net   2/6

GOULD. Concerning Lafcadio Hearn. By G. M. Gould, M.D. With 5 Illustrations. Demy 8vo, cloth.   net 8/6

GRATTAN. Henry Grattan. (The Gladstone Prize Essay in the University of Oxford, 1902.) By Percy M. Roxby, Scholar of Christ Church. With Frontispiece. Cr. 8vo, cloth.   net   3/6

GRAY. Wise Words and Loving Deeds. See under "Lives Worth Living."

HAECKEL. Haeckel. His Life and Work By Wilhelm Bölsche. Translated and with an Introduction and Supplementary Chapter by Joseph McCabe With four Coloured Frontispieces and many other Illustrations. Demy 8vo, cloth. net 15/-

HARDY. The Love Affairs of Some Famous Men. By the Rev. E. J Hardy, M A Imp. 16mo, cloth. 6/-
Cheaper Edition, cr 8vo cloth. 3/6

HARVEY William Harvey. By D'Arcy Power With Photogravure Frontispiece. (Masters of Medicine Vol. 2) Large cr 8vo, cloth 3/6

HELMHOLTZ. Hermann von Helmholtz. By Prof. John G McKendrick. With Photogravure Frontispiece (Masters of Medicine. Vol 7) Large cr. 8vo, cloth. 3/6

HILL Sir Rowland Hill The Story of a Great Reform Told by his Daughter, Eleanor C. Smyth With a Photogravure Frontispiece and 16 other Illustrations Large cr 8vo cloth net 5/-

HOLYOAKE Bygones Worth Remembering. A Sequel to "Sixty Years of an Agitator's Life" By George Jacob Holyoake. With a Photogravure Frontispiece, and 18 other Portraits. 2 vols. Demy 8vo, cloth 21/-

Also Reformer's Bookshelf 2 vols Large cr 8vo, cloth. 7/-
—— Sixty Years of an Agitator's Life. George Jacob Holyoake's Autobiography 2 vols. (Reformer's Bookshelf.) Large cr 8vo, cloth. 7/-
Also in Unwin's Half-Crown Standard Library. 1 vol cloth net 2/6

HORRIDGE Lives of Great Italians. By Frank Horridge. Illustrated Large cr. 8vo, cloth 7/6
Prize Edition 3 6

HUNTER. John Hunter. By Stephen Paget. With Photogravure Frontispiece (Masters of Medicine Vol 1) Large cr 8vo, cloth 3/6

IRVING Sir Henry Irving A Biography. By Percy Fitzgerald With a Photogravure Frontispiece and 35 other Illustrations. Demy 8vo, cloth. net 10/6

JAPP. Master Missionaries. See under "Lives Worth Living"
—— Labour and Victory. See under "Lives Worth Living."
—— Good Men and True. See under "Lives Worth Living"

JULIAN The Apostate. A Historical Study. By Gaetano Negri Translated by the Duchess Lita-Visconti-Arese With an Introduction by Professor Pasquale Villari. Illustrated. 2 vols. Demy 8vo, cloth net 21/-

KEENE (Charles). By Joseph Pennell and W. H Chesson. See under "Art"

KERR. Commissioner Kerr—An Individuality. By G Pitt-Lewis, K C With Photogravure and half-tone Portraits Demy 8vo, cloth net 10/6

KRUGER. The Memoirs of Paul Kruger. Four Times President of the South African Republic. Told by Himself Translated by A Teixeira de Mattos With Portraits and Map 2 vols Demy 8vo, cloth gilt 32/-
Also a *Fine Edition* on Japan paper Price on application

LAURENSON. Memoirs of Arthur Laurenson. Edited by Catherine Spence With Portrait Cr 8vo, cloth 7/6

LEAR The Letters of Edward Lear (Author of "The Book of Nonsense") to Chichester Fortescue, Lord Carlingford, and Frances, Countess Waldegrave (1848 to 1864). Edited by Lady Strachey (of Sutton Court) With a Photogravure Frontispiece, 3 Coloured Plates, and many other Illustrations. Demy 8vo, cloth net 15/

LINCOLN. Abraham Lincoln. A History. By John G Nicolay and Colonel John Hay With many full-page Illustrations, Portraits and Maps 10 vols. Royal 8vo, cloth.   120/-

"LIVES WORTH LIVING," THE, Series of Popular Biographies. Illustrated Cr 8vo, cloth extra, gilt edges   per vol 3/6

(1) **Leaders of Men.** By H A Page
(2) **Wise Words and Loving Deeds.** By E Conder Gray.
(3) **Master Missionaries.** Studies in Heroic Pioneer Work By A H Japp.
(4) **Labour and Victory.** By A. H. Japp, LL D
(5) **Heroic Adventure** Chapters in Recent Explorations and Discovery Illustrated
(6) **Great Minds in Art.** By William Tirebuck

(7) **Good Men and True.** By Alex H Japp, LL D
(8) **Famous Musical Composers.** By Lydia Morris
(9) **Oliver Cromwell and His Times.** By G. Holden Pike
(10) **Captain John Brown.** By John Newton.
(11) **Story of Thomas Carlyle.** By A S Arnold
(12) **Wesley and His Preachers.** By G. Holden Pike.
(13) **Dr Parker & His Friends** By G. Holden Pike.

McCARTHY. British Political Leaders By Justin McCarthy Illustrated from Photographs. Large cr 8vo, cloth, gilt top   net 7/6
Popular Edition.   net 3/6

—— **Portraits of the Sixties.** By Justin McCarthy, M P, Author of "A History of our Own Times," &c. Illustrated. Demy 8vo, cloth net 15/-

MACHIAVELLI. Life and Times of Niccolo Machiavelli. By Professor Pasquale Villari Revised Edition. Translated by Linda Villari Illustrated Demy 8vo, cloth   7/6
Also in Unwin's Half-Crown Standard Library 1 vol., cloth. net 2/6

MADDISON. The Life of W Randal Cremer, M.P. By Fred Maddison, M P, and Howard Evans.   net 5/-

MAITLAND. Sir Thomas Maitland: The Mastery of the Mediterranean By Walter Frewen Lord With Frontispiece and Maps (Builders of Greater Britain. Vol. 2) Large cr. 8vo, cloth.   5/-

MASTERS OF MEDICINE. Edited by C Louis Taylor. Cr 8vo, cloth each 3/6

For full Titles see under:

(1) **John Hunter**
(2) **William Harvey.**
(3) **Sir James Y. Simpson.**
(4) **William Stokes.**
(5) **Sir Benjamin Brodie.**
(6) **Hermann von Helmholtz.**
(7) **Claude Bernard.**
(8) **Thomas Sydenham.**

MAUDE. Oriental Campaigns and European Furloughs The Autobiography of an Indian Mutiny Veteran By Colonel Edwin Maude, late H.M. 2nd (Leinster) Regiment With a Photogravure Frontispiece Demy 8vo, cloth   net 7/6

MOFFAT. The Lives of Robert and Mary Moffat. By their Son, John Smith Moffat Illustrated Cr 8vo, cloth   6/-
Also in Unwin's Half-Crown Standard Library 1 vol., cloth net 2/6

MORRIS. Famous Musical Composers. See under "Lives Worth Living."

NAPOLEON. Napoleon's Last Voyages Being the Diaries of Admiral Sir Thomas Usher, R N., K C B (on board the "Undaunted") and John R Glover, Secretary to Rear-Admiral Cockburn (on board the "Northumberland"). New Edition, with Introduction and Notes by J Holland Rose, Litt D, Author of "Life of Napoleon I.," &c. Illustrated Demy 8vo, cloth net 10/6

NORTHCOTE (James). By Stephen Gwynn See under "Art"

O'NEILL. Owen Roe O'Neill. By J. F. Taylor, K.C. (New Irish
Library. Vol. 8.) Small cr. 8vo.   Paper covers, 1/- ; cloth   2/-

PAGE. Leaders of Men. See under "Lives Worth Living."

PARKER. Dr. Parker and his Friends. By G. Holden Pike. With
Portraits. Cr. 8vo, cloth.   net   5/-
Also "Lives Worth Living" Series, cr. 8vo, cloth.   3/6

PHILLIP. Admiral Phillip ; the Founding of New South Wales. By
Louis Becke and Walter Jeffery. With Frontispiece and Maps.
(Builders of Greater Britain. Vol. 6.) Large cr. 8vo, cloth.   5/-

PLOWDEN. Grain or Chaff ? The Autobiography of a Police Magistrate. By A. C. Plowden. With Photogravure Frontispiece. Demy
8vo, cloth gilt.   net   16/-
Popular Edition, cloth.   6/-

PORTER. Life and Letters of Mr. Endymion Porter. By Dorothea
Townshend. Illustrated. Demy 8vo, cloth.   12/-

PRAED. My Australian Girlhood. By Mrs. Campbell Praed. With
many Illustrations. Demy 8vo, cloth.   16/-
Popular Edition, cloth.   net   6/-

RAFFLES. Sir Stamford Raffles ; England in the Far East. By Hugh
E. Egerton. With Frontispiece and Maps. (Builders of Greater
Britain. Vol. 8.) Large cr. 8vo, cloth.   5/-

RALEGH. Sir Walter Ralegh ; the British Dominion of the West. By
Martin A. S. Hume. With Frontispiece and Maps. (Builders of
Greater Britain. Vol. 1.) Large cr. 8vo, cloth.   5/-
Also in Unwin's Half-Crown Standard Library. 1 vol., cloth. net 2/6

RODIN. The Life of Auguste Rodin. By Frederick Lawton. With
many Illustrations. Demy 8vo, cloth.   net   15/-

ROSS. Three Generations of Englishwomen : Memoirs and Corre-
spondence of Mrs. John Taylor, Mrs. Sarah Austin, and Lady Duff
Gordon. By Janet Ross. New Edition, Revised and Augmented.
With Portraits. Large cr. 8vo, cloth.   7/6

ROSSETTI. Letters of Dante Gabriel Rossetti to William Alling-
ham (1854-70). Edited by George Birkbeck Hill, D.C.L., LL.D.
Illustrated. Demy 8vo, cloth.   12/-

SARSFIELD. Life of Patrick Sarsfield. By Dr. John Todhunter.
(New Irish Library. Vol. 7.)   Paper covers, 1/- ; cloth   2/-

SAVONAROLA. The Life and Times of Girolamo Savonarola. By
Prof. Pasquale Villari. Translated by Linda Villari. Fully Illus-
trated. Large cr. 8vo, cloth.   7/6
Also in Unwin's Half-Crown Standard Library. 1 vol., cloth. net 2/6

SECCOMBE. Lives of Twelve Bad Men. Edited by Thomas
Seccombe, M.A. Second Edition. Cr. 8vo, cloth.   8/-

SEGANTINI (Giovanni). By Luigi Villari. See under "Art."

de SEGOVIA (Pablo). By F. de Quevedo. Illustrated by Daniel
Vierge. See under "Art."

SEYMOUR. The "Pope" of Holland House. By Lady Seymour.
Biographical Introduction and Supplementary Chapter by W. P.
Courtney. With a Photogravure Frontispiece and 8 other Illus-
trations. Demy 8vo, cloth.   net 10/6

SHEEHY-SKEFFINGTON. Michael Davitt : Revolutionary, Agitator, and Labour Leader. By F. Sheehy-Skeffington. With
an Introduction by Justin McCarthy and a Portrait. Demy 8vo,
cloth.   net   7/6

SHERVINTON. The Shervintons—Soldiers of Fortune. By Kathleen Shervinton. Illustrated. Small demy 8vo. net 10/6

SIMPSON. Sir James Y. Simpson. By H. Laing Gordon. With Photogravure Frontispiece. (Masters of Medicine. Vol. 3.) Large cr. 8vo, cloth. 3/6

SIMPSON. The Autobiography of William Simpson, R.I. (Crimean Simpson). Edited by George Eyre-Todd. Illustrated with many Reproductions of his Pictures. Royal 8vo, cloth. net 21/-
Also a *Fine Edition*, limited to 100 copies, printed on Arnold's unbleached, hand-made paper, with Plates on Japan paper. net 42/-

SKIPSEY (Joseph). A Memoir. See "Watson."

SMITH. Forty Years of Washington Society. From the Letters and Journals of Mrs. Samuel Harrison Smith (Margaret Bayard). Edited by Gaillard Hunt. With numerous Illustrations and Portraits. Demy 8vo, cloth. net 10/6

STANSFELD. James Stansfeld. By Jessie White Mario. Demy 8vo, cloth. 21/-

STOKES. William Stokes. By Sir William Stokes. With Photogravure Frontispiece. (Masters of Medicine. Vol. 4.) Large cr. 8vo, cloth. 3/6

SULLIVAN. Barry Sullivan and his Contemporaries. By Robert M. Sillard. 2 vols. Illustrated. Demy 8vo. net 21/-

SWANWICK. Anna Swanwick. A Memoir and Recollections. By Mary L. Bruce. Illustrated with a Photogravure Portrait, and five others in half-tone. Cr. 8vo, cloth. net 6/-

SWIFT. Unpublished Letters of Dean Swift. Edited by George Birkbeck Hill, D.C.L., LL.D. Illustrated. Demy 8vo, cloth. 12/-
—— Swift in Ireland. By Richard Ashe King, M.A. (New Irish Library.) Small cr. 8vo. Paper covers, 1/- ; cloth 2/-

SYDENHAM. Thomas Sydenham. By J. F. Payne. With Photogravure Frontispiece. (Masters of Medicine. Vol. 8.) Large cr. 8vo, cloth. 3/6

TAYLOR (Mrs. John). See Ross, "Three Generations."

TETLEY. Old Times and New. By J. George Tetley, D.D., Canon Residentiary of Bristol. With Frontispiece. Demy 8vo, cloth. net 7/6

TIREBUCK. Great Minds in Art. See under "Lives Worth Living."

TOURGUENEFF. Tourgueneff and his French Circle. Edited by H. Halpérine-Kaminsky. Translated by Ethel M. Arnold. Cr. 8vo, cloth. 7/6

TREHERNE, Spencer Perceval. A Biography. By Philip Treherne. With portraits. Cr. 8vo, cloth. net 5/-

TROWBRIDGE (W. R. H.). Works. See under "History."

TROWBRIDGE. Mirabeau the Demi-God. Being the True and Romantic Story of his Life and Adventures By W. R. H. Trowbridge. With a Photogravure Frontispiece and 32 other Illustrations. Demy 8vo, cloth. net 15/-

VAMBERY. The Story of My Struggles. The Memoirs of Arminius Vambéry, C.V.O. With Photogravure and other Illustrations. 2 vols. Demy 8vo, cloth. net 21/-
Popular Edition in 1 vol. Demy 8vo, cloth. net 7/6
—— Arminius Vambery: His Life and Adventures. By Himself. Imperial 16mo, cloth. 6/-
Boys' Edition, cr. 8vo, cloth gilt, gilt edges. 5/-

VERNON. Admiral Vernon and the Navy. A Memoir and Vindication, with Sundry Sidelights. By Douglas Ford. Illustrated. Demy 8vo, cloth. net 10/6

VINCENT. Twelve Bad Women : A Companion Volume to "Twelve
Bad Men." Edited by Arthur Vincent. Illustrated. Large cr. 8vo,
cloth.   6/-
WAKEFIELD. Edward Gibbon Wakefield ; the Colonisation of South
Australia and New Zealand. By R. Garnett, C.B., LL.D. With
Frontispiece and Maps. (Builders of Greater Britain. Vol. 4.)
Large cr. 8vo, cloth.   5/-
WALPOLE. Essays Political and Biographical. By Sir Spencer
Walpole, K.C.B. Edited by Francis Holland. With a Memoir by his
Daughter, and a Photogravure Frontispiece. Demy 8vo, cloth. net 10/6
—— **Studies in Biography.** By Sir Spencer Walpole, K.C.B. With
Photogravure Frontispiece. Demy 8vo, cloth.   net 15/-
WASHINGTON. From Slave to College President. Being the
Life Story of Booker T. Washington. By G. Holden Pike. With
Frontispiece. Cr. 8vo, half-bound cloth.   1/6
—— **The Youth of George Washington.** Told in the form of an Auto-
biography. By S. Weir Mitchell. Large cr. 8vo, cloth.   6/-
WATSON. The Savage Club. A Medley of History, Anecdote and
Reminiscence. By Aaron Watson. With a chapter by Mark
Twain, and a Photogravure Frontispiece, 4 Coloured Plates, and
64 other Illustrations. Medium 8vo, cloth.   net 21/-
WATSON. Joseph Skipsey, a Memoir. By the Rt. Hon. Robert
Spence Watson. With 3 Portraits. Crown 8vo, cloth.   net   2/6
WESLEY and his Preachers : Their Conquest of Britain. By
G. Holden Pike. Fully Illustrated. Cr. 8vo, cloth.   7/6
Also "Lives Worth Living " Series.   3/6
WILBERFORCE. The Private Papers of William Wilberforce.
Collected and Edited by A. M. Wilberforce. Illustrated. Demy
8vo, cloth.   12/-
WILKINSON. The Personal Story of the Upper House. By
Kosmo Wilkinson. Demy 8vo, cloth.   16/-

**UNWIN'S HALF-CROWN STANDARD LIBRARY OF HISTORY
AND BIOGRAPHY.** Illustrated. Large cr. 8vo, cloth. each, net   2/6

(1) The Life of Richard Cobden. By the Right Hon.
John Morley.

(2) The Life of Girolamo
Savonarola. By Professor
Pasquale Villari.

(3) The Life of Niccolò
Machiavelli. By Professor
Pasquale Villari.

(4) The Lives of Robert and
Mary Moffat. By John
Smith Moffat.

(5) The History of Florence
(for the first two centuries).
By Prof. Pasquale Villari.

(6) English Wayfaring Life
in the Middle Ages (XIVth
Century). By J. J. Jusse-
rand.

(7) Lord Beaconsfield. By
T. P. O'Connor.

(8) Rome and Pompeii :
Archæological Rambles.
By Gaston Boissier.

(9) Holyoake : Sixty Years
of an Agitator's Life. By
George Jacob Holyoake.

(10) Sir Walter Ralegh. By
Martin A. S. Hume.

(11) The Dawn of the Nineteenth Century in Eng-
land. By John Ashton.

(12) Life of Goethe. By
Heinrich Düntzer.

(13) Charles Bradlaugh. By
Hypathia Bradlaugh Bonner

(14) Augustus. The Life and
Times of the Founder of the
Roman Empire. By E. S.
Shuckburgh.

ADVENTURE SERIES, THE. Popular Re-issue. Large cr. 8vo, fully
Illustrated, cloth. Per vol. 3/6

(1) **Adventures of a Younger Son.** By Edward J. Trelawny. Introduction by Edward Garnett.

(2) **Madagascar ; or, Robert Drury's Journal during his Captivity on that Island.** Preface and Notes by Captain S. P. Oliver, R.A.

(3) **Memoirs of the Extraordinary Military Career of John Shipp.** Written by Himself. Introduction by H. Manners Chichester.

(4) **The Buccaneers and Marooners of America.** Edited and Illustrated by Howard Pyle.

(5) **The Log of a Jack Tar.** Being the Life of James Choyce, Master Mariner. Edited by Commander V. Lovett Cameron.

(6) **Ferdinand Mendez Pinto, the Portuguese Adventurer.** New Edition. Annotated by Prof. Arminius Vambéry.

(7) **Adventures of a Blockade Runner.** By William Watson. Illustrated by Arthur Byng, R.N.

(8) **The Memoirs and Travels of Count de Benyowsky in Siberia, Kamtschatka, Japan, the Liukiu Islands, and Formosa.** Edited by Captain S. P. Oliver, R.A.

(9) **The Life and Adventures of James P. Beckwourth.** New Edition. Edited and with Preface by C. G. Leland (" Hans Breitmann ")

(10) **A Particular Account of the European Military Adventurers of Hindustan (1784-1803).** Compiled by Henry Compton. New and Cheaper Edition. Maps and Illustrations.

(11) **A Master Mariner.** The Life of Captain Robert W. Eastwick. Edited by Herbert Compton.

(12) **Kolokotrones: Klepht and Warrior.** Translated from the Greek by Mrs. Edmonds. Introduction by M. Gennadius.

(13) **Missing Friends.** The Adventures of an Emigrant in Queensland.

The following Volumes are done at 5/- only. 5/-

The Escapes of Latude and Casanova from Prison. Edited, with Introduction, by P. Villars.

The Story of the Filibusters. By James Jeffrey Roche. And, The Life of Colonel David Crockett.

The following Volumes are done at 7/6 each. 7/6

The Women Adventurers. Edited by Menie Muriel Dowie.

The Life and Adventures of James Beckwourth. Mountaineer, Scout, Pioneer, and Chief of the Crow Nation of Indians. Edited by Charles G. Leland (" Hans Breitmann ").

A Particular Account of the European Military Adventurers of Hindustan (1784-1803). Compiled by Henry Compton. New and Cheaper Edition. Maps and Illustrations.

Famous Prison Escapes of the Civil War. Edited by G. W. Cable.

HISTORY and HISTORICAL LITERATURE.

ARCHER and KINGSFORD. The Crusades: The Story of the Latin Kingdom of Jerusalem. By T. A. Archer and Charles Lethbridge Kingsford. Third Impression. With 58 Illustrations and 3 Maps. (Story of the Nations. Vol. 40.) Large cr. 8vo, cloth.   5/-

ASHTON. The Dawn of the Nineteenth Century in England: A Social Sketch of the Times. By John Ashton. Third Edition. Illustrated. Large cr. 8vo, cloth.   7/6

Cheap Edition, " England 100 Years Ago."   3/6

Also in Unwin's Half-Crown Standard Library. 1 vol., cloth.   net   2/6

BARING-GOULD. Germany. By S. Baring-Gould, M.A. Seventh Impression. With 108 Illustrations and Maps. (Story of the Nations. Vol. 3.) Large cr. 8vo, cloth.   5/-

BARRY. The Papal Monarchy: From Gregory the Great to Boniface VIII. (590-1303). By William Barry, D.D. With 61 Illustrations and Maps. (Story of the Nations. Vol. 58.) Large cr. 8vo, cloth.   5/-

BATESON. Mediæval England (1066-1350). By Mary Bateson, Associate and Lecturer of Newnham College, Cambridge. With 93 Illustrations. (Story of the Nations. Vol. 62.) Large cr. 8vo, cloth.   5/-

BEARNE. Heroines of French Society in the Court, the Revolution, the Empire, and the Restoration. By Mrs. Bearne. With many Illustrations. Large cr. 8vo, cloth.   net   10/6

—— **A Leader of Society at Napoleon's Court** (Laura Permon). By Mrs. Bearne. Fully Illustrated. Large cr. 8vo, cloth.   10/6

—— **Lives and Times of the Early Valois Queens.** By Mrs. Bearne. Illustrated by E. H. Bearne. Small demy, cloth.   10/6

—— **Pictures of the Old French Court.** By Mrs. Bearne. Second Edition, Revised. Illustrated. Small demy 8vo, cloth.   10/6

—— **A Royal Quartette.** By Mrs. Bearne. Fully Illustrated. Large cr. 8vo, cloth.   net   10/6

—— **A Sister of Marie Antoinette.** The Life Story of Maria Carolina, Queen of Naples. By Mrs. Bearne. Fully Illustrated. Large cr. 8vo, cloth.   net   10/6

—— **A Queen of Napoleon's Court: The Life Story of Désirée Bernadotte.** By Mrs. Bearne. Fully Illustrated. Large cr. 8vo, cloth.   10/6

BENJAMIN. Persia. By S. G. W. Benjamin, late U.S. Minister to Persia. Fourth Edition. With 56 Illustrations and Maps. (Story of the Nations. Vol. 17.) Large cr. 8vo, cloth.   5/-

BIRCH. History of Scottish Seals, from the Eleventh to the Seventeenth Century. By Walter de Gray Birch, LL.D., F.S.A., of the British Museum. With many Illustrations derived from the finest and most interesting examples extant. Vol. 1, The Royal Seals of Scotland. Crown 4to, buckram, gilt top.   net   12/6

Also a *Fine Edition* on large paper.   net   21/-

BLISS. Turkey and the Armenian Atrocities. By Edwin M. Bliss. Introduction by Frances E. Willard. Cloth gilt.   10/6

BLUNT. Secret History of the English Occupation of Egypt. Being a Personal Narrative of Events. By Wilfrid Scawen Blunt. Second Edition, Revised, with an Introduction by Sir William F. Butler, K.C.B. With a Photogravure Frontispiece. Demy 8vo, cloth. net 15/-

BOISSIER (Gaston). The Country of Horace and Virgil. See under "Geography."

—— Rome and Pompeii. See under "Geography."

BOURINOT. Canada. By Sir John Bourinot, K.C.M.G. With 63 Illustrations and Maps. New Edition, with a new Map, and revisions and a supplementary chapter by Edward Porritt. (Story of the Nations. Vol. 45.) Large cr. 8vo, cloth. 5/-

BOXALL. The Anglo-Saxon : A Study in Evolution. By George E. Boxall. Crown 8vo, cloth. 5/-

—— The History of the Australian Bushrangers. By G. E. Boxall. Large cr. 8vo, cloth. net 5/-

BOYESEN. A History of Norway. From the Earliest Times. By Professor Hjalmar H. Boyesen. With a Chapter by C. F. Keary. With 77 Illustrations and Maps. (Story of the Nations. Vol. 55.) Large cr. 8vo, cloth. 5/-

BRADLEY. The Goths. From the Earliest Times to the End of the Gothic Dominion in Spain. By Henry Bradley. Fifth Edition. With 35 Illustrations and Maps. (Story of the Nations. Vol. 12.) Large cr. 8vo, cloth. 5/-

BRERETON. The Literary History of the Adelphi and its Neighbourhood. By Austin Brereton. With a new Introduction, a Photogravure Frontispiece, and 26 other full-page Illustrations. Demy 8vo, cloth. net 10/6

BROOKS. Dames and Daughters of the French Court. By Geraldine Brooks. With a Photogravure Frontispiece and 10 other Illustrations. Large cr. 8vo, cloth. net 8/6

BROWNE. Bonaparte in Egypt and the Egyptians of To-day. By Haji A. Browne. With Frontispiece. Demy 8vo, cloth. net 10/6

BUEL (Clarence C.). See "Johnson."

BUTLER. The Lombard Communes. A History of the Republics of North Italy. By W. F. Butler. With Maps and Illustrations. Demy 8vo, cloth. net 15/-

BUTLER. Wellington's Operations in the Peninsula (1808-1814). By Captain Lewis Butler. With Maps. 2 vols. Demy 8vo, cloth. net 32/-

Also in Six paper Parts. each, net 5/-

CARSE. All the Monarchs of Merry England. William I. to Edward VII. By Roland Carse. With 40 full-page Coloured Illustrations by W. Heath Robinson. 252 pages, bound in full leather and gold-blocked. 15/-

—— The Monarchs of Merry England. William I. to Richard III. By Roland Carse. With 20 full-page Coloured Illustrations by W. Heath Robinson. 124 pages, bound in full cloth. 6/-

Also bound in art picture boards cloth back. 5/-

—— More Monarchs of Merry England. Henry VII. to Edward VII. By Roland Carse. With 20 full-page Coloured Pictures by W. Heath Robinson. 128 pages, bound in full cloth. 6/-

Also bound in picture boards, cloth back. 5/-

—— The Monarchs of Merry England. In Four Parts, each containing 10 full-page Coloured Illustrations by W. Heath Robinson. 60 pages, bound in art picture boards, cloth back.

Part	1. William I. to Henry III.	2/6
,,	2. Edward I. to Richard III.	2/6
,,	3. Henry VII. to Elizabeth.	2/6
,,	4. James I. to Edward VII.	2/6

CESARESCO. Lombard Studies. By Countess Evelyn Martinengo Cesaresco Photogravure Frontispiece, and many other Illustrations Demy 8vo, cloth.   16/-

CHURCH. Carthage; or, the Empire of Africa By Professor Alfred J Church, M A Eighth Edition With the Collaboration of Arthur Gilman, M.A. With 43 Illustrations and Maps (Story of the Nations Vol 4) Large cr 8vo, cloth   5/-

—— **Early Britain.** By Professor Alfred J. Church, M.A., Author of "Carthage," &c Sixth Impression. With 57 Illustrations and Maps (Story of the Nations Vol 21) Large cr 8vo, cloth.   5/-

CLAYDEN. England Under the Coalition: The Political History of England and Ireland from 1885 to 1892 By P W Clayden Small demy 8vo, cloth   12/-

CLERIGH History of Ireland to the Coming of Henry II By Arthur Ua Clerigh, M A, K C Demy 8vo, cloth   net 10/6

COLERIDGE The Story of a Devonshire House. By Lord Coleridge, K.C Illustrated. Demy 8vo, cloth.   net 15/-

COPINGER. The Manors of Suffolk. Notes on their History and Devolution and their Several Lords. The Hundreds of Babergh and Blackbourn By W. A. Copinger, LL D, F S A, F R S A Illustrated. Folio, cloth   net 21/-

CRICHFIELD The Rise and Progress of the South American Republics. By George W. Crichfield. Illustrated 2 vols Royal 8vo, cloth.   net 25/-

DAVIDS Buddhist India By T. W Rhys Davids, LL D, Ph D. With 57 Illustrations and Maps. (Story of the Nations Vol. 61.) Large cr 8vo, cloth.   5/-

DAVIS The Patriot Parliament of 1689, with its Statutes, Votes and Proceedings. By Thomas Davis Edited by Ch G Duffy Third Edition. (New Irish Library Vol. 1) Small cr 8vo
                              Paper covers, 1/- ; cloth   2/-

DIEULAFOY. David the King An Historical Inquiry By Marcel Auguste Dieulafoy. (Membre de l'Institut) Translated by Lucy Hotz Small demy 8vo, cloth   net 7/6

DODGE. From Squire to Prince: Being the Rise of the House of Aiksena By Walter Phelps Dodge Illustrated Demy 8vo, cloth 10/3

DOUGLAS China. By Prof Robert K Douglas. Third Edition. With a new preface and a chapter on recent events. With 51 Illustrations and a Map (Story of the Nations Vol 51) Large cr 8vo, cloth   5/-

DUFFY (B). The Tuscan Republics (Florence, Siena, Pisa, and Lucca) with Genoa. By Bella Duffy. With 40 Illustrations and Maps (Story of the Nations Vol. 32) Large cr. 8vo, cloth   5/-
Also Tourist Edition in Baedeker Binding   5/-

DUFFY (Ch. G.) Young Ireland : A Fragment of Irish History By the Hon Sir Charles Gavan Duffy. Illustrated. Two Parts, in stiff wrapper   each 2/-
In one Volume, demy 8vo, cloth   5/-

EDWARDS. A Short History of Wales By Owen M. Edwards, Lecturer on Modern History at Lincoln College, Oxford. With Maps Cr 8vo, cloth   2/-

—— **Wales.** By Owen M. Edwards. With 47 Illustrations and 7 Maps. (Story of the Nations Vol 56) Large cr 8vo, cloth   5/-

ESCOTT. Society in the Country House Anecdotal Records of Six Centuries By T H S Escott, Author of "King Edward and His Court," &c With Photogravure Frontispiece Demy 8vo, cloth   16/-

FITZGERALD. Lady Jean : The Romance of the Great Douglas Cause. By Percy Fitzgerald, F.S.A. With Photogravure Frontispiece and other Illustrations. Demy 8vo, cloth. net 12/-

FORREST. The Development of Western Civilization. By J. Dorsey Forrest. Large cr. 8vo, cloth. net 9/-

FOSTER. The Stuarts. Being Outlines of the Personal History of the Family from James V. to Prince Charles Edward. By J. J. Foster, F.S.A. Illustrated with 30 full-page Photogravure Plates. Cloth. net 25/-

FRAZER. British India. By R. W. Frazer, LL.D. Third Edition. With 30 Illustrations and Maps. (Story of the Nations. Vol. 46.) Large cr. 8vo, cloth. 5/-

FREEMAN. Sicily : Phœnician, Greek, and Roman. By Prof. Edward A. Freeman, M.A., Hon. D.C.L., LL.D., Oxford. Third Edition. With 45 Illustrations. (Story of the Nations. Vol. 31.) Large cr. 8vo, cloth. 5/-
Also Tourist Edition in Baedeker Binding. 5/-

GANNON. A Review of Irish History in Relation to the Social Development of Ireland. By John P. Gannon. 268 pp., cr. 8vo, green buckram. 6/-

GARDNER. A History of Jamaica. From its discovery by Christopher Columbus to the year 1872. By W. J. Gardner. Large cr. 8vo. net 7/6

GILMAN. Rome : From the Earliest Times to the End of the Republic. By Arthur Gilman, M.A. Third Edition. With 43 Illustrations and Maps. (Story of the Nations. Vol. 1.) Large cr. 8vo, cloth. 5/-

—— The Saracens : From the Earliest Times to the Fall of Bagdad. By Arthur Gilman, M.A. Fourth Edition. With 57 Illustrations and Maps. (Story of the Nations. Vol. 9.) Large cr. 8vo, cloth. 5/-

GOMME. The Governance of London. Studies of the place of London in English Institutions. By G. Lawrence Gomme, F.S.A. With Maps. Demy 8vo, cloth. net 15/-

GORDON. The Old Bailey and Newgate. By Charles Gordon. With about 100 Illustrations and a Frontispiece in tint. Med. 8vo, cloth. net 21/-

—— Old Time Aldwych, Kingsway, and Neighbourhood. By Charles Gordon. Fully Illustrated and with Map. Medium 8vo, cloth, net 21/-
Popular Edition. Fully illustrated and with Map. Medium 8vo, cloth. net 7/6

GRAY. The Buried City of Kenfig. By Thomas Gray. With a Map and Illustrations. Demy 8vo, cloth. net 10/6

GRIFFITHS. Famous British Regiments. By Major Arthur Griffiths. Fully Illustrated. Cr. 8vo, cloth gilt. 2/6

HALE. Mexico. By Susan Hale. Third Impression. With 47 Illustrations and Maps. (Story of the Nations. Vol. 27.) Large cr. 8vo, cloth 5/-

HANNAH. A Brief History of Eastern Asia. By I. C. Hannah, M.A. Cr. 8vo, cloth. 7/6

HASEN. Contemporary American Opinion of the French Revolution. By Charles Downer Hasen. Demy 8vo, cloth. net 8/6

HERTZ. English Public Opinion after the Restoration. By Gerald Berkeley Hertz. Cr. 8vo, cloth. net 3/6

HOLYOAKE (G.T.). History of Co-operation. See under " Politics."

HOSMER. The Jews : In Ancient, Mediæval, and Modern Times. By Prof. James K. Hosmer. Seventh Edition. With 37 Illustrations and Maps. (Story of the Nations. Vol. 2.) Large cr. 8vo, cloth. 5/-

HOUGHTON. Hebrew Life and Thought. Being Interpretative Studies in the Literature of Israel. By Louis Seymore Houghton. Large cr. 8vo, cloth. net 6/6

HOWARD. A History of Matrimonial Institutions. By George Elliott Howard, Ph.D., University of Chicago. 3 vols. Super royal 8vo.   net 42/-

HUG and STEAD. Switzerland. By Lina Hug and Richard Stead, B.A. Third Impression. With over 54 Illustrations, Maps, &c. (Story of the Nations. Vol. 26.) Large cr. 8vo, cloth.   5/-
Also Tourist Edition in Baedeker Binding.   5/-

HUME. Modern Spain (1878-1898). By Martin A. S. Hume, F.R.H.S., Second Impression. With 37 Illustrations and a Map. (Story of the Nations. Vol. 53.) Large cr. 8vo, cloth.   5/-

HUNGARY. Its People, Places and Politics. The Journey of the Eighty Club in 1906. With 60 Illustrations. Demy 8vo, cloth.   10/6

JAMAICA (A History of). See "Gardner."

JAMES. The Siege of Port Arthur. Records of an Eye-Witness. By David H. James, Special War Correspondent for the London *Daily Telegraph* with the Third Japanese Army. With 4 Maps and Plans and 16 Illustrations. Demy 8vo, cloth.   net 10/6

JANE. The Coming of Parliament. (England from 1350 to 1660.) By L. Cecil Jane. With 51 Illustrations and 1 Map. (Story of the Nations. Vol. 63.) Large cr. 8vo, cloth.   5/-

JENKS. Parliamentary England. The Evolution of the Cabinet System. By Edward Jenks, M.A. With 47 Illustrations. (Story of the Nations. Vol. 60.) Large cr. 8vo, cloth.   5/-

JESSOPP. Arcady: for Better, for Worse. By Augustus Jessopp, D.D. Seventh Edition. Cr. 8vo, limp cloth, silk sewn.   3/6

—— **Before the Great Pillage,** with other Miscellanies. By Augustus Jessopp, D.D., Cr. 8vo, cloth.   7/6
New Cheap Edition, cr. 8vo, cloth.   3/6

—— **The Coming of the Friars,** and other Mediæval Sketches. By Augustus Jessopp, D.D. Cr. 8vo, limp cloth, silk sewn.   3/6

—— **Frivola, Simon Ryan and other Papers.** By Augustus Jessopp, D.D. Cr. 8vo, limp cloth.   3/6

—— **One Generation of a Norfolk House.** A contribution to Elizabethan History. By Augustus Jessopp, D.D. Large cr. 8vo, cloth.   7/6

—— **Random Roaming,** and other Papers. With Portrait. By Augustus Jessopp, D.D. Cr. 8vo, limp cloth, silk sewn.   3/6

—— **Studies by a Recluse:** In Cloister, Town, and Country. By Augustus Jessopp, D.D. Cr. 8vo, limp cloth, silk sewn.   3/6

—— **The Trials of a Country Parson:** Some Fugitive Papers. By Augustus Jessopp, D.D. Cr. 8vo, limp cloth, silk sewn.   3/6

JEWETT. The Story of the Normans. Told Chiefly in Relation to their Conquest of England. By Sarah Orne Jewett. Third Impression. With 35 Illustrations and Maps. (Story of the Nations. Vol. 29.) Large cr. 8vo, cloth.   5/-

JOHNSON and BUEL. Battles and Leaders of the American Civil War. By Robert U. Johnson and Clarence C. Buel. An Authoritative History written by Distinguished Participants on both sides, and Edited by the above. Four volumes, royal 8vo, elegantly bound. Fully Illustrated.   105/-

JONES (David Brynmor). See "Welsh People."

JONES (H. S.) The Roman Empire, B.C. 29—A.D. 476. By H. Stuart Jones, M.A. With a Map and many Illustrations. (Story of the Nations. Vol. 65.) Large cr. 8vo, cloth.   5/-

JUSSERAND. English Wayfaring Life in the Middle Ages (XIVth Century). By J. J. Jusserand, Conseiller d'Ambassade. Translated from the French by Lucy A. Toulmin Smith. With over 60 Illustrations. Large cr. 8vo, cloth. 7/6
Also in Unwin's Half-crown Standard Library. 1 vol. Cloth. net 2/6

—— A French Ambassador at the Court of Charles II., Le Comte de Cominges. From his unpublished Correspondence. By J. J. Jusserand, Conseiller d'Ambassade. Second Edition. Large cr. 8vo, cloth. 7/6

—— The Romance of a King's Life. By J. J. Jusserand. With Illustrations. Fcap. 8vo, cloth. 6/-

LANE-POOLE. The Barbary Corsairs. By Stanley Lane-Poole. With Additions by J. D. J. Kelly. Fourth Edition. With 39 Illustrations and Maps. (Story of the Nations. Vol. 22.) Large cr. 8vo, cloth. 5/-

—— Mediæval India under Mohammedan Rule (A.D. 712-1764). By Stanley Lane-Poole. With 59 Illustrations. (Story of the Nations. Vol. 59.) Large cr. 8vo, cloth. 5/-

—— The Moors in Spain. By Stanley Lane-Poole. With Collaboration of Arthur Gilman, M.A. Eighth Edition. With 29 Illustrations and Maps. (Story of the Nations. Vol. 6.) Large cr. 8vo, cloth. 5/-

—— Turkey. By Stanley Lane-Poole. Assisted by E. J. W. Gibb and Arthur Gilman. New Edition. With a new chapter on recent events. (1908.) With 43 Illustrations, Maps, &c. (Story of the Nations. Vol. 14.) Large cr. 8vo, cloth. 5/-

LATANE. The Diplomatic Relations of the United States and Spanish America. By John H. Latane. Large cr. 8vo, cloth. net 6/6

LAWLESS. Ireland. By the Hon. Emily Lawless. Seventh Impression. With some Addition by Mrs. Arthur Bronson. With 58 Illustrations and Maps. (Story of the Nations. Vol. 10.) Large cr. 8vo, cloth. 5/-

LEBON. Modern France (1789-1895). By André Lebon. With 26 Illustrations and a Chronological Chart of the Literary, Artistic, and Scientific Movement in Contemporary France. (Story of the Nations. Vol. 47.) Large cr. 8vo, cloth. 5/-

LEE. Studies in the Eighteenth Century in Italy. By Vernon Lee. New Edition, with a new Preface, a Photogravure Frontispiece, and 40 other Illustrations selected by Dr. Guido Biagi, of the Laurentian Library, Florence. Super royal 8vo, half-bound. net 21/-

LEYDS. The First Annexation of the Transvaal. By W. J. Leyds, LL.D., formerly State Secretary of the South African Republic. Demy 8vo, cloth. net 21/-

LILLY. Renaissance Types. By W. S. Lilly. Demy 8vo, cloth. 16/-

LITTLE. Mediæval Wales, Chiefly in the Twelfth and Thirteenth Centuries. By A. G. Little, M.A., F.R.Hist.S. With Maps and Plans. Cr. 8vo, cloth. net 2/6

LONERGAN. Forty Years of Paris. By W. F. Lonergan. With 32 Portraits of Leading Frenchmen. Demy 8vo, cloth. net 10/6

McCARTHY. Modern England (Vol. I.). Before the Reform Bill. By Justin McCarthy, M.P. Author of " The History of Our Own Times," &c. With 31 Illustrations. (Story of the Nations. Vol. 50.) Large cr. 8vo, cloth. 5/-

—— Modern England (Vol. II.). From the Reform Bill to the Present Time. By Justin McCarthy, M.P. Second Edition. With 46 Illustrations. (Story of the Nations. Vol. 52.) Large cr. 8vo, cloth. 5/-

MACKINTOSH. Scotland : From the Earliest Times to the Present Day. By John Mackintosh, LL.D., Author of "History of Civilisation in Scotland," &c. Fifth Impression. With 60 Illustrations and Maps. (Story of the Nations. Vol. 25.) Large cr. 8vo, cloth.   5/-

MAHAFFY. Alexander's Empire. By John Pentland Mahaffy, D.D. With Collaboration of Arthur Gilman, M.A. With 43 Illustrations and Maps. (Story of the Nations. Vol. 5.) Eighth Impression. Large cr. 8vo, cloth.   5/-

—— **An Epoch in Irish History :** Trinity College, Dublin, Its History and Fortunes (1591-1660). By J. P. Mahaffy, D.D., Mus. Doc. Dublin ; Hon. D.C.L., Oxon. ; sometime Professor of Ancient History in the University of Dublin. Demy 8vo, cloth.   16/-
Cheap Edition. Demy 8vo, cloth.   net   7/6

—— **The Particular Book of Trinity College, Dublin.** A facsimile in collotype of the original copy. Edited by J. P. Mahaffy, D.D. A Companion Volume to "An Epoch in Irish History." Demy 4to.   net   63/-

—— **The Progress of Hellenism in Alexander's Empire.** By John Pentland Mahaffy, D.D. Large cr. 8vo, cloth.   net   5/-

—— **The Silver Age of the Greek World.** By J. P. Mahaffy. Large cr. 8vo, cloth.   net   13/6

MARIO. The Birth of Modern Italy. The Posthumous Papers of Jessie White Mario. Edited with Introduction, Notes, and Epilogue, by the Duke Litta-Visconti-Aresc. Illustrated. Demy 8vo, cloth. net   12/6

MASPERO. New Light on Ancient Egypt. By G. Maspero, Director-General of the Service of Antiquities in Egypt. Translated by Elizabeth Lee. Illustrated. Demy 8vo, cloth.   net   12/6

MASSEY. Ancient Egypt, the Light of the World. A Work of reclamation and Restitution in Twelve Books. By Gerald Massey. With Diagrams, 2 vols. Super royal 8vo, cloth.   net   42/-

MASSON. Mediæval France : From the Reign of Hugues Capet to the Beginning of the Sixteenth Century. By Gustave Masson, B.A. Fifth Edition. With 48 Illustrations and Maps. (Story of the Nations. Vol. 16.) Large cr. 8vo, cloth.   5/-

MAURICE. Bohemia : From the Earliest Times to the Fall of National Independence in 1620 ; with a Short Summary of later Events. By C. Edmund Maurice. Second Impression. With 41 Illustrations and Maps. (Story of the Nations. Vol. 43.) Large cr. 8vo, cloth.   5/-

MILFORD. Haileybury College. By Rev. L. S. Milford. Illustrated.   net   7/6

MILLER. The Balkans : Roumania, Bulgaria, Servia and Montenegro. By William Miller, M.A., Oxon. New Edition, with a new chapter containing their History from 1896 to 1908. With 39 Illustrations and Maps. (Story of the Nations. Vol. 44.) Large cr. 8vo, cloth.   5/-

—— **Mediæval Rome :** From Hildebrand to Clement VIII. 1073-1535. By William Miller, M.A. With 35 Illustrations. (Story of the Nations. Vol. 57.) Large cr. 8vo, cloth.   5/-

MONARCH SERIES, THE.
Humorous Rhymes of Historical Times. By Roland Carse. With Illustrations in colour and black and white by W. Heath Robinson. Size 8½ in. by 11 in. (For titles of volumes see under "Carse.")

MOORE. The Story of the Isle of Man. By A. W. Moore, M.A. Illustrated. Cr. 8vo, cloth.   1/-

MORFILL. Poland. By W R Morfill, M A, Professor of Russian and
Slavonic Languages in the University of Oxford Third Impression
With 50 Illustrations and Maps (Story of the Nations Vol 33)
Large cr 8vo, cloth   5/-

—— **Russia.** By W. R. Morfill, M A. Fourth Edition. With 60 Illustrations and Maps (Story of the Nations Vol 23) Large cr 8vo, cloth   5/-
War Edition Brought up to date and with Supplementary Chapters
on the Present Situation, and Large War Map. Cloth.   5/-

MORRISON The Jews Under Roman Rule By W. D Morrison
Second Impression With 61 Illustrations and Maps (Story of the
Nations Vol. 24.) Large cr. 8vo, cloth.   5/-

MURRAY Japan. By David Murray, Ph D LL D, late Adviser to
the Japanese Minister of Education. Third Edition With 35
Illustrations and Maps (Story of the Nations Vol 37) Large
cr 8vo, cloth.   5/-
War Edition, with New Chapter by Joseph H Longford, formerly
British Consul at Nagasaki, and Large War Map. Cloth.   5/-

NEEDHAM Somerset House, Past and Present. By Raymond
Needham and Alexander Webster With Photogravure Frontispiece and many Illustrations Demy 8vo, cloth.   21/-

NEGRI Julian the Apostate A Historical Study By Gaetano Negri.
Translated by the Duchess Litta Visconti Arese. With an Introduction by Professor Pasquale Villari. Illustrated 2 vols Demy
8vo, cloth   net 21/-

O'BRIEN Irish Memories. By R. Barry O'Brien, Author of " The
Life of Charles Stuart Parnell." With Plans. Cr 8vo, cloth net   3/6

O CONNOR. The Parnell Movement · Being the History of the Irish
Question from the Death of O'Connell to the Suicide of Pigott. By
T. P. O'Connor, M P Cr 8vo. Paper covers, 1/- , cloth boards   2/-

OMAN. The Byzantine Empire By C W C Oman, M A , F S A ,
Oxford Third Edition With 44 Illustrations and Maps (Story
of the Nations Vol 30) Large cr 8vo, cloth.   5/-

ORSI. Modern Italy (1748-1898) By Pietro Orsi. Professor of
History in the R. Liceo Foscarini, Venice Translated by Mary
Alice Vialls With over 40 Illustrations and Maps (Story of the
Nations Vol. 54) Large cr. 8vo, cloth.   5/-

PAIS Ancient Italy Historical and Geographical Investigations in
Central Italy, Magna Græcia, Sicily, and Sardinia By Ettore Pais,
Professor in the University of Rome, formerly Director of the
Naples Museum Translated by C. D Curtis Demy 8vo, cloth net   21/-

**Patriot Parliament of 1689, with its Statutes, Votes and Pro-
ceedings, The** (New Irish Library. Vol. 1) See under
' Thomas Davis "

POTT. A Sketch of Chinese History. By the Rev F. L. Hawks Pott,
D D Demy 8vo, cloth   net 6/-

PUSEY. The Past History of Ireland. By S. E. Bouverie-Pusey
Small cr. 8vo. Paper covers   1/-

RAGOZIN Assyria: From the Rise of the Empire to the Fall of
Nineveh (Continued from "Chaldea.") By Zénaïde A Ragozin
Sixth Edition With 81 Illustrations and Maps (Story of the
Nations Vol 13) Large cr 8vo, cloth   5/-

—— **Chaldea .** From the Earliest Times to the Rise of Assyria Treated
as a General Introduction to the Study of Ancient History. By
Zénaïde A. Ragozin. Seventh Impression With 80 Illustrations
and Maps (Story of the Nations Vol 11) Large cr 8vo, cloth   5/-

RAGOZIN. Media, Babylon, and Persia : From the Fall of Nineveh to the Persian War. Including a Study of the Zend-Avesta, or Religion of Zoroaster. By Zénaïde A. Ragozin. Fourth Edition. With 71 Illustrations and Maps. (Story of the Nations. Vol. 19.) Large cr. 8vo, cloth.　　　　　　　　　　5/-

—— Vedic India. As Embodied Principally in the Rig-Veda. By Zénaïde A. Ragozin. Third Edition. With 36 Illustrations and Maps. (Story of the Nations. Vol. 41.) Large cr. 8vo, cloth.　5/-

RAWLINSON. Ancient Egypt. By Prof. George Rawlinson, M.A. Tenth Edition. With 50 Illustrations and Maps. (Story of the Nations. Vol. 7.) Large cr. 8vo, cloth.　　　　　　　5/-

—— Parthia. By Prof. George Rawlinson, M.A. Third Impression. With 48 Illustrations and Maps. (Story of the Nations. Vol. 34.) Large cr. 8vo, cloth.　　　　　　　　　　　　5/-

—— Phœnicia. By Prof. George Rawlinson, M.A. Third Edition. With 47 Illustrations and Maps. (Story of the Nations. Vol. 18.) Large cr. 8vo, cloth.　　　　　　　　　　　　5/-

RHYS (John). See "Welsh People."

RODWAY. The West Indies and the Spanish Main. By James Rodway, F.L.S. Third Impression. With 48 Illustrations and Maps. (Story of the Nations. Vol. 42.) Large cr. 8vo, cloth.　5/-

ROGERS. Holland. By Prof. James E. Thorold Rogers. Fifth Edition. With 57 Illustrations and Maps. (Story of the Nations. Vol. 15.) Large cr. 8vo, cloth.　　　　　　　　　　　5/-

—— The Industrial and Commercial History of England. By Prof. Thorold Rogers. 2 vols. (Reformer's Bookshelf.) Large cr. 8vo, cloth.　　　　　　　　　　　　　　　　7/-

ROWBOTHAM. Tales from Plutarch. By F. Jameson Rowbotham. Fully Illustrated. Cr. 8vo, cloth.　　　　　　　　　5/-

SCAIFE. The War to Date (to Majuba Day.) By A. H. Scaife. Illustrated. Cr. 8vo, cloth.　　　　　　　　　　3/6

SEIGNOBOS. History of Ancient Civilization. By Charles Seignobos, Doctor of Letters of the University of Paris. Large cr 8vo, cloth. net 5/-

—— History of Mediæval Civilization and of Modern to the End of the Seventeenth Century. Large cr. 8vo, cloth.　　　net 5/-

—— History of Contemporary Civilization.　　　　net 5/-

SERGEANT. The Franks. From their Origin as a Confederacy to the Establishment of the Kingdom of France and the German Empire. By Lewis Sergeant. Second Edition. With 40 Illustrations and Maps. (Story of the Nations. Vol. 48.) Large cr. 8vo, cloth.　　　　　　　　　　　　　　　　5/-

SHUCKBURGH. Augustus. The Life and Times of the Founder of the Roman Empire (B.C. 63—A.D. 14.) By E. S. Shuckburgh Demy 8vo, cloth gilt. Illustrated.　　　　　　　16/-
Popular Edition. Illustrated. Large cr. 8vo, cloth.　　net 5/-
Also in Unwin's Half-Crown Standard Library. One vol., cloth. net 2/6

—— The Story of Greece, from the Coming of the Hellenes to A.D. 14. By E. S. Shuckburgh. With 2 Maps and about 70 Illustrations. (Story of the Nations. Vol. 64.) Large cr. 8vo, cloth.　5/-

THE SOUTH AMERICAN SERIES. See under "Geography."

STANLEY. Before and After Waterloo. By Edward Stanley, sometime Bishop of Norwich. Edited by J. H. Adeane and Maud Grenfell. With 5 Photogravures and 5 Coloured Plates, and 27 other Illustrations. Medium 8vo, cloth.　　　　net 18/-

STEPHENS. Portugal. By H. Morse Stephens, M.A., Oxford. New Edition with a new Chapter by Major Martin Hume and 5 new illustrations. With 44 Illustrations and Maps. (Story of the Nations. Vol. 28.) Large cr. 8vo, cloth.　　　　　　5/-

STORY OF THE NATIONS, THE. The volumes occupy about 400 pages each, and contain respectively, besides an Index and Coloured Map, a great many Illustrations. The size is large cr. 8vo. There are published now (Autumn, 1908) 65 volumes, which are to be had in the following bindings :—

Ordinary Edition. Fancy cloth, gold lettered.	**5/-**
Half morocco, gilt.	net **10/6**
Subscription Edition. Special cloth binding. On Subscription only.	

Subscription Edition.—A set of 65 volumes, newly printed on specially prepared paper, and containing 2,500 full-page and other Illustrations. Now offered cloth bound for a preliminary payment of 15s., and 18 subsequent monthly payments of 10s. each, or a cash payment of £9 5s. 3d. ; or bound in half morocco, for a preliminary payment of 25s. and 17 further payments of 20s. each, or a cash payment of £17 7s. Delivered free in the London Postal district.

LIST OF VOLUMES.

[*For full Titles see under Authors' names.*]

(1) **Rome :** From the Earliest Times to the End of the Republic. By Arthur Gilman, M.A.

(2) **The Jews.** By Prof. James K. Hosmer.

(3) **Germany.** By S. Baring-Gould, M.A.

(4) **Carthage.** By Professor Alfred J. Church, M.A.

(5) **Alexander's Empire.** By John Pentland Mahaffy, D.D.

(6) **The Moors in Spain.** By Stanley Lane-Poole.

(7) **Ancient Egypt.** By Prof. George Rawlinson, M.A.

(8) **Hungary.** By Professor Arminius Vambéry.

(9) **The Saracens :** From the Earliest Times to the Fall of Bagdad. By Arthur Gilman, M.A.

(10) **Ireland.** By the Hon. Emily Lawless.

(11) **Chaldea:** From the Earliest Times to the Rise of Assyria. By Zénaïde A. Ragozin.

(12) **The Goths.** By Henry Bradley.

(13) **Assyria :** From the Rise of the Empire to the Fall of Nineveh. (Continued from "Chaldea.") By Zénaïde A. Ragozin.

(14) **Turkey.** By Stanley Lane-Poole.

(15) **Holland.** By Prof. J. E. Thorold Rogers.

(16) **Mediæval France.** By Gustave Masson, B.A.

(17) **Persia.** By S. G. W. Benjamin.

(18) **Phœnicia.** By Prof. George Rawlinson, M.A.

(19) **Media, Babylon and Persia :** From the Fall of Nineveh to the Persian War. By Zénaïde A. Ragozin.

(20) **The Hansa Towns.** By Helen Zimmern.

(21) **Early Britain.** By Prof. Alfred J. Church, M.A.

(22) **The Barbary Corsairs.** By Stanley Lane-Poole.

(23) **Russia.** By W. R. Morfill, M.A.

(24) **The Jews under Roman Rule.** By W. D. Morrison.

(25) **Scotland.** By John Mackintosh, LL.D.

(26) **Switzerland.** By Lina Hug and R. Stead.

(27) **Mexico.** By Susan Hale.

(28) **Portugal.** By H. Morse Stephens, M.A.

(29) **The Normans.** By Sarah Orne Jewett.

(30) **The Byzantine Empire.** By C. W. C. Oman, M.A.

(31) **Sicily:** Phœnician, Greek, and Roman. By Prof. E. A. Freeman.

STORY OF THE NATIONS, THE.—*continued.*

(32) **The Tuscan Republics, with Genoa.** By Bella Duffy.

(33) **Poland.** By W. R. Morfill.

(34) **Parthia.** By Prof. Geo. Rawlinson.

(35) **The Australian Commonwealth.** (New South Wales, Tasmania, Western Australia, South Australia, Victoria, Queensland, New Zealand.) By Greville Tregarthen.

(36) **Spain:** Being a Summary of Spanish History from the Moorish Conquest to the Fall of Granada (711-1492 A.D.). By Henry Edward Watts.

(37) **Japan.** By David Murray, Ph.D., LL.D.

(38) **South Africa.** By George McCall Theal.

(39) **Venice.** By Alethea Wiel.

(40) **The Crusades:** The Story of the Latin Kingdom of Jerusalem. By T. A. Archer and C. L. Kingsford.

(41) **Vedic India.** By Zénaïde A. Ragozin.

(42) **The West Indies and the Spanish Main.** By James Rodway, F.L.S.

(43) **Bohemia:** From the Earliest Times to the Fall of National Independence in 1620; with a Short Summary of later Events. By C. Edmund Maurice.

(44) **The Balkans.** By W. Miller, M.A.

(45) **Canada.** By Sir John Bourinot, C.M.G.

(46) **British India.** By R. W. Frazer, LL.D.

(47) **Modern France.** By André Lebon.

(48) **The Franks.** By Lewis Sergeant.

(49) **Austria.** By Sidney Whitman.

(50) **Modern England before the Reform Bill.** By Justin McCarthy.

(51) **China.** By Prof. R. K. Douglas.

(52) **Modern England under Queen Victoria.** By Justin McCarthy.

(53) **Modern Spain, 1878-1898.** By Martin A. S. Hume.

(54) **Modern Italy, 1748-1898.** By Prof. Pietro Orsi.

(55) **Norway.** By Professor Hjalmar H. Boyesen.

(56) **Wales.** By Owen Edwards.

(57) **Mediæval Rome, 1073-1535.** By William Miller.

(58) **The Papal Monarchy:** From Gregory the Great to Boniface VIII. By William Barry, D.D.

(59) **Mediæval India under Mohammedan Rule.** By Stanley Lane-Poole.

(60) **Parliamentary England:** From 1660-1832. By Edward Jenks.

(61) **Buddhist India.** By T. W. Rhy Davids.

(62) **Mediæval England.** By Mary Bateson.

(63) **The Coming of Parliament.** (England 1350-1660.) By L. Cecil Jane.

(64) **The Story of Greece** (from the Earliest Times to A.D. 14.) By E. S. Shuckburgh.

(65) **The Story of the Roman Empire** (B.C. 29 to A.D. 476). By H. Stuart Jones.

THEAL. **The Beginning of South African History.** By Dr. George McCall Theal. With Maps and Illustrations. Demy 8vo, cloth. 16/-

—— **A Little History of South Africa.** By Dr. George McCall Theal. Third Edition. Cr. 8vo. 1/6

—— **South Africa.** (The Cape Colony, Natal, Orange Free State, South African Republic, Rhodesia, and all other Territories south of the Zambesi.) By Dr. George McCall Theal. D.Lit., LL.D. Ninth Impression (Sixth Edition). With 39 Illustrations and Maps. (Story of the Nations. Vol. 38.) Large cr. 8vo, cloth. 5/-

THOMAS. Roman Life under the Cæsars. By Emile Thomas. Numerous Illustrations. Small demy 8vo, cloth. 7/6

TREGARTHEN. The Australian Commonwealth. (New South Wales, Tasmania, Western Australia, South Australia, Victoria, Queensland, New Zealand.) By Greville Tregarthen. Fourth Impression. With 36 Illustrations and Maps. (Story of the Nations. Vol. 35.) Large cr. 8vo, cloth. 5/-

TROWBRIDGE. Court Beauties of Old Whitehall. By W. R. H. Trowbridge. With a Photogravure Frontispiece and many other Illustrations. Demy 8vo, cloth. net 15/-

—— **Mirabeau, the Demi-God.** Being the True and Romantic Story of his Life and Adventures. By W. R. H. Trowbridge. With a Photogravure Frontispiece and 32 other Illustrations. Demy 8vo, cloth. net 15/-

—— **Seven Splendid Sinners.** By W. R. H. Trowbridge. With a Photogravure Frontispiece and other Illustrations. Demy 8vo, cloth. net 15/-

TURQUAN. The Sisters of Napoleon. Edited from the French of Joseph Turquan by W. R. H. Trowbridge. Illustrated. Demy 8vo, cloth. net 16/-

VAMBÉRY. Hungary : In Ancient, Mediæval, and Modern Times. By Prof. Arminius Vambéry. With Collaboration of Louis Heilprin. Seventh Edition. With 47 Illustrations and Maps. (Story of the Nations. Vol. 8.) Large cr. 8vo, cloth. 5/-

VILLARI. The Barbarian Invasions of Italy. By Prof. Pasquale Villari. Translated by Linda Villari. With Frontispiece and Maps. 2 vols. Demy 8vo. 32/-

—— **The History of Florence.** (The First Two Centuries of Florentine History.) By Prof. Pasquale Villari. Translated by Linda Villari. Illustrated. Demy 8vo, cloth. 7/6

Also in Unwin's Half-Crown Standard Library. 1 vol., cloth. net 2/6

—— **Studies Historical and Critical.** By Professor Pasquale Villari, Author of "Girolamo Savonarola," &c. With 7 Photogravure Plates. Demy 8vo, cloth. net 15/-

VOIGT. Fifty Years of the History of the Republic in South Africa (1795-1845). By J. C. Voigt, M.D. With Coloured Maps, Sketches, and Diagrams. Maps and Plans. 2 vols. Demy 8vo. net 25/-

WATTS. Spain : Being a Summary of Spanish History from the Moorish Conquest to the Fall of Granada (711-1492, A.D.). By Henry Edward Watts. Third Edition. With 36 Illustrations and Maps. (Story of the Nations. Vol. 36.) Large cr. 8vo, cloth. 5/-

WEBSTER (Alexander). See "Needham."

WELSH PEOPLE, THE : Their Origin, Language, and History. Being Extracts from the Reports of the Royal Commission on Land in Wales and Monmouthshire. Edited, with Additions, Notes and Appendices, by John Rhys, Principal of Jesus College, and Professor of Celtic in the University of Oxford, and David Brynmor Jones, K.C., M.P. Second Edition, Revised. Demy 8vo, cloth. 16/-
Also a cheap Edition. Large cr. 8vo, cloth. net 5/-

WHITMAN. Austria. By Sidney Whitman. With the Collaboration of J. R. McIlraith. Third Edition. With 35 Illustrations and a Map. (Story of the Nations. Vol. 49.) Large cr. 8vo, cloth. 5/-

WHITTY. St. Stephen's in the Firties. By E. M. Whitty. With an
Introduction by Justin McCarthy. And Notes by H. M. Williams.
With Frontispiece. Demy 8vo, cloth.   net 10/6
   Also in Reformer's Bookshelf. Large cr. 8vo, cloth.   3/6
WIEL. Venice. By Alethea Wiel. Fourth Edition. With 61 Illustra-
tions and Maps. (Story of the Nations. Vol. 39.) Large cr. 8vo,
cloth.   5/-
   Also Tourist Edition in Baedeker Binding.   5/-
WILKINSON. The Personal Story of the Upper House. See under
"Biography."
ZIMMERN. The Hansa Towns. By Helen Zimmern. Third Edition.
With 51 Illustrations and Maps. (Story of the Nations. Vol. 20.)
Large cr. 8vo. cloth.   5/-
—— Heroic Tales. Retold from Firdusi the Persian. By Helen
Zimmern. With two etchings by L. Alma-Tadema, R.A., and a
Prefatory Poem by Edmund W. Gosse. Third Edition. Cr, 8vo,
cloth.   5/-
—— Old Tales from Rome. By Alice Zimmern, Author of "Old
Tales from Greece." Cr. 8vo, cloth. Fully illustrated.   5/-

POLITICS, ECONOMICS, FREE TRADE, &c.

ALBRIGHT. The Churches and the Liquor Traffic. By Mrs. W.
A. Albright. Cr. 8vo. paper cover.   net 6d.
ARONSON. The Working of the Workmen's Compensation Act,
1906. By V. R. Aronson, Barrister-at-law. Demy 8vo, cloth. net 15/-
BAMFORD'S Passages in the Life of a Radical. Edited, and with
an Introduction, by Henry Duckley ("Verax"). 2 vols. (Reformer's
Bookshelf.) Large cr. 8vo, cloth.   7/-
BARNETT. Towards Social Reform. By A. S. Barnett, M.A., Canon
of Westminster. Cr. 8vo, cloth.   net 5/-
BENTLEY. The Process of Government. A Study of Social
Pressures. By Arthur F. Bentley. Demy 8vo, cloth.   net 12/6
BLISS (Rev. E. M.). Turkey and the Armenian Atrocities. See
under "History."
BLUNT. Atrocities of Justice under British Rule in Egypt. By
Wilfred Scawen Blunt. Paper cover.   net 1/-
BOWACK. Another View of Industrialism. By William Mitchell
Bowack. Large cr. 8vo, cloth.   net 6/-
BOWEN. The Statutes of Wales. Collected, arranged and edited by
Ivor Bowen, Barrister-at-law, of the South Wales Circuit. Demy
8vo, cloth.   net 21/-
BOWLES. National Finance : An Imminent Peril. By Thomas
Gibson Bowles. Paper cover.   6d.
—— National Finance. In 1908 and after. By Thomas Gibson Bowles.
Paper Boards.   net 1/-
—— The Public Purse and the War Office. By T. Gibson Bowles.
Royal 8.o, paper cover.   net 6d.
BOXALL. The Awakening of a Race. By George E. Boxall. Large
cr. 8vo, cloth.   net 7/6
BRADLAUGH (Charles). A Record of his Life. See under
"Biography."

COX. Mr, Balfour's Pamphlet: A Reply. By Harold Cox. Medium 8vo, paper covers. net **2d.**

—— **The Policy of Free Imports.** By Harold Cox. A Paper read at Liverpool on February 16th, 1903, to the New Century Society. Large cr. 8vo. Paper covers, **1d.** ; cloth, net **6d.**

—— **Protection and Employment.** By Harold Cox, formerly Secretary of the Cobden Club. Paper covers. **6d.**

CROMPTON. Our Criminal Justice. By Henry Crompton. With an Introduction by Sir Kenelm Digby, K.C.B. net **6d.**

DANSON. Economic and Statistical Studies, 1840-1890. By John Towne Danson. With a brief memoir by his daughter, Mary Norman Hill, and an Introduction by E. C. K. Gonner, M.A., Brunner, Professor of Economic Science, Liverpool University. With a Photogravure Frontispiece, 2 other Portraits, and 31 Plates. Small royal 8vo, cloth. net **21/-**

DAVENPORT. Value and Distribution. A Critical and Constructive Study. By Herbert Joseph Davenport, Associate Professor of Political Economy in the University of Chicago. Demy 8vo, cloth. net **15/-**

DAWSON. The Evolution of Modern Germany. See under "Travel."

DEWSNUP. American Railway Organization and Working. Lectures by Prominent Railway Men. Edited by Ernest R. Dewsnup. Large cr. 8vo, cloth. net **9/-**

DIETZEL. Retaliatory Duties. By H. Dietzel. Professor at the University of Bonn. Translated by D. W. Simon, D.D., and W. Osborne Brigstocke, Member of the Unionist Free Trade Club. Cr. 8vo, cloth. net **2/6**

ELIAS. The Political Advertiser. By Frank Elias. Illustrated. Fcap. 4to, paper covers. net **1/-**

ELLIOTT. Corn Law Rhymes and Other Verses. By Ebenezer Elliott. 12mo. Paper covers, **2d.** ; cloth limp **6d.**

ESCOTT. The Story of British Diplomacy : Its Makers and Movements. By T. H. S. Escott, Author of "Society in the Country House," &c., &c. With a Photogravure Frontispiece. Demy 8vo, cloth. **16/-**

Failure of Lord Curzon, The. A Study in Imperialism. An Open Letter to the Earl of Rosebery. By "Twenty-eight Years in India." Cr. 8vo, cloth. net **2/6**

GEBUZA. The Peril in Natal. By Gebuza. Demy 8vo, paper covers. net **3d.**

GOMME. The Governance of London. Studies of the place of London in English Institutions. By G. Lawrence Gomme, F.S.A., Clerk to the London County Council. With Maps. Demy 8vo, cloth. net **15/-**

GOULD. The Modern Chronicles of Froissart. Told and Pictured by Sir F. Carruthers Gould. With special Cover Design, Decorated Title, and 44 Illustrations. Fifth Impression. Fcap. 4to. **3/6**

—— **Froissart in 1902.** Told and Pictured by Sir F. Carruthers Gould. With special Cover Design and Coloured Frontispiece. Fcap. 4to. **3/6** Also a *Fine Edition* (limited to 50 copies) on Japan paper, numbered and signed. net **21/-**

—— **F.C.G.'s Froissart, 1903-1906.** Told and Pictured by Sir F. Carruthers Gould. With special Cover Design, and 50 Illustrations. Fcap. 4to, cloth. net **2/6** Also a *Fine Edition* (limited to 50 copies) on Japan paper, numbered and signed. net **21/-**

See also "Lawson"

GOULD The Gould-en Treasury. With 34 Illustrations by Sir F. Carruthers Gould. Fcap 4to   Paper, net 1/-, cloth, net   2,6

GRANT. Free Food and Free Trade. By Daniel Grant, Ex-M P, Paper covers.   2d.

HALDANE. Army Reform and Other Addresses. By the Right Hon. Richard Burton Haldane, M P Large cr 8vo, cloth   net   7/6

Heart of the Empire, The. Studies in Problems of Modern City Life in England. Large cr. 8vo, cloth.   net   7/6
Cheap Edition, cloth.   net   3,6

HIRST. National Credit and the Sinking Fund. How to make £500,000,000. By Francis W. Hirst Paper covers.   6d.

HOBHOUSE. Democracy and Reaction. By L T. Hobhouse. Cr. 8vo, cloth   5/-
A'so a revised Edition in paper covers.   net   1/-
—— **The Labour Movement** By L. T. Hobhouse, M.A. (Reformer's Bookshelf), large cr. 8vo, cloth   3/6
Also a New and Cheaper Edition. Cr. 8vo, paper covers.   net   1/-

HODGSON To Colonise England. A Plea for a Policy By W B Hodgson, C F G Masterman and Other Writes Edited by A G. Gardiner Cr. 8vo   Paper, net 2/6, cloth, net   3,6

HOGAN. The Gladstone Colony. By James Francis Hogan, M P Demy 8vo, cloth   7/6
Also (Reformer's Bookshelf), cloth.   3/6

HOLYOAKE. Sixty Years of an Agitator's Life George Jacob Holyoake's Autobiography. 2 vols (Reformer's Bookshelf) cloth   7/-
Also n 1 vol (Unwin's Half-Crown Standard Library)   net   2,6
—— **The History of Co-operation.** Its Literature and its Advocates. By G J Holyoake Illustrated 2 vols. Demy 8vo, cloth   net 21/-
Also a Popular Edition in 1 vol Illustrated. Large cr 8vo, cloth.   net   7,6
—— **Bygones Worth Remembering.** See under "Biography."
—— **Public Speaking and Debate.** A Manual for Advocates and Agitators. By George Jacob Holyoake. New Edition Paper covers, net 1/-, cloth, net   2/-

HOWE. The City, the Hope of Democracy By Frederic C Howe, Ph D. Large cr 8vo, cloth   net   7/6
—— **The British City.** By F C. Howe Author of "The City, the Hope of Democracy." Large cr 8vo, cloth.   net   7/6

HOWELL Labour Legislation, Labour Movements, and Labour Leaders By George Howell Demy 8vo, cloth   10/6
Also 2 vols. Large cr. 8vo, cloth. (Reformer's Bookshelf)   7/-

Hungry Forties, The. An Account of Life under the Bread Tax from the Letters of Living Witnesses With an Introduction by Mrs Cobden Unwin Illustrated Large cr 8vo, cloth.   6/-
Also (Reformer's Bookshelf), cloth.   3/6
People's Edition Paper covers.   6d.

JEPHSON. The Sanitary Evolution of London. By Henry Jephson Demy 8vo, cloth.   net   6/-

JERNIGAN China's Business Methods and Policy. By T. R. Jernigan, Ex-Consul-General of the United States of America at Shanghai Demy 8vo, cloth   net 12/-

KING Electoral Reform. An Inquiry into our System of Parliamentary Representation. By Joseph King. Cr. 8vo, cloth.   net   2'6

KITSON. The Cause of Industrial Depression. A Lecture delivered at the New Reform Club. By Arthur Kitson. Paper covers.   6d.

Labour and Protection. Essays by Various Writers. (John Burns, G. J. Holyoake, &c.) Edited by H. W. Massingham. Large cr. 8vo, cloth.   6/-
Also (Reformer's Bookshelf).   3/6

LANE. Patriotism under Three Flags : A Plea for Rationalism in Politics. By Ralph Lane. Cr. 8vo, cloth.   6/-

LATANE. The Diplomatic Relations of the United States and Spanish America. By J. H. Latane, Ph.D. Demy 8vo, cloth. net   6/6

LAWSON. Cartoons in Rhyme and Line. By Sir Wilfrid Lawson, Bart., M.P. Illus. by Sir F. Carruthers Gould. Fcap. 4to, cloth. net   4/6
Edition de Luxe, signed by Author and Artist. Printed on hand-made paper.   net 21/-

LEVASSEUR. The American Workman. By Prof. R. Levasseur. Translated by Thomas S. Adams, and Edited by Theodore Marburg. Demy 8vo, cloth.   net 12/6

LLOYD. The Swiss Democracy. A Study of a Sovereign People. By H. D. Lloyd and John A. Hobson. Large cr. 8vo, cloth.   net 6/-

LOW. The Governance of England. By Sidney Low, B.A., late Lecturer on Modern History, King's College, London. Demy 8vo, cloth.   net 7/6

Cheap Edition. Large cr. 8vo, cloth.   net 3/6

—— The Increase of the Suburbs. By Sidney Low. Cr. 8vo, paper covers.   net 6d.

LUNN. Municipal Lessons from Southern Germany. By Henry S. Lunn, M.D., J.P. With an Introduction by the Rt. Hon. Sir John Gorst, and 7 Illustrations. Medium 8vo, cloth.   2/-

von MACH. The Bulgarian Exarchate : Its History and the Extent of its Authority in Turkey. From the German of Richard von Mach. With a Map. Demy 8vo, cloth.   net 3/6

MACY. Party Organisation and Machinery in the United States. By Jesse Macy, Professor of Political Science at Iowa College. Cr. 8vo, cloth.   net 6/-

McCLELLAND. The Fiscal Problem. With Diagrams. By J. McClelland. Cr. 8vo.   Paper covers, 1/- ; cloth   2/-

MALLET (Sir Louis). See Welby (" Cobden's Work ").

MEAKIN (B.). Model Factories and Villages. Ideal Conditions of Labour and Housing. By Budgett Meakin, Lecturer on Industrial Betterment. With about 200 Illustrations. Large cr. 8vo, cloth.   7/6

MEAKIN (W.). The Life of an Empire. By Walter Meakin, B.A., LL.B. Large cr. 8vo, cloth.   net 6/-

MILYOUKOV. Russia and Its Crisis. By Professor Paul Milyoukov. With 6 Maps. Demy 8vo, cloth.   net 18/6

MOLINARI. The Society of To-Morrow : A Forecast of its Political and Economic Organisation. By G. de Molinari, Membre de l'Institut and Editor of *Le Journal des Économistes*. Translated by P. H. Lee-Warner. With a Prefatory Letter by Frédéric Passy, and an Introduction by Hodgson Pratt. Cr. 8vo, cloth.   6/-

MOREL. Red Rubber. The Story of the Rubber Slave Trade on the Congo. By E. D. Morel. With an Introduction by Sir Harry H. Johnston, G.C.M.G., K.C.B., and a Frontispiece. Cr. 8vo.
    Paper boards, net 2/6 ; cloth, net   3/6
Popular Edition, paper covers.   net   1/-

MORLEY (John). Life of Richard Cobden. See under " Biography."

NOEL. The Labour Party: What it is and What it Wants. By the Rev. Conrad Roden Noel. Cr. 8vo. Paper, net 1/- ; cloth, net 2/-

O'BRIEN. England's Title in Ireland. A Letter Addressed to the Lord Lieutenant. By R. Barry O'Brien. Paper covers. 6d.

—— Irish Memories. By R. Barry O'Brien. See under " History."

O'CONNOR (T. P.). The Parnell Movement. See under "History."

O'DONNELL. The Causes of Present Discontents in India. By C. J. O'Donnell, M.P. Demy 8vo, cloth. net 2/6

RAVENSHEAR. The Industrial and Commercial Influence of the English Patent System. By A. F. Ravenshear. Large Cr. 8vo. net 5/-

REFORMER'S BOOKSHELF, THE. Large cr. 8vo, cloth. each 3/6

The Labour Movement. By L. T. Hobhouse, M.A. Preface by R. B. Haldane, M.P.

Sixty Years of an Agitator's Life. G. J. Holyoake's Autobiography. 2 vols.

Bamford's Passages in the Life of a Radical. Edited and with an Introduction by Henry Dunckley. 2 vols.

The Economic Interpretation of History. By Professor Thorold Rogers. 2 vols.

The Industrial and Commercial History of England. By Professor Thorold Rogers. 2 vols.

Charles Bradlaugh : A Record of his Life and Work. By his Daughter Hypathia Bradlaugh Bonner. 2 vols.

The Inner Life of the House of Commons. Selected from the Writings of William White.

The Life of Richard Cobden. By John Morley. 2 vols.

The Political Writings of Richard Cobden. A New Edition. With Preface by Lord Welby, and Introduction by Sir Louis Mallet and William Cullen Bryant, and a Bibliography. With Frontispieces. 2 vols.

The Gladstone Colony. By James Francis Hogan, M.P.

British Industries under Free Trade. Edited by Harold Cox.

My Life in Two Hemispheres. By Sir Charles Gavan Duffy, K.C.M.G. 2 vols.

Labour Legislation, Labour Movements, and Labour Leaders. By George Howell. With Frontispiece. 2 vols.

St. Stephen's in the Fifties. By E. M. Whitty. With an Introduction by Justin McCarthy.

The Crowd: A Study of the Popular Mind. By Gustave Le Bon.

Juvenile Offenders. By W. Douglas Morrison, LL.D.

Bygones Worth Remembering. A Sequel to "Sixty Years of an Agitator's Life." By George Jacob Holyoake. With a Photogravure Frontispiece and 18 other Portraits. 2 vols.

The Hungry Forties. An account of Life Under the Bread Tax. With an Introduction by Mrs. Cobden Unwin. Illustrated.

ROGERS. The Economic Interpretation of History : Lectures on Political Economy and its History, delivered at Oxford, 1887-1888. By Professor Thorold Rogers. 2 vols. (Reformer's Booksl. lf.) Large cr. 8vo, cloth. 7/-

—— The Industrial and Commercial History of England. See under " Historical Literature."

RUSSELL. The Uprising of the Many. By Charles E. Russell. With 32 Illustrations. Large cr. 8vo, cloth. net 5/-

SABATIER. Disestablishment in France. By Paul Sabatier. Translated (with an Introduction) by Robert Dell. With Portraits of the Author and the Abbé Loisy ; and the complete text (both in French and English) of the Law for the Separation of the Churches and the State, with explanatory notes. Cr. 8vo, cloth. net 3/6

SCHREINER. The Political Situation. By Olive Schreiner and C
S. Cronwright Schreiner. Cr. 8vo, cloth.   1/6

SHAW. Municipal Government in Continental Europe. By Albert
Shaw   Demy 8vo, cloth   net   7/6
—— Municipal Government of Great Britain. By Albert Shaw.
Demy 8vo, cloth   net   7/6

SIBLEY Criminal Appeal and Evidence By N. W. Sibley, B A,
LL M Trin H Camb and B A London ; Barrister-at-Law of
Lincoln's Inn , Joint Author of "International Law as Interpreted
during the Russo-Japanese War," and "The Aliens Act, 1905 "
Demy 8vo, cloth   net 15/-

SMALL. General Sociology: An Exposition of the Main Development in Sociological Theory, from Spencer to Ratzenhofer. By
Albion W Small, Professor and Head of the Department of Sociology in the University of Chicago Demy 8vo, cloth.   net 18/-

—— Adam Smith and Modern Sociology A Study in the Method-
ology of the Social Sciences By Albion W. Small, Professor and
Head of the Department of Sociology in the University of Chicago
Cloth   net   5/6

SMITH (Goldwin). My Memory of Gladstone. See under "Biography."

SMITH. International Law as Interpreted during the Russo-
Japanese War   By F E Smith, B C L , and N W Sibley, LL.M
Second Edition, Revised   Royal 8vo, cloth.   net 25/-

SPELLING Bossism and Monopoly   By T. C. Spelling. Large
cr 8vo, cloth   net   7/6

STEAD   Peers or People ? The House of Lords Weighed in the
Balances and Found Wanting   An Appeal to History.   By W. T.
Stead   Cr 8vo   Paper boards, net 2/6 , cloth, net   3/6

STEVENI. The Scandinavian Question. By William Barnes Steveni
With a Map   Large cr. 8vo, cloth.   net   3/6

STOPES The Sphere of "Man" in Relation to that of "Woman"
in the Constitution   By Mrs C. C Stopes, Author of "British
Freewomen."   Large cr. 8vo, paper covers.   net   6d.

SVENSKE Sweden's Rights and the Present Political Position.
By Anders Svenske   Cloth   net   2/8

TAYLOR. Side-Lights on Protection. The History of a Vanished
Industry. By Austin Taylor, M P   Paper covers.   6d.

TWAIN   King Leopold's Soliloquy A Defence of his Congo Rule.
By Mark Twain. With a Preface and Appendices by E D Morel,
Author of "Red Rubber " Cr. 8vo.   Paper, net 1/- ; cloth, net   1/6

VILLARI. Russia Under the Great Shadow. By Luigi Villari.
With 84 Illustrations Demy 8vo, cloth.   net 10/6

VILLARI (Pasquale) Niccolo Machiavelli. See under "Biography."

VILLIERS (B.). The Opportunity of Liberalism. By Brougham
Villiers Paper covers.   net   1/-

—— The Case for Woman's Suffrage A volume of essays by Mrs.
Henry Fawcett, Mrs. Pankhurst, J Keir Hardie, M P., Miss Eva
Gore Booth, Miss Ll. Davies, Miss Margaret McMillan, and others.
Edited with an Introduction by Brougham Villiers Cr. 8vo.
                               Paper boards, net 2/6 , cloth, net   3/6

—— The Socialist Movement in England. By Brougham Villiers,
Author of "The Opportunity of Liberalism." Demy 8vo. cloth net 10/6

VILLIERS (Ch. P.). Fiscal Reformation Sixty Years Ago : Passages from the Speeches of the Rt. Hon. Charles Pelham Villiers, M.P. for Wolverhampton, 1835-1898. Selected by Wilbraham Villiers Cooper. Paper covers. 1/-

WATSON. The National Liberal Federation from its Commencement to the General Election of 1906. By R. Spence Watson, LL.D., President of the Federation 1890-1902. With a Photogravure Frontispiece from a Portrait by Sir George Reid, and an Introduction by the Right Honourable Augustine Birrell. Cr. 8vo, cloth. net 5/-

WELBY and MALLET. Cobden's Work and Opinions. By Lord Welby and Sir Louis Mallet. Imitation Calf covers. net 3d.

WHITE. The Inner Life of the House of Commons : Selected from the Writings of William White, with a Prefatory Note by his Son, and an Introduction by Justin McCarthy. 2 vols. (Reformer's Bookshelf.) Cr. 8vo, cloth. 7/-

WILKINSON. The Personal Story of the Upper House. See under "Biography."

[For reference see also "Biography" and "History."]

GEOGRAPHY, TRAVEL, MOUNTAINEERING, &c.

ADAMS. The New Egypt. By Francis Adams. Large cr. 8vo, cloth. 5/-

ANGLO-ITALIAN LIBRARY, THE. Each volume fully illustrated. Large cr. 8vo, cloth. net 5/-

    With Shelley in Italy. A Selection of Poems and Letters relating to His Life in Italy. Edited, with an Introduction, by Anna Benneson McMahan.

    With Byron in Italy. A Selection of Poems and Letters relating to His Life in Italy. Edited by Anna Benneson McMahan.

    Romola. By George Eliot. A Historically Illustrated Edition. Edited, with Introduction and Notes, by Guido Biagi, Librarian of the Laurentian and Riccardi Libraries, Florence. 2 vols.

    The four volumes may also be obtained in Florentine white vellum binding. Price 10, 6 net each.

BAKER. Moors, Crags, and Caves of the High Peak and the Neighbourhood. By Ernest A. Baker, M.A. With about 40 Illustrations and 2 Maps. Demy 8vo, cloth gilt. net 6/-

BANFIELD. The Confessions of a Beachcomber. Scenes and Incidents in the Career of an Unprofessional Beachcomber in Tropical Queensland. By E. J. Banfield. With a Map and 48 Illustrations. Demy 8vo, cloth. net 15/-

BINDLOSS (Harold). Wide Dominion. See Overseas Library. No. 7.

BLOND (Mrs. Aubrey Le). See under "Le Blond."

BOISSIER. The Country of Horace and Virgil. By Gaston Boissier. Translated by D. Havelock Fisher. Large cr. 8vo, cloth. 7/6

—— Rome and Pompeii. By Gaston Boissier. Translated by D. Havelock Fisher. (The only authorised version in English of "Les Promenades Archæologiques.") Maps and Plans. Large cr. 8vo, cloth. 7/6

    Also in Unwin's Half-Crown Standard Library. Cloth. net 2/6

BUCHANAN   The Real Australia   By A J Buchanan   Cr 8vo.   6/-

BULFIN (W.).   Tales of the Pampas.   See Overseas Library   No 10.

CADDICK.   A White Woman in Central Africa.   By Helen Caddick
16 Illustrations   Cr 8vo, cloth   6/-

CAIRD   Romantic Cities of Provence.   By Mona Caird, Author of
"The Pathway of the Gods," &c , &c.   Illustrated with Sketches by
Joseph Pennell and Edward M Synge   Small royal 8vo, cloth   net 15/-

CAYLEY   The Bridle Roads of Spain (Las Alforjas)   By George
John Cayley   New edition   With an Introduction by Martin Hume,
M A , and Recollections of the Author by Lady Ritchie and Mrs.
Cobden Sickert, and a Photogravure Frontispiece   La. cr 8vo, net   7/6

CESARESCO   Lombard Studies.   By Countess Evelyn Martinengo
Cesaresco   Photogravure Frontispiece and many other Illustrations.   Demy 8vo, cloth.   16/-

CLIFFORD (Hugh).   A Corner of Asia.   See Overseas Library.   No. 5.

CONWAY,   Climbing and Exploration in the Karakoram-
Himalayas.   By Sir William Martin Conway, M.A , F.S A., F R.G S.
300 Illustrations by A D. McCormick, and Maps.   Super royal 8vo,
cloth   net 31/6
Supplementary Volume.   With Frontispiece of the Author.   Super
royal 8vo, cloth.   net 15/-

CONWAY AND COOLIDGE'S CLIMBERS' GUIDES.   Edited by
Sir William M Conway and Rev W A B Coolidge.   Gilt lettered,
with pocket, flap, and pencil   32mo, limp cloth, each.   10/-

(1) **The Central Pennine Alps.** By Sir William Martin Conway.	(7) **The Mountains of Cogne.** By George Yeld and W. A. B Coolidge. With Map.
(2) **The Eastern Pennine Alps** By Sir William Martin Conway	(8) **The Range of the Todi.** By W A B Coolidge.
(3) **The Lepontine Alps** (Simplon and Gotthard). By W A B Coolidge and Sir William M Conway	(9) **The Bernese Oberland.** Vol 1 From the Gemmi to the Monchjoch By G Hasler
(4) **The Central Alps of the Dauphiny.** By W. A B Coolidge, H. Duhamel, and F Perrin Second Edition. Thoroughly revised. Small 8vo, cloth 7/6 net.	(10) **The Bernese Oberland.** Vol 2 From the Monchjoch to the Grimsel By W A B Coolidge
(5) **The Chain of Mont Blanc** By Louis Kurz	(11) **The Bernese Oberland.** Vol 3 The West Wing By H Dübi.
(6) **The Adula Alps of the Lepontine Range** By W. A. B. Coolidge	(12 & 13) **The Bernese Oberland.** Vol. 4 (Parts 1 and 2) From the Grimsel to the Uri Rothstock. By H. Dübi

Also a Series of Six Coloured Maps of the Alps of the Dauphiny,
mounted on linen, and strongly bound in cloth case, the set   4/6

COOLIDGE (W. A. B).   See under Conway and Coolidge's Climbers'
Guides

CORNABY.   China under the Searchlight.   By W A Cornaby.   Cr.
8vo, cloth   6/-

CORNISH.   The Panama Canal To-day.   By Vaughan Cornish
Cloth   6/-

DAVENPORT.   China from Within : A Study of Opium Fallacies and
Missionary Mistakes   By Arthur Davenport   Cr 8vo, cloth.   6/-

DAVIDSON. Present-Day Japan. By Augusta M. Campbell Davidson, M.A. Fully Illustrated. Medium 8vo, cloth. — 21/-
Cheap Edition (Modern Travel Series), cloth. — 5/-

DAVIS. The Congo and the Coasts of Africa. By Richard Harding Davis. Illustrated. Large cr. 8vo, cloth. — net 6/-

DAWSON. The Evolution of Modern Germany. By W. Harbutt Dawson, Author of " German Life in Town and Country." — net 21/-

DEASY. In Tibet and Chinese Turkestan. By Captain H. H. P. Deasy. Being the Record of Three Years' Exploration. With Appendices, Maps, and 80 Illustrations. Demy 8vo, cloth gilt. net — 21/-
Also a Cheap Edition. — net 6/-

DIGBY. "Prosperous" British India. By William Digby, C.I.E. With Diagrams and Maps. Demy 8vo, cloth. — 12/6

DUTT. The Norfolk and Suffolk Coast. By W. A. Dutt. With about 40 Illustrations. Cr. 8vo, cloth. — 6/-

ECKENSTEIN. The Karakorams and Kashmir : The Story of a Journey. By Oscar Eckenstein. Cr. 8vo, cloth gilt. — 6/-

ELIOT. Romola. By George Eliot. A historically illustrated edition. Edited, with Introduction and Notes, by Guido Biagi, Librarian of the Laurentian and Riccardi Libraries, Florence. With 160 Illustrations. 2 vols. (The Anglo-Italian Library.) — each, net 5/-

ENOCK. The Andes and the Amazon. Life and Travel in Peru. By C. Reginald Enock, F.R.G.S. With a Map and numerous Illustrations. Medium 8vo, cloth. — 21/-

—— **Peru.** Its Former and Present Civilization, Topography and Natural Resources, History and Political Conditions, Commerce and Present Conditions. By C. Reginald Enock, F.R.G.S. With an Introduction by Martin Hume, a Map, and numerous Illustrations. (The South American Series.) Demy 8vo, cloth. — net 10/6

—— **Mexico.** By C. Reginald Enock, F.R.G.S. (Volume 3 of the South American Series.) Demy 8vo, cloth. — net 10/6

Everyday Life in Cape Colony. By a late Resident. Illustrated. Cr. 8vo, cloth. — 3/6

FARGE. An Artist's Letters from Japan. See under "La Farge."

FINDLAY. Big Game Shooting and Travel in South and East Africa. By Frederick R. N. Findlay. Fully Illustrated, and with Map. Medium 8vo. — net 15/-

FITZ-GERALD. Climbs in the New Zealand Alps : Being an Account of Travel and Discovery. By E. A. Fitz-Gerald, F.R.G.S. Cloth, size 9½ by 6½. — net 31/6

FOREMAN. The Philippine Islands. A Political, Ethnographical, Social and Commercial History of the Philippine Archipelago. By John Foreman, F.R.G.S. With Maps and Illustrations. Royal 8vo, cloth. — net 25/-

GAGGIN (John). Among the Man-Eaters. See Overseas Library. No. 8.

GRAHAM (Cunningham). The Ipane : The Ipane. See Overseas Library. No. 1.

GRIBBLE. The Early Mountaineers : The Stories of their Lives. By Francis Gribble. Fully Illustrated. Demy 8vo, cloth gilt. — 21/-

HALL. Pre-Historic Rhodesia. An Examination of the Ethnological and Archæological Evidences as to the Origin and Age of the Rock Mines and Stone Buildings, with a Gazetteer of Mediæval South-East Africa. By R. N. Hall. With Illustrations, Maps and Plans. Medium 8vo, cloth. — net 12/6

HARDY. John Chinaman at Home. By the Rev. E. J. Hardy, Author of "How to be Happy though Married." With 36 Illustrations. Demy 8vo, cloth. — net 10/6
Cheap Edition (Modern Travel Series), cloth. — 5/-

HARVIE-BROWN. Travels of a Naturalist in Northern Europe. By J. A. Harvie-Brown. See under "Natural History."

HAWKESWORTH. Australian Sheep and Wool. A Practical and Theoretical Treatise. By Alfred Hawkesworth, Lecturer in Charge of "Sheep and Wool" Department, Technical College, Sydney. Second Edition, Revised and Enlarged. With 55 Illustrations. Demy 8vo, cloth.   net   7/6

HERRING. Among the People of British Columbia: Red, White, Yellow and Brown. By Frances E. Herring. Fully Illustrated from Original Photographs. Cr. 8vo, cloth.   net   6/-

—— In the Pathless West. By Frances E. Herring. With 14 Illustrations. Cr. 8vo, cloth.   net   6/-

HEYWOOD. Guide to Siena. History and Art. By William Heywood and Lucy Olcott. Cr. 8vo, cloth.   net   6/-

HILL. Cuba and Porto Rico: With the other Islands of the West Indies. By Robert T. Hill. 500 pages, with 250 Illustrations and Maps. Demy 8vo.   16/-

HINDLIP. British East Africa: Past, Present, and Future. By Lord Hindlip, F.R.G.S., F.Z.S. Cr. 8vo, cloth.   net   3/6

—— Sport and Travel: Abyssinia and British East Africa. By Lord Hindlip, F.R.G.S., F.Z.S. With Maps and more than 70 Illustrations. Demy 8vo, cloth.   net 21/-

HOBBES. Imperial India: Letters from the East. By John Oliver Hobbes. Cr. 8vo.   Paper covers, 1/- ; cloth   2/-

HOBSON. Canada To-Day. By J. A. Hobson, M.A., Author of "The Evolution of Modern Capitalism," &c. Cr. 8vo, cloth.   net   3/6

HONEYMAN. Bright Days in Merrie England. By C. Van Doren Honeyman. Cr. 8vo, cloth.   6/-

INDICUS. Labour and other Questions in South Africa. By "Indicus." Cr. 8vo, cloth.   3/6

JAVELLE. Alpine Memories. By Emile Javelle. Small demy, cloth.   7/6

JEBB. By Desert Ways to Baghdad. By Louisa Jebb. With many Illustrations from Photographs taken by the Author. Demy 8vo, cloth.   net 10/6

JERNIGAN. China's Business Methods and Policy. See under "Politics."

JOHNSON. Tramps Round the Mountains of the Moon and through the Back Gate of the Congo State. By T. Broadwood Johnson, M.A., of the Uganda Mission. With 30 Illustrations from Photographs. Large cr. 8vo, cloth.   6/-

KERR. From Charing Cross to Delhi. By S. Parnell Kerr. With 65 Illustrations. Demy 8vo, cloth.   net 10/6

KING. Mountaineering in the Sierra Nevada. By Clarence King. Cr. 8vo, cloth.   net   6/-

KURZ (Louis). See under Conway and Coolidge's Climbers' Guides.

LA FARGE. An Artist's Letters from Japan. With many Illustrations. Demy 8vo, cloth.   16/-

LE BLOND. Adventures on the Roof of the World. By Mrs. Aubrey Le Blond (Mrs. Main). With over 100 Illustrations. Demy 8vo, cloth.   net 10/6
Cheap Edition (Modern Travel Series), cloth.   5/-

—— True Tales of Mountain Adventure for Non-Climbers, Young and Old. By Mrs. Aubrey Le Blond (Mrs. Main). With numerous Illustrations and Frontispiece. Demy 8vo, cloth.   net 10/6
Cheap Edition (Modern Travel Series) cloth.   5/-

LE BLOND. Mountaineering in the Land of the Midnight Sun. By Mrs. Aubrey Le Blond (Mrs. Main). With many Illustrations and a Map. Demy 8vo, cloth. net **10/6**

LENTHERIC. The Riviera, Ancient and Modern. By Charles Lentheric. Translated by C. West. With 9 Maps and Plans. Large cr. 8vo, cloth. **7/6**

LITTLE. In the Land of the Blue Gown. By Mrs. Archibald Little, Author of "Intimate China." With over 100 Illustrations. Medium 8vo. net **21/-**
Also a Cheaper Edition. Cloth. net **7/6**

—— Round About My Peking Garden. By Mrs. Archibald Little. Author of "Li Hung Chang, His Life and Times," "A Marriage in China," &c., &c. Fully Illustrated. Demy 8vo, cloth. net **15/-**

LLOYD. In Dwarf-Land and Cannibal Country. By Albert B. Lloyd. Illustrated and with 3 Maps. Demy 8vo. net **21/-**
Also a Cheaper Edition. Cloth. net **7/6**

—— Uganda to Khartoum. Life and Adventure on the Upper Nile. By Albert B. Lloyd. With a preface by Victor Buxton. With a Map and 81 Illustrations. Demy 8vo, cloth. net **10/6**

LUMSDEN. Through Canada in Harvest Time : A Study of Life and Labour in the Golden West. By James Lumsden. Fully Illustrated, and with Map. Large cr. 8vo, cloth gilt. **6/-**

MAC (J.) Little Indabas. See Overseas Library. No. 9.

MACDONALD. In Search of El Dorado : A Wanderer's Experiences. By Alexander Macdonald. With 32 Illustrations. Demy 8vo, cloth. net **10/6**
Cheap Edition (Modern Travel Series), cloth. **5/-**

McMAHAN. Byron in Italy. A Selection of Poems and Letters relating to His Life in Italy. Edited by Anna Benneson McMahan. With more than 60 Illustrations from Photographs. Large cr., 8vo, cloth. net **5/-**

—— With Shelley in Italy. A Selection of Poems and Letters relating to His Life in Italy. Edited, with an Introduction, by Anna Benneson McMahan. With 64 Illustrations from Photographs. Large cr. 8vo, cloth. net **5/-**

MALLIK. Impressions of a Wanderer. By Manmath C. Mallik, of the Middle Temple, Barrister-at-Law. Crown 8vo, cloth. net **5/-**

MILLER. Travels and Politics in the Near East. By William Miller, Author of "The Balkans." With 100 Illustrations and a Map. Demy 8vo, cloth. **21/-**

MODERN TRAVEL SERIES, THE. Each Volume illustrated. Large cr. 8vo, cloth. **5/-**

(1) True Tales of Mountain Adventure. By Mrs. Aubrey le Blond (Mrs. Main). With many illustrations from photographs by the Author.

(2) In Search of El Dorado. A Wanderer's Experiences. By Alexander Macdonald, F.R.G S. With an Introduction by Admiral Moresby. With 32 Illustrations.

(3) Adventures on the Roof of the World. By Mrs. Aubrey le Blond (Mrs. Main). With more than 100 illustrations.

(4) John Chinaman at Home. By the Rev. E. J. Hardy, Author of "How to be Happy though Married," lately Chaplain to H.M. Forces at Hong Kong. With 36 Illustrations.

(5) Present Day Japan. By A. M. Campbell Davidson. With 32 Illustrations.

(6) Links in my Life on Land and Sea. By Commander J. W. Gambier, R.N. With a Frontispiece.

de **MONTAGNAC** (Noel). **Negro Nobodies.** See Overseas Library. No. 6.

MOSSO. Life of Man on the High Alps : Studies made on Monte Rosa. By Angelo Mosso. Translated from the Second Edition of the Italian by E. Lough Kiesow, in Collaboration with F. Kiesow. With numerous Illustrations and Diagrams. Royal 8vo, cloth. **21/-**

MUMMERY. Mes Escalades Dans les Alpes et le Caucase. Par A. F. Mummery. Traduit de l'Anglais par Maurice Paillon. With a new Preface and Notice on Mummery as a Climber. Illustrated by a Portrait of the Author in Collotype, 24 full-page Plates, and 4 Maps. Paper covers. **net 9/-**

—— **My Climbs in the Alps and Caucasus.** By A. F. Mummery. With Photogravure, Coloured and Half-Tone Illustrations by Joseph Pennell and others. New Edition, with Introductions by Mrs. Mummery and J. A. Hobson. Super-royal 8vo, cloth. **net 21/-**

NORMAN. The Peoples and Politics of the Far East. Travels and Studies in the British, French, Spanish, and Portuguese Colonies, Siberia, China, Japan, Korea, Siam, and Malaya. By Sir Henry Norman, M.P. With many Illustrations. Sixth Impression. Small demy 8vo, cloth. **7/6**

—— **The Real Japan.** By Sir Henry Norman, M.P. Profusely Illustrated. Large cr. 8vo. **net 5/-**

NORMAN-NERUDA. The Climbs of Norman-Neruda. Edited, with an Account of his last Climb, by May Norman-Neruda. Demy 8vo, cloth. **21/-**

OBER. A Guide to the West Indies and Bermudas. By F. A. Ober. With Maps and many Illustrations. Small cr. 8vo, cloth. **net 8/6**

OGILVIE. My Life in the Open. By Will H. Ogilvie, Author of " Fair Girls and Gray Horses." With Portrait. Large cr. 8vo, cloth. **net 5/-**

OLCOTT. Guide to Siena. See Heywood.

OVERSEAS LIBRARY, THE. At the End of this Section.

PARIS-PARISIEN. A Complete Guide to Paris. French Text. I.—What to See. II.—What to Know. III.—Parisian Ways. IV.— Practical Paris. Large demy 12mo, limp leather. **6/-**

PINNOCK. Wander Years Round the World. By James Pinnock. With over 70 Illustrations and about 20 special Maps. Demy 8vo, cloth. **net 21/-**

PULLEN-BURRY. Jamaica as it is. By B. Pullen-Burry. With a Map and 8 Illustrations. Cr. 8vo, cloth. **net 6/-**

—— **Ethiopia in Exile : Jamaica Revisited.** By B. Pullen-Burry. Cr. 8vo, cloth. **6/-**

QUIN (Ethel). **Well-Sinkers.** See Overseas Library. No. 4.

REY. The Matterhorn. By Guido Rey. Illustrated by Edoardo Rubino. With a Preface by Edmondo de Amicis. Translated from the Italian by J. E. C. Eaton. With 14 Coloured Plates, 23 Pen Drawings, and 11 Photographs. Super royal 8vo, cloth. **net 21/-** *Fine Paper Edition* (Limited to Fifteen Copies.) Price on application.

RODGERS. The Scenery of Sherwood Forest. With some Account of the Eminent Families once resident there, and an Essay on Robin Hood. By Joseph Rodgers. With Illustrations of the Magnificent Trees and Characteristic Scenery, from Drawings by the Author, and with Portraits in Photogravure. Super royal 8vo, cloth. **net 21/-**

RODWAY (James). In Guiana Wilds. See Overseas Library. No 3.

ROOSEVELT. Ranch Life and the Hunting Trail. By Theodore Roosevelt, late President of the United States. Illustrated by Frederick Remington. Royal 8vo, cloth. 10/6

SCIDMORE. Java: The Garden of the East. By Eliza Ruhamah Scidmore. With nearly 40 full-page Illustrations. Cr. 8vo. 7/6

—— Winter India. By Eliza Ruhamah Scidmore. Fully Illustrated. Medium 8vo, cloth. net 10/6

SCOTT-ELLIOTT. Chile. By G. F. Scott-Elliott, F.R.G.S. With an Introduction by Martin Hume. Illustrated. (The South American Library. Vol. 1.) Demy 8vo, cloth. net 10 6

SEARELLE. Tales of the Transvaal. By Luscombe Searelle. Illustrated by P Frenzeny, and after Photographs. 8vo, cloth. 2/6

SEYMOUR. Saunterings in Spain—Barcelona, Madrid, Toledo, Cordova, Seville, Granada. By Major-General Seymour. Illustrated. Demy 8vo, cloth. net 10/6

SIBREE. Madagascar before the Conquest. By James Sibree. Illustrated. With Map. Demy 8vo, cloth. 16/-

SMITH. Budapest. The City of the Magyars. By T. Berkeley Smith. Fully Illustrated. Cr. 8vo, cloth. net 5/-

THE SOUTH AMERICAN SERIES. Edited by Martin Hume. Each Volume Illustrated. Demy 8vo, cloth. net 10/6
   Vol. 1. Chile. By G. F. Scott-Elliot, F.R G.S
   Vol. 2. Peru. By C. Reginald Enock, F.R.G.S.
   Vol. 3. Mexico. By C. Reginald Enock, F.R.G.S.

STEAD. Japan, Our New Ally By Alfred Stead. With an Introduction by the Marquis Ito. Fully Illustrated. Cr. 8vo, cloth. net 6/-

STEIN. Sand-Buried Ruins of Khotan. By M. Aurel Stein, Indian Educational Service. With over 120 Illustrations and a Photogravure Frontispiece and large Map. Medium 8vo, cloth. net 21/-

STRASBURGER. Rambles on the Riviera. By Eduard Strasburger, F.R.S., D.C.L. Oxon. With 87 Coloured Illustrations by Louise Reusch. Demy 8vo, cloth. net 21/-

STRATILESCO. From Carpathian to Pindus: Pictures of Roumanian Country Life. By Tereza Stratilesco. With two Maps and many illustrations. Demy 8vo, cloth. net 15/-

STREET. A Philosopher in Portugal. By Eugène E. Street, F.S.A. Cr. 8vo, buckram. net 5/-

SUTCLIFFE. By Moor and Fell. Landscape and Lang-Settle Talk in West Yorkshire. By Halliwell Sutcliffe, Author of "Ricroft of Withens," &c. With many Illustrations. Cr. 8vo, cloth. 6/-

SYMONDS. Days Spent on a Doge's Farm. By Margaret Symonds (Mrs. Vaughan). With a Photogravure Frontispiece and many other Illustrations from Sketches and Photographs. New Edition. Demy 8vo, cloth. net 10/6

TAINE. Journeys through France: Being the Authorised Translation of "Carnets de Voyage." By Adolphe Hippolyte Taine. Cr. 8vo, cloth. 7/6

TAYLOR. Vacation Days in Hawaii and Japan. By Charles M. Taylor. Illustrated. Large cr. 8vo, cloth. net 7/6

TOWNSEND. Along the Labrador Coast. By Charles Wendell Townsend, M.D. With 40 Illustrations and a Map. Large cr. 8vo, cloth. net 5'.

TURNBULL. Tales from Natal. By A. R R. Turnbull Cr 8vo, cloth   3/6

TURNER Siberia : A Record of Travel, Climbing, and Exploration. By Samuel Turner, F.R.G.S. With more than 100 Illustrations and 2 Maps Demy 8vo, cloth   net 21/-

VANDERLIP. In Search of a Siberian Klondike By Washington B Vanderlip and H B. Hulbert. With 48 Illustrations. Large cr. cloth.   net   7/6

VILLARI. Russia Under the Great Shadow. By Luigi Villari, Author of "Giovanni Segantini," "Italian Life in Town and Country," &c With 84 Illustrations Demy 8vo, cloth   net 10/6

—— Fire and Sword in the Caucasus By Luigi Vallari. Illustrated. Demy 8vo, cloth   net 10/6

WALLIS. The Advance of our West African Empire. By Captain Braithwaite Wallis. Fully Illustrated. Medium 8vo, cloth   21/-

WATSON (JOHN). Woodlanders and Field Folk Sketches of Wild Life in Britain See "Natural History."   net   5/-

WEBSTER. Through New Guinea and the Cannibal Countries. By H Cayley-Webster Very fully Illustrated from Photographs, and with Maps, Diagrams, and Photogravure Frontispiece. Medium 8vo, cloth gilt   21/-

WELLBY. Through Unknown Tibet By Captain M S Wellby Photogravure and many other Illustrations, also Maps and Appendices of Flora, &c Medium 8vo, cloth gilt   21/-

WERNER (A). Captain of the Locusts See Overseas Library. No. 2.

WILSON The Climber's Note Book. By Claude Wilson, M D Waistcoat pocket size Buckram, gilt   net   1/-

de WINDT Through Savage Europe By Harry de Windt, Author of "Siberia as it is," "From Paris to New York by Land," &c , &c. With more than 90 Illustrations Demy 8vo, cloth.   net 10/6

WOODS Washed by Four Seas By H C Woods, F R G S , formerly of the Grenadier Guards. With an Introduction by Sir Martin Conway, 66 Photographs and a Map Demy 8vo, cloth.   net   7/6

WORKMAN. In the Ice World of Himalaya. By Fanny Bullock Workman and William Hunter Workman With 4 large Maps and nearly 100 Illustrations Demy 8vo, cloth gilt   16/-

Cheap Edition, with 2 Maps and 65 Illustrations.   6/-

—— Through Town and Jungle . Fourteen Thousand Miles Awheel among the Temples and People of the Indian Plain By William Hunter Workman and Fanny Bullock Workman. With Map and 202 Illustrations. Super royal 8vo, cloth   net 21/-

WRIGHT A Handbook of the Philippines. By Hamilton M. Wright Illustrated. Cr. 8vo, cloth.   net   7/6

YELD. Scrambles in the Eastern Graians. By George Yeld. Editor of the *Alpine Journal* Illustrated, and with a Map Large cr 8vo   7/6

Yorkshire Ramblers' Club Journal, The. Edited by Thomas Gray. Illustrated. 8vo, paper covers   net   2/-

ZIMMERMAN. Spain and her People. By Jeremiah Zimmerman With many Illustrations. Demy 8vo, cloth   net   8/6

ZURBRIGGEN. From the Alps to the Andes. Being the Autobiography of a Mountain Guide. By Mattias Zurbriggen. Translated by Mary Alice Vialls Fully Illustrated. Demy 8vo, cloth   net 10/6

[For reference see also "History."]

OVERSEAS LIBRARY, THE. Decorative Cover by W. H. Cowlishaw.
Cr. 8vo. Paper covers, 1/6 ; cloth, each   2/-

(1) **The Ipane.** By R. B. Cunninghame Graham.
(2) **The Captain of the Locusts, and Other Stories.** By A. Werner.
(3) **In Guiana Wilds.** By James Rodway.
(4) **The Well-Sinkers.** By Ethel Quin.

(5) **A Corner of Asia.** By Hugh Clifford.
(6) **Negro Nobodies.** By Nöel de Montagnac.
(7) **A Wide Dominion.** By Harold Bindloss.
(8) **Among the Man-Eaters.** By John Gaggin.
(9) **Little Indabas.** By J. Mac.
(10) **Tales of the Pampas.** By W. Bulfin.

NATURAL HISTORY, SCIENCE, &c.

BASTIAN. The Nature and Origin of Living Matter. By H. Charlton Bastian, M.A., M.D. (London), F.R.S., F.L.S., Emeritus Professor of the Principles and Practice of Medicine, and of Clinical Medicine at University College, London. With 76 Illustrations. Medium 8vo, cloth.   net   12/6

BEAVAN. Animals I Have Known. By Arthur H. Beavan. With about 50 Illustrations. Cr. 8vo, cloth.   5/-
Cheap Edition. (Unwin's Nature Books. Vol. 10.) Cloth.   2/-

—— Birds I Have Known. By Arthur H. Beavan. With 39 Illustrations. Cr. 8vo, cloth.   5/-
Cheap Edition. (Unwin's Nature Books. Vol. 9.) Cloth.   2/-

—— Fishes I Have Known. By Arthur H. Beavan. With about 40 Illustrations. Cr. 8vo, cloth.   5/-
Cheap Edition. (Unwin's Nature Books. Vol. 11.) Cloth.   2/-

BELL. Health at its Best v. Cancer and other Diseases. By Robert Bell, M.B., M.D., F.F.P.S., &c., formerly Senior Physician to the Glasgow Hospital for Women, Author of "Cancer : Its Cause and Treatment without Operation," &c., &c. Cr. 8vo, cloth.   net   5/-

BLIND. The Ascent of Man. An Edition de Luxe, limited to 250 Copies. By Mathilde Blind. With an Introduction by Alfred Russel Wallace. Heliogravure Medallion Portrait printed on Japan paper. Fcap. 4to.   10/6

BOXALL. The Evolution of the World and of Man. By G. E. Boxall. Cr. 8vo, cloth.   5/-

BRIGHTWEN. Glimpses into Plant Life : An Easy Guide to the Study of Botany. By Mrs. Brightwen. Illustrated. Cr. 8vo, cloth.   3/6
Cheap Reissue. (Unwin's Nature Books. Vol. 4.) Cloth.   2/-

—— Inmates of my House and Garden. By Mrs. Brightwen. With 32 Illustrations by Theo. Carreras. Crown 8vo, imitation leather, in box.   5/-
Also a Cheap Edition. (Unwin's Nature Books. Vol. 3.) Cloth.   2/-

—— More about Wild Nature. By Mrs. Brightwen. With Portrait of the Author and many other full-page Illustrations. Cr. 8vo, imitation leather, gilt lettered, gilt edges, in box.   5/-
Also a Cheap Edition. (Unwin's Nature Books. Vol. 2.) Cloth.   2/-

—— Quiet Hours with Nature. By Mrs. Brightwen. Fully Illustrated. Cr. 8vo, cloth.   5/-
Also a Cheap Edition. (Unwin's Nature Books. Vol. 7.) Cloth.   2/-

BRIGHTWEN. Wild Nature Won by Kindness. By Mrs. Brightwen.
Revised Edition, with additional Illustrations. Cr. 8vo, imitation
leather, gilt lettered, gilt edges, in box.   5/-

Also a Cheap Edition. (Unwin's Nature Books. Vol. i.) Cloth.   2/-

—— Last Hours with Nature. By Mrs. Brightwen, F.Z.S., F.E.S.,
Edited by W. H. Chesson. With Illustrations. Cr. 8vo, cloth. **net**   2/6

THE BRIGHTWEN SERIES. See " Unwin's Nature Books."

CESARESCO. The Psychology and Training of the Horse. By
Count Eugenio Martinengo Cesaresco. With Photogravure Frontispiece. Demy 8vo, cloth.   **net 10/6**

CHAMBERLAIN. Methods in Plant Histology. By Charles J. Chamberlain, A.M, Ph.D. With many Illustrations from Photomicro-
graphs. Demy 8vo, cloth.   **net 10/6**

DITTRICH. The Horse: A Pictorial Guide to its Anatomy. 110
Drawings (reproduced by Photo. Lithography) by Hermann Dittrich,
with Explanatory Notes by Prof. Ellenberger and Prof. Baum. In
portfolio, 4to.   **net 30/-**

FLAMMARION. Astronomy for Amateurs. By Camille Flammarion.
Authorised Translation by Francis A. Welby. With 84 Illustrations. Cr. 8vo, cloth.   6/-

—— Mysterious Psychic Forces. An Account of the Author's Investigations in Psychical Research, together with those of other European
Savants. By Camille Flammarion. With 21 Illustrations. Demy
8vo, cloth,   **net** 8/6

GEEN. What I Have Seen While Fishing. By Philip Geen. See
under " Varia."

GUYER. Animal Micrology. Practical Exercises in Microscopical
Methods. By Michael F. Guyer, Ph.D. Demy 8vo, cloth.   **net** 9/-

HARTING. Recreations of a Naturalist. By J. E. Harting. With
numerous Illustrations. Demy 8vo, cloth.   **net 15/-**

HARVIE-BROWN. Travels of a Naturalist in Northern Europe. By
J. A. Harvie-Brown, F.R.S.E., F.Z.S. With 4 Maps, 2 Coloured
Plates, and many Illustrations. 2 vols. Small royal 8vo, cloth.
                                                                  net 63/-

HULME. That Rock Garden of Ours. By F. E. Hulme, F.L.S., F.S.A.
With Coloured Illustrations. Demy 8vo, cloth.   **net 10/6**

INGERSOLL. The Wit of the Wild. By Ernest Ingersoll. Illustrated. Cr. 8vo, cloth.   **net** 5/-

IRVING. How to Know the Starry Heavens. An Invitation to the
Study of Suns and Worlds. By Edward Irving. With Charts,
Coloured Plates, Diagrams, and many Engravings of Photographs.
Demy 8vo, cloth.   **net** 8/6

LOEB. Studies in General Physiology. By Jacques Loeb. With
numerous Illustrations. 2 vols., royal 8vo, cloth.   **net 31/6**

MILLS. The Dog Book: The Origin, History, Varieties, Breeding,
Education, and General Management of the Dog in Health, and his
Treatment in Disease. By Wesley Mills, M.A., M.D., D.V.S., &c.
With 43 full-page Cuts, one Coloured Plate, and numerous other
Illustrations. Large cr. 8vo, cloth.   10/6

NEWMAN. Bird Skinning and Bird Stuffing. By Edward Newman.
Cr. 8vo.   1/-

OPPENHEIM. The Face and How to Read it. By Annie Isabella
Oppenheim, F.B.P.S. Illustrated. Cr. 8vo, cloth.   **net** 2/6

PARSONS. The Nature and Purpose of the Universe. By John Denham Parsons. Demy 8vo, cloth. net 21/-

PIKE. In Bird-Land with Field-Glass and Camera. By Oliver G. Pike. With over 80 Photographs of British Birds. Photogravure Frontispiece. Cr. 8vo, cloth gilt. 6/-

Cheap Reissue. (Unwin's Nature Books. Vol. 5.) Cr. 8vo. cloth. 2/-

RICHMOND. In My Lady's Garden. By Mrs. Richmond (late Garden Editor of *The Queen*). With a Coloured Frontispiece and other Illustrations. Demy 8vo, cloth. net 10/6

RUDAUX. How to Study the Stars. By L. Rudaux. Profusely Illustrated. Cloth. net 5/-

SCHMIDT. Pain: Its Causation and Diagnostic Significance in Internal Diseases. By Dr. Rudolph Schmidt. Translated and Edited by Karl M. Vogel, M.D., and Hans Zinsser, A.M., M.D., Demy 8vo, cloth. net 12/6

SNELL. The Camera in the Fields. A Practical Guide to Nature Photography. By F. C. Snell. With 80 Illustrations. Cr. 8vo, cloth. 5/-

Cheap Re-issue. (Unwin's Nature Books. Vol. 12.) 2/-

—— Nature Studies by Night and Day. By F. C. Snell. With about 90 Photographs taken direct from Nature. Cr. 8vo, cloth. 5/-

SOLLAS. The Age of the Earth, and other Geological Studies. By W. J. Sollas, LL.D., D.Sc., F.R.S., Professor of Geology in the University of Oxford. Illustrated. Demy 8vo, cloth. net 10/6

Cheap Edition. Large cr. 8vo, cloth. net 6/-

STRACHEY. Cat and Bird Stories from "The Spectator." With an Introduction by John St. Loe Strachey. Cr. 8vo, cloth. 5/-

—— Dog Stories from "The Spectator." With an Introduction by J. St. Loe Strachey. Cr. 8vo, cloth. 5/-

STUTTARD. The Butterfly : Its Nature, Development, and Attributes. By John Stuttard. Illustrated. Fcap. 8vo, limp cloth. 1/-

THOMPSON. The Mental Traits of Sex. An Experimental Investigation of the Normal Mind in Men and Women. By Helen Bradford Thompson, Ph.D. With many Diagrams. Large cr. 8vo, cloth. net 6/-

UNWIN. Future Forest Trees. The Importance of German Experiments in the Introduction of North American Trees. By A. Harold Unwin, D. Oec. Publ. (Munich). With 4 Illustrations. Demy 8vo, cloth. net 7/6

UNWIN'S NATURE BOOKS (Formerly The Brightwen Series.) Each volume fully Illustrated. Cr. 8vo, cloth. each 2/-

(1) **Wild Nature Won by Kindness.** By Mrs. Brightwen.
(2) **More about Wild Nature.** By Mrs. Brightwen.
(3) **Inmates of my House and Garden.** By Mrs. Brightwen.
(4) **Glimpses into Plant Life.** By Mrs. Brightwen.
(5) **In Birdland with Field-Glass and Camera.** By Oliver G. Pike.
(6) **Bird Life in Wild Wales.** By J. A. Walpole-Bond.
(7) **Quiet Hours with Nature.** By Mrs. Brightwen.
(8) **Nature's Story of the Year.** By Charles A. Witchell.
(9) **Birds I Have Known.** By Arthur H. Beavan.
(10) **Animals I have Known.** By Arthur H. Beavan.
(11) **Fishes I Have Known.** By Arthur H. Beavan
(12) **The Camera in the Fields.** By F. C. Snell.

WALPOLE-BOND. **Bird Life in Wild Wales.** By J. A. Walpole-Bond. With 60 Illustrations from photographs by Oliver G. Pike. Large cr. 8vo, cloth.   7/6

Cheap Re-issue. (Unwin's Nature Books. Vol. 6.)   2/-

WESTELL. **British Bird Life.** By W. Percival Westell, M.B.O.U., F.R.H.S., &c. With over 60 Illustrations. With an Introduction by Sir Herbert Maxwell, Bart. Large cr. 8vo, cloth.   5/-
Cheap Edition, Large cr. 8vo, cloth.   3/6

WATSON. **Woodlanders and Field Folk.** Sketches of Wild Life in Britain. By John Watson, author of "Poachers and Poaching," and Blanche Winder. Illustrated. Large cr. 8vo, cloth.   net   5/-

WITCHELL. **Nature's Story of the Year.** By Charles A. Witchell. Fully Illustrated. Cr. 8vo, cloth.   5/-

Cheap Re-issue. (Unwin's Nature Books. Vol. 8.) Cr. 8vo, cloth.   2/-

RELIGION and EDUCATION.

ALLARDYCE. **Stops ; or, How to Punctuate.** A Practical Handbook for Writers and Students. By Paul Allardyce. Fcap. 8vo, cloth.   1/-

BADHAM. **St. Mark's Indebtedness to St. Matthew.** By F. P. Badham. Cr. 8vo, cloth.   3/6

BENSON. **The Religion of the Plain Man.** By Father Robert Hugh Benson. Cr. 8vo, cloth.   net   2/6

BERRY. **How to Become a Teacher.** By T. W. Berry. Fcap. 8vo, cloth.   1/-

BLYTH. **The Last Step to Religious Equality.** By Edmond Kell Blyth. Cr. 8vo, paper covers.   6d.

BOUSSET. **What is Religion ?** By Professor W. Bousset. Translated by F. B. Low. Cr. 8vo, cloth.   net   5/-

—— **The Faith of a Modern Protestant.** By Professor W. Bousset. Translated by F. B. Low. Cr. 8vo, cloth.   net   2/6

BRAY. **The Town Child.** By Reginald A. Bray, L.C.C., Author of "The Children of the Town" in "The Heart of the Empire," "The Boy and the Family" in "The Studies of Boy Life," &c. Demy 8vo, cloth.   net   7/6

BRIDGETT. **A History of the Holy Eucharist in Great Britain.** By T. E. Bridgett, C.S.S.R. A New Revised and Illustrated Edition. Edited, with notes, by Herbert Thurston, S.J. Royal Folio, cloth. net   21/-

BROWN. **The Social Message of the Modern Pulpit.** By Charles Reynolds Brown. Cr. 8vo, cloth.   net   5/-

BURTON. **The Life of Christ.** An Aid to Historical Study, and a Condensed Commentary on the Gospels. By Ernest de Witt Burton and Shailer Mathews, Professors in the University of Chicago. Large cr. 8vo, cloth.   net   5/-

CAMPBELL. **Thursday Mornings at the City Temple.** By the Rev. R. J. Campbell, M.A. Cr. 8vo, cloth.   net   5/-

COX. **The Bird's Nest,** and Other Sermons for Children of all Ages. By Samuel Cox, D.D. Fourth Edition, imp. 16mo, cloth.   3/6

—— **Expositions.** By Samuel Cox, D.D. In 4 vols. Demy 8vo, cloth, each.   7/6

DILLON The Original Poem of Job. Translated from the Restored Text. By E. J. Dillon, Doc Orient Lang, Author of "The Sceptics of the Old Testament," &c To which is appended "The Book of Job According to the Authorised Version." Crown 8vo, cloth. 5/-

ELPHINSTONE. The Power of Character, and Other Studies. By Lady Elphinstone. With a Preface by Canon J. G Tetley. Cr 8vo, cloth net 3/6

FOSTER (G. B) The Finality of the Christian Religion By George Burman Foster, Professor of the Philosophy of Religion, Chicago Demy 8vo, cloth net 13/-

GARDINER. The Bible as English Literature. By J H Gardiner. Cr. 8vo, cloth net 5/-

GEORGE. Seventeenth Century Men of Latitude Precursors of Liberal Theology By E. A George With Portraits Cr. 8vo, cloth net 3 6

GILMAN. University Problems in the United States. By Daniel Coit Gilman, LL D Demy 8vo, 320 pp , cloth 10/6

HALL. Christian Belief Interpreted by Christian Experience. By Charles Cuthbert Hall With an Introductory Note by the Vice-Chancellor of the University of Bombay. Demy 8vo, cloth. net 6/6

HARDY. Doubt and Faith. By Rev. E. J Hardy, M A Cr. 8vo, cloth. 6/-

HARPER. Religion and the Higher Life. By William Rainy Harper, D D., LL D Large cr. 8vo, cloth net 6/-

—— The Trend in Higher Education in America. By William Rainy Harper, D.D , LL.D Cr. 8vo, cloth. net 7/6

HENSON. Christ and the Nation. Westminster and other Sermons By H Hensley Henson, Canon of Westminster, and Rector of St. Margaret's Cr. 8vo, cloth net 5/-

HERBERT (George). A Country Parson. See under "Philosophy, Essays," &c

—— The Temple. Sacred Poems By George Herbert Facsimile Reprint of the First Edition (1633). With an Introduction by J H. Shorthouse, Author of ' John Inglesant " Fcap 8vo net 3/6

HILL. The Aspirate ; or, the Use of the Letter " H " in English, Latin, Greek, and Gaelic By Geoffry Hill, M A Cr 8vo, cloth. net 3/6

HORTON. Revelation and the Bible. By R F Horton, M A , D D. Third Edition Cr 8vo, cloth 3/6

—— Inspiration and the Bible: An Inquiry. By R F Horton, M A , D D. Crown 8vo, cloth. 3/6

Popular Edition, cr 8vo Paper, net, 1/- , cloth, net 2/-

HOWARD. A History of Matrimonial Institutions. By George Elliott Howard, Ph D See under "History."

HYDE. The Religious Songs of Connacht. By Douglas Hyde, LL D , M R.I A , Author of "A Literary History of Ireland," "Love Songs of Connacht," &c 2 vols Cr 8vo, cloth net 10/-

JEPHSON. Christian Democracy. A Church for Our Day. By Julie Jephson. Cr 8vo, paper covers. 6d.

KING. The Psychology of Child Development By Irving King With an Introduction by John Dewey. Cr. 8vo, cloth. net 5/-

KO. Elementary Handbook of the Burmese Language. By Taw Sein Ko, M R A S., F A I , F S A Boards. net 3/9

KRUGER. The Papacy The Idea and its Exponents By

LEIGH. Our School Out of-Doors. By the Hon M. Cordelia Leigh, Author of "Simple Lessons from Nature," &c. Illustrated. Cr. 8vo, cloth   2/-

LUCAS and ABRAHAMS. A Hebrew Lesson-Book. By Alice Lucas and Israel Abrahams   Cr 8vo, cloth   net   1/-

MACPHAIL. Essays in Puritanism. By Andrew Macphail Large cr. 8vo, cloth.   6/-

MARK. The Teacher and the Child. Elements of Moral and Religious Teaching in the Day School, the Home, and the Sunday School By H Thiselton Mark, Master of Method, the Owens College, Manchester   With Frontispiece.   Cr. 8vo, cloth.   net   1/-

MARTIN'S Up-To-Date Tables . Weights, Measures, Coinage. For Use throughout the Empire   By Alfred J Martin, F S I   With 18 Diagrams and 3 Maps   Demy 16mo, cloth   net   2/6

——Up-to-Date Beginners' Table Book. For Schools and Home Teaching   Twenty-ninth Thousand. In paper covers   1d.

MATHEWS The Messianic Hope in the New Testament. By Shailer Mathews. Demy 8vo, cloth.   net   10/6

MAZZINI (Joseph)   See Stubbs.

NEGRI   Julian the Apostate. By Gaetano Negri. See under " Biography "

OMAN. The Mystics, Ascetics, and Saints of India. By John Campbell Oman. Fully Illustrated. Medium 8vo, cloth.   net   14/-

Cheaper Edition. Demy 8vo, cloth.   net   7/6

—— The Brahmans, Theists and Muslims of India   By John Campbell Oman, D.Lit   Illustrated   Medium 8vo, cloth,   net   14/-

—— Cults, Customs, and Superstitions of India. Being a Revised and Enlarged Edition of "Indian Life, Religious and Social' By J. Campbell Oman, D Lit , M R A.S. Illustrated. Demy 8vo, cloth.   net   14/-

PARKER. The Complete Works of Theodore Parker. Crown 8vo, cloth.   each   5/-

(1) A Discourse of Matters Pertaining to Religion
(2) The World of Matter and the Spirit of Man.
(3) The American Scholar.
(4) The Transient and Permanent in Christianity.
(5) Ten Sermons on Religion.
(6) Historic Americans.
(7) The Sins and Safeguards of Society
(8) Social Classes in a Republic
(9) Prayers, Poems and Parables
(10) Lessons from the World of Matter and of Man
(11) Theism and Atheism
(12) The Divine Presence.
(13) The Slave Power.
(14) The Law of God and the Statutes of Man.
(15) The Rights of Man in America.
(16) A Minister's Experience.

PAULSEN   German Education, Past and Present. By Friedrich Paulsen, Ph D   Translated by T. Lorenz, Ph D. Crown 8vo, cloth   net   5/-

PFLEIDERER. Religion and Historic Faiths. By Otto Pfleiderer, D D , Professor of Theology in the University of Berlin   Crown 8vo, cloth   net   5/-

—— Christian Origins   By Otto Pfleiderer, D.D   Crown 8vo, cloth. net   5/-

—— The Development of Christianity. By Otto Pfleiderer. Cr. 8vo, cloth   net   5/-

PHILPOTT. London at School : The Story of the School Board, 1870—1904. By Hugh B. Philpott. Illustrated. Cr. 8vo, cloth. 6/-

PIKE. Wesley and his Preachers. By G. Holden Pike. See under " Biography."

RAVENSTEIN. A Pocket German-English Conversation-Dictionary. By G. E. Ravenstein. (Meyer's Sprachführer.) 500 pages. 16mo, cloth. net 2/6

ROBINSON. The Golden Sayings of the Blessed Brother Giles of Assisi. Newly Translated and Edited, together with a Sketch of his Life, by Father Paschal Robinson, of the Order of Friars Minor. With 6 Illustrations. Crown 8vo, cloth. net 5/-

SABATIER. Modernism. The Jowett Lectures of 1908. By Paul Sabatier. With a Preface and Notes, and the full text of the Encyclicals *Pieni l' Animo, Lamentabili,* and *Pascendi Dominici Gregis.* Translated by C. A. Miles. Crown 8vo, cloth. net 5/-

—— Disestablishment in France. See under " Politics."

SELLECK. The New Appreciation of the Bible. A Study of the Spiritual Outcome of Biblical Criticism. By W. C. Selleck, D.D. Crown 8vo, cloth. net 6/6

STUBBS. "God and the People!" The Religious Creed of a Democrat. Being Selections from the Writings of Joseph Mazzini. By Charles William Stubbs (Dean of Ely). Second Edition. Cr. 8vo. 3/6

TYRRELL. The Programme of Modernism. A Reply to the Encyclical *Pascendi* of Pius X. Translated from the second Italian Edition (with the author's latest additions), by George Tyrrell, M.A. With an Introduction by A. L. Lilley, M.A., Vicar of St. Mary's, Paddington Green. Crown 8vo, cloth. net 5/-

UNWIN'S THEOLOGICAL LIBRARY.
    Crown 8vo, cloth. Each Volume. net 5/-
1 Modernism. The Jowett Lectures of 1908. By Paul Sabatier.
2 What is Religion ? By Professor W. Bousset.
3 The Bible as English Literature. By Professor J. H. Gardiner.
4 The Programme of Modernism. A Reply to the Encyclical Pascendi of Pius X.
5 Christian Origins. By Professor Otto Pfleiderer.
6 Religion and Historic Faiths. By Professor Otto Pfleiderer.
7 The Development of Christianity. By Otto Pfleiderer.

WAGNER. Courage. By Charles Wagner, Author of "The Simple Life," &c. Medium 12mo. Paper, net 1/- ; cloth, net 2/-

—— Towards the Heights. By Charles Wagner. Medium 12mo. Paper, net 1/- ; cloth, net 2/-

WARING. Christianity and its Bible. By Henry F. Waring. Large cr. 8vo, cloth. net 4/6

WILLIAMS. Psalms and Litanies, Counsels and Collects for Devout Persons. By Rowland Williams, D.D. New Edition. Cr. 8vo, cloth. 3/6

—— Stray Thoughts from the Note-Books of Rowland Williams, D.D. New Edition. Cr. 8vo, cloth. 3/6

WORSLEY. Concepts of Monism. A Critical Comparison of all Systems of Monism, both Asiatic and European. By A. Worsley. Demy 8vo, cloth net 21/-

    See also under "Biography" for Oliver Cromwell, Robert and Mary Moffat, Dr. Parker, Girolamo Savonarola, Wesley, and others. Also Japp [" Master Missionaries,"] &c.

DOMESTIC LITERATURE.

BOLAND. The Century Invalid Cookery Book. By Mary A. Boland. Edited by Mrs. Humphrey ("Madge" of *Truth*). Cr. 8vo, cloth.   3/6

DAVIES. The Housewife's What's What. A Hold-All of Useful Information for the House. By Mary Davies. Large cr. 8vo, cloth. net   6/-
Popular Edition, large cr. 8vo, cloth   net   2/6

FORSTER. Chelsea Window Gardening; or, Some Notes on the Management of Pot Plants and Town Gardens. By L. M. Forster. Cr. 8vo, paper covers.   2d.

GUARRACINO. "Please, M'm, the Butcher!" A Complete Guide to Catering for the Housewife of Moderate Means, with Menus of all Meals for a Year, numerous Recipes, and Fifty-two additional Menus of Dinners without Meat. Illustrated. By Beatrice Guarracino. Large cr. 8vo, cloth.   net   6/-
Cheap Edition, cloth.   net   2/6

HARDY. The Business of Life: A Book for Everyone. By the Rev. E. J. Hardy, M.A. Square imperial 16mo, cloth.   3/6
Presentation Edition, bevelled boards, gilt edges, in box.   7/6

—— The Five Talents of Woman: A Book for Girls and Young Women. By the Rev. E. J. Hardy, M.A. Popular Edition, small cr. 8vo, cloth.   3/6
Presentation Edition, bevelled boards, gilt edges, in box.   7/6

—— How to be Happy though Married: Being a Handbook to Marriage. By the Rev. E. J. Hardy, M.A. Presentation Edition, imperial 16mo, white vellum, cloth, extra gilt, bevelled boards, gilt edges, in box.   7/6
Popular Edition, cr. 8vo, cloth, bevelled boards.   3/6
Large cr. 8vo, green cloth with white label, flat back.   net 2/6
New Edition, 83rd thousand, small cr. 8vo, cloth.   net 1/-
Small cr. 8vo, paper cover.   1/-
Also a Sixpenny Edition.   6d.

—— How to Get Married. By the Rev. E. J. Hardy, Author of "How to be Happy though Married." Cr. 8vo, paper covers.   net 1/-

—— "Manners Makyth Man." By the Rev. E. J. Hardy, M.A. Presentation Edition, imperial 16mo, cloth, bevelled boards, gilt edges, in box.   7/6
   cloth, 6/-
Popular Edition, small square 8vo, cloth.   3/6

—— The Sunny Days of Youth: A Book for Boys and Young Men. Square imperial 16mo, cloth.   3/6
Presentation Edition, elegantly bound, bevelled boards, gilt edges, in box.   7/6

HARLAND and HERRICK. The National Cook-Book: A Thousand Recipes carefully prepared in the light of the Latest Methods of Cooking and Serving. By Marian Harland and Christine Terhune Herrick. 12mo, cloth.   7/6

HUMPHREY. Manners for Girls. By Mrs. Humphrey. Long 8vo, cloth, decorated cover.   1/-

PINK. Gardening for the Million. By Alfred Pink. Large cr. 8vo,
cloth. net 2/6

—— **Recipes for the Million :** A Handy-Book for the Household. By
Alfred Pink. Twelfth Thousand. Cr. 8vo, cloth. 2/6

Quickest Guide to Breakfast, Dinner, and Supper, The. By Aunt
Gertrude. Paper boards. 1/-

READ. The Way to Keep Well. Practical Home Hints on Common
Ailments. By C. Stanford Read, M.B. (Lond.), London County
Council Lecturer. Cr. 8vo, cloth. net 2/6

RONALD. The Century Cook-Book. By Mary Ronald. Fully
Illustrated. Demy 8vo, cloth. 7/6

—— **Luncheons :** A Cook's Picture Book. A Supplement to "The
Century Cook-Book." With many Illustrations. By Mary Ronald.
Large cr. 8vo, cloth. net 6/-

TUCKER. Mother, Baby, and Nursery : A Manual for Mothers. By
Genevieve Tucker, M.D. Illustrated. Large cr. 8vo, cloth.
Paper covers, 1/- ; cloth. 3/6

WHADCOAT. Every Woman's Own Lawyer. A Legal Adviser for
Ladies. By Gordon Cuming Whadcoat, Solicitor, Author of " The
Balance," and other novels. Cr. 8vo, cloth. net 3/4

WOOD. Quotations for Occasions. Compiled by Katharine B. Wood.
Large cr, 8vo cloth. 3/6

BOOKS for CHILDREN.

BRENTANO. New Fairy Tales from Brentano. By Kate Freiligrath
Kroeker. A New Edition. With Coloured Frontispiece and eight
Illustrations by F. C. Gould. Fcap. 4to, cloth. 3/6

BYLES. The Boy and the Angel : Discourses for Children. By Rev.
John Byles. Cr. 8vo, cloth. 3/6

—— **The Legend of St. Mark : A New Series of Sunday Morning
Talks to Children.** By Rev. John Byles. Crown 8vo, cloth. 3/6

CHILDREN'S LIBRARY, THE. Illustrated. Fcap. 8vo. The following
in cloth, Pinafore binding, floral edges. each 2/6

BASILE. **The Pentamerone ;**
or, the Story of Stories. By
Giambattista Basile. Translated from the Neapolitan
by John Edward Taylor.
New Edition, revised and
edited by Helen Zimmern.
Illustrated by George Cruikshank.

BECKMAN. **Pax and Carlino.**
By Ernest Beckman.

COLLODI. **The Story of a
Puppet.** By C. Collodi.
Translated from the Italian
by M. A. Murray. Illus-
trated by C. Mazzanti.

DAUDET. **The Pope's Mule,
and Other Stories.** By
Alphonse Daudet. Trans-
lated by A. D. Beavington-
Atkinson and D. Havers.
Illustrated by Ethel K.
Martyn.

DEFOE. **The Adventures of
Robinson Crusoe.** Edited
with Illustrations by George
Cruikshank.

DROSINES. **Stories from
Fairyland.** By Georgios
Drosines. Illustrated by
Thomas Riley.

CHILDREN'S LIBRARY, THE—*continued*

EIVIND. Finnish Legends. Adapted by R. Eivind. Illustrated from the Finnish text.

EVANS Sea Children. By S. Hope Evans. Illustrated

HAUFF. The Little Glass Man, and Other Stories. Translated from the German of Wilhelm Hauff Illustrated by James Pryde.

HUEFFER. The Feather. By Ford H Hueffer. Frontispiece by Madox Brown

HUGESSEN. The Magic Oak Tree, and Other Fairy Stories. By Knatchbull Hugessen (Lord Brabourne), Author of "Prince Marigold," "Queer Folk" &c

MORRIS Cornish Whiddles for Teenin' Time. By Mrs. Frank Morris. Illustrated by Arch K Nicolson

WILLIAMS. Tales from the Mabinogion. By Meta Williams.

Popular Re-issue, Fcap 8vo, decorated bindings   Illustrated   each   **1/-**

BROOKFIELD. Æsop's Fables for Little People. Told by Mrs. Arthur Brookfield. Pictured by Henry J. Ford.

BECKMAN Pax and Carlino. By Ernest Beckman Illustrated by Florence K Upton

CAPUANA Once Upon a Time By Luigi Capuana. Illustrated by C Mazzanti.

COLLODI. The Story of a Puppet; or, The Adventures of Pinocchio Illustrated by C. Mazzanti

DAUDET La Belle Nivernaise. By Alphonse Daudet. Illustrated by Montegut.

DROSINES Stories from Fairyland By Georgios Drosines Illustrated by Thomas Riley.

HOFFMANN Nutcracker and Mouse King, and Other Stories By E. T. A. Hoffmann Translated from the German by Ascott R Hope.

HUEFFER. The Brown Owl. By Ford H. Hueffer Illustrated by Madox Brown

MOLESWORTH. An Enchanted Garden. By Mrs. Molesworth Illustrated by J. W. Hennessey.

O'GRADY. Finn and His Companion. By Standish O'Grady. Illustrated by Jack B Yeats

VOLKHOVSKY The China Cup, and Other Stories By Felix Volkhovsky. Illustrated by Malischeff

YEATS. Irish Fairy Tales Edited by W. B. Yeats. Illustrated by Jack B. Yeats

CHILDREN'S STUDY, THE. Long 8vo, cloth, gilt top, with Photogravure Frontispiece.   each   **2/6**

(1) Scotland. By Mrs Oliphant
(2) Ireland. Edited by Barry O'Brien
(3) England. By Frances E. Cooke
(4) Germany. By Kate Freiligrath Kroeker

(5) Old Tales from Greece. By Alice Zimmern, Author of "Old Tales from Rome."
(6) France. By Mary Rowsell.
(7) Rome. By Mary Ford.
(8) Spain. By Leonard Williams
(9) Canada. J N. McIlwraith.

COX. The Brownies in the Philippines. By Palmer Cox. Large 4to. Copiously illustrated.   **6/-**

DEFOE The Adventures of Robinson Crusoe. By Daniel Defoe Newly Edited after the Original Editions. 19 full-page Illustrations by Kauffmann Large cr. 8vo, cloth extra, gilt edges   **5/-**

DODGE. The Disdainful Maiden. A Fairy Story. By W. Phelps Dodge, Author of "Piers Gaveston," &c. Parchment, grey covers, cr 12mo   **2/-**

Lightning Source UK Ltd.
Milton Keynes UK
UKHW022359090223
416721UK00001B/115